The
Rational Expectations Revolution
in Macroeconomics

The Rational Expectations Revolution in Macroeconomics

Theories and Evidence

DAVID K.H. BEGG

The Johns Hopkins University Press
Baltimore, Maryland

Printed in Great Britain

First published in the United States of America, 1982, by
The Johns Hopkins University Press, Baltimore, Maryland 21218
by arrangement with
Philip Allan Publishers Limited, Deddington, Oxford, UK.

Library of Congress Cataloging in Publication Data

Begg, David K.H.
   The rational expectations revolution in
   macroeconomics.
   1. Economic development — Mathematical models
   I. Title
   330'.01   HD82   82–47785

   ISBN 0-8018-2882-3 hardcover
   ISBN 0-8018-2882-1 paperback

To my Mother and Father

Contents

Preface

The Rational Expectations Hypothesis asserts that individuals do not make systematic mistakes in forecasting the future. In the last decade this innocuous proposition has transformed macroeconomics, not merely by providing an exciting set of results which challenge the old conventional wisdom on every front, but also by encouraging a reassessment of the very methodology of theoretical and empirical macroeconomic analysis. The purpose of this book is to offer a comprehensive evaluation of this research.

This book is about economics, not mathematics. The exposition draws heavily on my experience in trying to convey the key insights of Rational Expectations analysis to undergraduates, business audiences and Civil Servants. The only knowledge which I assume is elementary algebra and a familiarity with the material of an introductory macroeconomics course. More technical analysis is confined to optional starred sections which may be omitted without loss of continuity. Suggestions for further reading are given in Notes on the Literature at the end of each chapter. An extensive reference bibliography is also provided.

I am conscious of my intellectual debt to Rudi Dornbusch, Stan Fischer, John Flemming and Jerry Hausman, and should like to take this opportunity to thank them for their kindness and encouragement. I should also like to thank Philip Allan for persuading me to write this book; John Flemming, Chris Gilbert, Andrew Harvey, Mark Precious, Peter Sinclair, Ken Wallis and Rod Whittaker for reading individual chapters; and especially Jim Poterba and Mike Wickens who read the entire manuscript. At every stage I have been helped immeasurably by Susie Symes, without whom my discussion would have been more narrow, yet less precise. For sharing my life as well as my thoughts over the last two years, I am most grateful of all to her.

1
Introduction

1.1 The Rational Expectations Revolution in Macroeconomics

Expectations formation is a central issue in macroeconomics. In the past, the adoption of various *ad hoc* assumptions about the process of expectations formation has allowed the development of simple macroeconomic models whose dynamic properties might be analysed. Yet *ad hoc* assumptions are troubling for they are arbitrary. The recent work on the hypothesis of Rational Expectations has commanded considerable attention because it seems to rely on a good optimising principle: individuals should not make systematic mistakes in forecasting the future. It is not appealing to assume that individuals make predictable errors yet take no action to revise their rule for forming expectations, but *ad hoc* expectations assumptions typically possess this property; only under Rational Expectations is the contradiction avoided.

Throughout the last decade, Rational Expectations has been a major theme of macroeconomic research. Its proponents claim that the hypothesis represents a vital breakthrough in the methodology of macroeconomics, with profound implications for all theoretical and empirical work. Why cannot specialist economists beat the Financial Times or Dow Jones Stock Market Index? Why are economists so frequently wrong about the change in the exchange rate? These questions are easily answered in the literature on Rational Expectations, which argues that such phenomena

1

are the predictable consequence of a world in which expectations are Rational and may be evidence of the success of economics rather than its failure.

However, the hypothesis has a wider significance than merely the provision of a riposte to popular complaints against the professional competence of economists. Many Monetarists have found in Rational Expectations the assumption for which they had long been searching, an elegant device for translating their intuitive beliefs into results which can be derived analytically within the market clearing models to which they subscribe. By allowing Monetarism a new academic respectability, Rational Expectations has had an important influence on economic policy. For example, the New Classical Macroeconomics[1] argues that demand management policies will have little effect on real variables even in the short run.

Critics of this New Macroeconomics fall into two groups: those who reject Rational Expectations as a plausible model of actual behaviour, and those who find the hypothesis attractive but nevertheless are troubled by the results it generates when applied within the market clearing Natural Rate models. It is both possible and important to distinguish between the assumption about expectations formation and the assumption about the structure of the underlying economic model in which the expectations assumption is embedded. Critics within the second group cited above have gradually realised that it is the structure of the underlying model, and in particular the assumption of market clearing under flexible prices, to which they really wish to object. The task of reassessing the role of Rational Expectations in models which do not assume continuous market clearing has only just begun.

The impact of the hypothesis of Rational Expectations has not been confined to theoretical macroeconomics. Empirical econometricians have constructed models of national economies to be used both for forecasting and for policy evaluation, in which the simulation of hypothetical

---

1. An excellent non-technical introduction is Grossman, H.I. (1980).

policies allows a better understanding of the likely consequences of adopting the policy. If expectations are Rational it is possible to show that the naive use of such econometric models for policy evaluation will generate totally misleading results. If actually adopted, a change in policy would alter individuals' expectations of the future. Unless the equations of the model are amended to reflect this revision of expectations, the policy simulation is likely to be quite worthless. The hypothesis of Rational Expectations not only exposes a problem which had previously gone unnoticed, but also provides a framework in which to predict the probable revision of expectations when a new policy is adopted.

Thus the hypothesis of Rational Expectations has had far reaching consequences in both theoretical and empirical macroeconomics. To accept the hypothesis is to concede a lasting revolution in the methodology of macroeconomics. The purpose of this book is threefold: to provide a consistent exposition of the Rational Expectations approach; to assess the plausibility of the assumption itself; and to present a selection of applications, both theoretical and empirical.

While the central idea of Rational Expectations is extremely simple, the technical analysis often seems forbidding to the non-mathematician since the solution procedure typically requires the consideration of the whole future path of the economy. Because this involves a degree of technical complexity, readers new to the literature are frequently so intent on mastering the techniques that they fail to develop any intuitive understanding of the approach. My intention is to provide a unified discussion which is comprehensive, yet accessible to the widest class of reader. The only knowledge which is assumed is elementary algebra and a familiarity with the material of an introductory macroeconomics course.[2] The reader I have in mind might be an undergraduate enrolled in an intermediate course in macroeconomics, or a working economist interested in recent developments in macroeconomics. Some readers, graduate students for example, or undergraduates reading mathe-

2. See, for example, Dornbusch and Fischer (1978).

matical economics, may require a more rigorous treatment. This additional material is presented in short sections beginning and ending with the symbol (**). Readers not wishing to pursue this level of rigour should simply omit these starred sections and may be assured that the important discussion takes place in the main text.

1.2 The Role of Expectations in Macroeconomic Theory

Before setting out the plan of the book, it is useful to review the role of expectations in macroeconomics for two reasons: first, in order to pre-empt the criticism that expectations formation is a peripheral issue which is not central to macroeconomics as we know it; secondly, to introduce the idea that many of the standard controversies in macroeconomics depend, at least in part, on differences in the implicit assumption about how expectations are formed.

Only at the simplest level do economists maintain the fiction that decisions may be modelled within the context of a single time period. Typically, decision makers' preferences extend over a longer horizon: they care about the future. In an economy without any stores of value, there might be no way in which individuals, by their current choices, could affect the opportunities available in subsequent periods; however, the existence of assets allows individuals to break the period by period equality of flow income and flow expenditure. They can save or dissave, thus altering the timing of expenditure and revenue across periods. Given a complete set of forward markets, individuals could currently make contracts for all future transactions at prices agreed, and therefore known, in the current period. In such a world there would be no need to form views about the future. In practice, imperfect and costly information gives rise to transactions costs and uncertainty which severely restrict the number of forward markets in operation. It is then essential to form views about the future to make sensible intertemporal decisions.

Since current decisions by individuals depend on their current evaluation of the future, such considerations must also influence the behaviour of economic aggregates which form the building blocks of macroeconomics. As a simple example, consider the aggregate consumption function. Introductory macroeconomics texts present several formulations: the simple Keynesian function $C = C(Y)$ which emphasises the dependence of current real consumption C on current real income Y; *ad hoc* generalisations of the form $C = C(Y, W)$ which recognise the additional influence of current real wealth W; and formal analyses of the intertemporal decision of consumers such as the Permanent Income Hypothesis $C = C(Y_p)$ which relates current consumption to permanent income Y_p, an appropriate average of current and expected future real incomes. Since expectations are not directly observable, a theory of expectations formation is required to make operational this last and most sophisticated version of the consumption function. In the next chapter, I will argue that Keynes(1936) adopted the device of treating expectations as exogenous and therefore independent of current variables. In the short run, with expected future incomes held exogenously constant by assumption, variation in current income is the most important source of variation in permanent income, which averages current and future incomes. This illustration makes two points. First, even theories which seem to deal only in current variables, such as the assertion that current consumption depends chiefly on current income, usually have an implicit assumption about expectations. In my judgment, that is a more charitable interpretation than one which asserts that the theories have positively denied that decisions are ever intertemporal. Secondly, when faced with conflicting theories, it is important to consider whether the differences are to be sought and understood chiefly in the differing expectations assumptions adopted.

Many other examples may be cited of the need to investigate the issue of expectations in macroeconomics. Let me briefly mention two. When wage contracts are set in nominal terms, but firms and workers, having no money illusion, care only about real wages, it will be necessary for wage bargainers to form views about the likely inflation rate over the duration of the contract in order to assess the expected real value of the nominal settlement. No discussion of the Phillips Curve or related issues can avoid this. Similarly, when rates of return in asset markets, whether for equities, bonds, or foreign exchange, depend in part on uncertain capital gains over the holding period, it will be necessary to model expectations formation if these markets are to be understood.

In short, it is impossible to provide a sensible treatment of macroeconomic theory without resort to some model of expectations formation. Sometimes this model is only implicit. It is better that the expectations assumption should be made explicit, even where it is almost embarrassingly simple. Not only does this avoid confusion and place the model clearly within a more general framework, it may also prevent inconsistency. If macroeconomics is the study of interdependent or simultaneous systems of relations, it cannot be satisfactory to treat expectations formation in an *ad hoc* manner which may vary from equation to equation.

1.3 Expectations and Empirical Macroeconomics

Economic theories should be confronted with economic data. A large part of the ensuing discussion is concerned with empirical work in macroeconomics. Econometricians consider how the theory of mathematical statistics can be used to provide rigorous criteria for the analysis of economic data. This analysis may be divided into four areas: quantification, testing, prediction, and policy evaluation. The purpose of this section is not merely to introduce these concepts to readers who are not familiar with econometrics, but also to argue that the issue of expectations formation is as important for empirical macroeconomics as it is for theoretical macroeconomics.

Some economists are reluctant to place any weight on the results of econometric analysis, believing that mathematical precision offers a misleading account of the complex world in which we live. I believe this view to be misconceived. Suppose we have a simple theory, for example that consumption C depends linearly on income Y. We write

$$C = b + cY + u \qquad (1.3.1)$$

where *b* and *c* are constants and *u* is a random disturbance whose average value is zero. By rewriting this equation as

$$u = C - (b + cY)$$

it becomes apparent that *u* is simply the extent to which our simple model $(b + cY)$ fails to provide an exact description of actual consumption. While it would be unreasonable to assert that consumption is exactly explained by the model $C = b + cY$, no such charge can be levelled against the random or stochastic formulation, for its point of departure is the recognition that the theory, by simplifying, ignores some influences on actual consumption.

The term *u* will only be truly random, in the sense of being completely unpredictable, if the underlying theory or model correctly captures all the systematic influences on consumption. If *u* includes important systematic influences which the theory has omitted, such as the effects of wealth or expected future incomes, the behaviour of *u* will not be purely random. For example, if wealth and expected future incomes are trending upwards over time, *u* will trend upwards also. Econometrics uses mathematical statistics to model the behaviour of the random term *u*. At the very least, this will provide two kinds of information. First, we will be able to measure the relative importance of the systematic terms $(b + cY)$ embodying the content of the economic theory against that of the random term *u* which reflects the state of our ignorance about remaining influences on consumption. Thus, we can derive some measure of the confidence we should place in our economic theory. Secondly, by examining the behaviour of the disturbance term *u* over time, we may be able to diagnose the presence of other influences and infer how our theory should be amended. Far from implying a false precision, econometrics becomes an indispensable tool in a complex world in which economic theory can provide only rules of thumb.

Thus in later chapters I examine empirical econometric evidence on macroeconomic models with Rational Expectations. To introduce the most important ideas, I continue to work with the example of the consumption function. The first problem facing an econometrician is *Model Selection*, the specification of the systematic and random components of the relation. Economic theory may indicate the variables on which consumption depends, but it rarely provides strong justification for a particular functional form. Equation (1.3.1) represents one particular model selection in which the systematic part $(b + cY)$ is linear in current income. No other variables are included, nor is a non-linear functional form, such as $C = \log Y$, adopted. Typically, the chosen functional form will be simple, but compatible with the *a priori* restrictions implied by the theory or by previous empirical work.

The second problem is *Estimation*, use of the data to determine particular values for the unknown constants b and c. Estimation theory provides criteria for choosing values for these parameters so that the resulting equation best fits the actual data at hand. Estimation is especially important in macroeconomics because a complete model of the economy will usually encompass different effects operating in different directions, so that theory alone cannot predict the outcome; indirect effects may outweigh direct effects and it is essential to know the relevant magnitudes.

The next problem is to *Test* the economic theory embodied in the systematic part of the equation. Suppose, for example, we wish to test the hypothesis that equation (1.3.1) is the correct model of consumption against the alternative hypothesis that consumption depends not only on income but also on current wealth. Thus, the more general hypothesis might be specified as

$$C = b + cY + dW + u \qquad (1.3.2)$$

where d is another constant and W denotes real wealth. Econometric testing proceeds as follows. First, estimate the more general model, here equation (1.3.2). Having selected values of b, c, and d to best fit the data, examine whether the estimated value of the constant d is sufficiently close to zero that we may ignore the influence of wealth on consumption as equation (1.3.1) asserts. The theory of statistical inference provides criteria for deciding how close to zero the estimated value of d must be before we may concede that wealth may legitimately be ignored. The most widely developed, and most widely used, set of statistical criteria for testing economic hypotheses takes the above form: specify and estimate a more general model than the economic theory asserts and examine whether the additional variables are redundant.

If we conclude that the data do indeed support equation (1.3.1), we may then proceed to use the estimated equation for *Forecasting*. Let b^* and c^* be the estimated values of the constants over our sample period. Assume also that we have confirmed that the residuals $(C - b^* - c^* Y)$ are zero on average and display no trend. We might then predict next period's consumption C_{+1} by first guessing the value of next period's income Y_{+1}, then using our estimated equation to predict consumption as $b^* + c^* Y_{+1}$. There are three reasons why such a forecast of consumption may prove inaccurate. First, since the basic equation (1.3.1) contains a genuinely random term, even a successful theory will not predict consumption exactly; it is only a simplification. Secondly, we may have failed to guess correctly the future value of income. Finally, we may have failed to estimate the systematic part of the consumption function correctly: either equation (1.3.1) has omitted an important variable and we have failed to detect this at the testing stage, or the econometric procedures used to estimate b and c have been inappropriate, leading to incorrect estimates of these parameters. Only in the third of these instances can it be said that the empirical econometrics is deficient. On many occasions, forecasting errors will arise because of one of the first two reasons and we must simply conclude that we have done the best we can in a world which is characterised by considerable uncertainty.

As mentioned earlier, we may use an estimated model for *Policy Evaluation*. First, we may use the model to predict what will occur if present policies are maintained unchanged, then we may alter the future path of one of the variables under government control and simulate the new prediction for the path of the economy. By comparing the two paths we can quantify the effects of the proposed policy change, thus allowing a more informed discussion about the desirability of adopting a different policy.

Having introduced the main themes of econometric research, we can now contemplate the role of expectations formation in empirical macroeconomics. Consider first the specification of the model to be estimated. Clearly, if the economic theory explicitly addresses the issue of expectations formation, the corresponding empirical work can do no less. However, when expectations formation is only implicit in the economic theory, the problem is more subtle. It may be convenient to develop theoretical models in which it is assumed that expectations are constant in the short run. Such models provide useful insights into short-run behaviour. However, if one wishes to apply these theories to actual data over time, it cannot be maintained that expectations were necessarily invariant over some long period. Because it requires a large number of data points to obtain estimates of unknown parameters, empirical economists cannot duck the issue of expectations formation even when the theorist can. In this sense, the requirement for a coherent theory of expectations formation is even more important in empirical macroeconomics.

Consider next the problem of estimating a model in which expectations formation is recognised. Individuals' expectations are unobservable and can be treated only by postulating a model relating these unobservable expectations to variables which can be observed and for which data exists. It is sometimes asserted that survey data on expectations could be used, rendering expectations immediately observable. We should simply ask individuals what they expect and record this information. However, if we wish to forecast some way into the future, we cannot now ask individuals what at some future date they will be expecting for a yet later date. Rather we have to model the process by which expectations are formed, forecast the variables on which these expectations depend, and hence derive a forecast of what expectations will be. Nor would survey data provide a reliable guide to policy evaluation in which we should have to collect data on what individuals would expect in some hypothetical situation about which they may not have thought very carefully. For these reasons, most economists believe it is preferable to attempt to model the process of expectations formation and estimate its unknown parameters.

Thirdly, consider the problem of testing an economic model. Precisely because the specification includes both a hypothesis about the underlying framework, for example that consumption depends on permanent income, and a hypothesis about the process by which expectations are formed, it is hard to separate these distinct aspects of the model. If we are confident that expectations formation has been correctly captured, we can use the data on aggregate behaviour to test whether the economic theory about the underlying structure is correct. However, this requires us to place considerable faith in the postulated model of expectations formation and further underlines the importance of this issue in empirical macroeconomics.

Finally, consider the problem of policy evaluation in which a hypothetical policy change alters the evolution of the economy. Whatever expectations were previously assumed are now likely to be inappropriate. Unless individuals were completely and permanently misled, they would surely revise their expectations if a new policy were adopted. For example, extrapolating the past may be a reasonable rule of thumb while policy is maintained unchanged; it would be completely inappropriate if a radically different policy were about to be introduced. Policy evaluation will be worthless unless it captures the dependence of expectations formation on the policy in force.

1.4 Summary of the Argument and Outline of the Remaining Chapters

Since people care about the future, macroeconomic theory cannot be discussed without reference to expectations formation. Competing macroeconomic models can frequently be related within a general framework once their differing expectations assumptions are recognised. Models of a macroeconomic system may be internally inconsistent unless the prior question of expectations formation is addressed explicitly. Empirical economists using data over a long period must model expectations formation as a process or decision rule, since reliable data on present and future expectations are not available, and must succeed in this modelling if theories about the underlying economic structure are to be understood and tested. Without a model of endogenous expectations revision, policy evaluation is likely to be highly misleading.

Taken together, these arguments provide the justification for a book on the role of expectations in macroeconomics. The discussion is organised as follows. In Chapter 2 I consider the meaning of the term expectations. I then examine treatments of expectations formation which were adopted before the hypothesis of Rational Expectations became fashionable. The insistence that macroeconomics is necessarily inter-temporal and must confront the issue of expectations formation dates back at least to Keynes. I will argue that he foresaw so many difficulties in developing a theory of endogenous expectations revision that he preferred to side-step the question by the simple expedient of treating expectations as exogenous in the short run. Within this framework, the consequences of a change in expectations could be analysed without reference to the causes of such changes. Much of Post-Keynesian macroeconomics may be viewed as an attempt to meet Keynes' challenge to elaborate an explicit theory of expectations revision. Drawing on the earlier theory of Static Expectations, the first important attempt to meet this challenge was the hypothesis of Adaptive Expectations. This hypothesis is studied and its limitations discussed.

In Chapter 3 I set out the theory of Rational Expectations which starts from the presumption that optimising individuals should not make systematic mistakes in expectations formation. Otherwise, there exists an incentive to diagnose the source of the systematic error and amend the basis of the forecasting rule. Economists may generate expectations within the model in order to reproduce this property by adopting the following strategy: pretend that individuals know the systematic part of the model and use this to form expectations. These expectations are Rational in the following sense: when these expectations are fed back into the model the actual evolution of the economy will imply that there are no systematic forecasting errors which could have been discovered by individuals using information available at the date they had to form expectations. Chapter 3 explains how economists may solve models to obtain Rational Expectations. The problem is first discussed in the context of a model in which there is perfect certainty. Rational Expectations then reduces to Perfect Foresight. Having set out the structure of the problem in this simpler case, uncertainty is then admitted and the additional complications are studied. The chapter concludes with a critique of the plausibility of Rational Expectations as a model of actual expectations formation.

In Chapter 4 I consider the implications of Rational Expectations for empirical macroeconomics. I begin by summarising the statistical properties which the hypothesis implies, testable properties which much of the empirical literature seeks to examine. After a brief discussion of the structure of macroeconomic models with Rational Expectations I then introduce the problem of statistical identification by which we mean the question of whether separate estimates of the unknown parameters can be disentangled from the data. Provided the parameters can be identified the issue of testing can then be addressed. Such testing may be of two kinds: testing the expectations hypothesis conditional on some underlying structure of the economic model, or testing the underlying structure conditional on a particular expectations hypothesis. Both questions are discussed. Finally, I set out the devastating criticism of conventional policy evaluation first noted by Lucas(1976) and discuss whether a satisfactory solution can be offered.

Chapter 4 provides a general introduction to empirical research in macroeconomic models with Rational Expectations and assumes no prior knowledge of econometric theory. Since some readers will wish a more rigorous treatment, Chapter 5 examines the extension of conventional econometric theory to models with Rational Expectations. Because this chapter assumes familiarity with the econometric theory of simultaneous equation systems, it is a starred chapter (**). For those who wish to follow the chapter, a bibliography of assumed material is provided. Any reader with some knowledge of econometric theory is encouraged to read this chapter. However, other readers may simply omit this chapter without loss of continuity: Chapter 4 is intended to provide an adequate introduction to the issues which are treated in the subsequent chapters.

Chapters 6—8 discuss particular applications of Rational Expectations in modern macroeconomics. In Chapter 6, I discuss the use of monetary and fiscal policies for the management or stabilisation of aggregate demand. Whereas the textbook IS/LM analysis typically assumes an elastic supply of goods, it is possible that the economy is always at its full employment or Natural level. If so, attempts to manipulate aggregate goods demand will have no effect on aggregate real output. Thus it is the specification of aggregate supply which lies at the heart of this debate about the efficacy of stabilisation policy. A model is presented in which stabilisation policy will have real effects under Adaptive Expectations, but not under Rational Expectations. The foundations of this Neutrality result are then examined in some detail. It is argued that the result depends heavily on the assumed structure of the underlying economic model. In particular, if markets fail to clear it is still possible to allow Rational Expectations, but policies will then have conventional Keynesian results. Empirical evidence on the Rational Expectations/Natural Rate model is examined.

Whereas the focus of Chapter 6 is really the behaviour of aggregate supply, Chapter 7 considers how the components of aggregate demand should be modelled when expectations are Rational. Under this hypothesis, the Permanent Income theory of consumption is shown to have a strikingly simple implication. The empirical evidence is examined and the extent to which it provides support for the joint theories is discussed. The implications for investment are then considered. Modern theories of investment behaviour seek to explain investment as the sluggish adjustment of actual capital to the desired capital stock. One particular justification for sluggish adjustment is that offered by Keynes (1936): speculation on the price of new capital goods leads some firms to postpone investment until bottlenecks in the capital goods industry ease and capital goods prices decline. This model provides a neat application of the Rational

Expectations hypothesis and its implications are examined. Empirical evidence is again discussed.

Chapter 8 considers the role of Rational Expectations in asset markets. Three markets are discussed: the market for equities, for government bonds, and for foreign exchange when currencies are floating. Expected capital gains play a crucial role in all these asset markets. If available information is used efficiently, the current asset price should already reflect all knowable information about the asset. Apart from considerations implied by risk aversion and the desire to diversify portfolios, all assets should yield the same expected return. The implications and empirical evidence are discussed for the three markets in turn. This discussion embraces familiar issues such as the Term Structure of bond interest rates and the various competing theories of the determination of floating exchange rates. The latter discussion is wide ranging, including such issues as the consequences of discovering an important natural resource such as oil, and argues that complicated dynamic properties may be obtained even in very simple models once sophisticated expectations formation is allowed.

In the concluding chapter, I offer a preliminary assessment of the Rational Expectations revolution in macroeconomics and suggest areas for further research.

2
Previous Treatments of Expectations Formation

In this chapter I discuss the treatment of expectations formation in macroeconomics before the formulation of the Rational Expectations hypothesis. After considering what one might mean by the term 'expectations', I examine the view set out by Keynes(1936) in the *General Theory*. While insisting that expectations formation was central to macroeconomic analysis, Keynes was reluctant to elaborate a theory of endogenous expectations revision; indeed, the problems which he foresaw in such an attempt bear directly on the recent literature on Rational Expectations and will be evaluated at greater length in Chapter 3. Nevertheless, some theory of expectations revision is essential. The first attempt to model systematic expectations revision in the light of new information was the hypothesis of Adaptive Expectations introduced by Cagan(1956) and Nerlove(1958). For nearly two decades, this hypothesis was widely adopted in theoretical and empirical macroeconomics. Having described the hypothesis, I draw attention to the shortcomings which eventually led many economists to seek a more plausible model of expectations formation.

2.1 The Meaning of Expectations

I can no longer avoid the question of what exactly is meant by the term 'expectations'. The discussion turns on what we

16

mean by uncertainty. Consider first a stylised example. A fair coin is to be tossed and all agree that the probability of a head is one half. Statisticians might approach this definition of probability either from the *ex ante* standpoint that the event of tossing a fair coin can be decomposed into two possible outcomes, each of which is equally likely; or from the *ex post* standpoint that half the outcomes would be heads if the coin were tossed sufficiently often. Suppose we assign the value zero to the outcome of a head and the value one to the outcome of a tail. The expected value of the outcome of a single toss is then one half. By this mathematical expectation, or mean, we denote the result of taking each conceivable outcome, here zero and unity, multiplying each outcome by the associated probability, and summing over all possible outcomes. Suppose next that we toss the coin ten times, adding the score for each outcome to obtain a total score. Since the different tosses are independent experiments, we can deduce that the mean total score is ten times one half. We may also define measures of the dispersion around this mean of five, indicating the probability that the total score will depart from five by various amounts. For example, the outcome of ten consecutive heads is very unlikely, but possible.

We wish to model individual behaviour in an uncertain world. Consider an individual faced with two alternative bets, each with the same mean but having different dispersions or degrees of riskiness of deviating from the mean value. If individuals reveal that they are indifferent between the two bets, we say that they are risk neutral: their preferences may be entirely described in terms of the mean or mathematical expectation of the uncertain event. If, for two bets having the same mean, individuals prefer the bet with the lower dispersion, we say that individuals exhibit risk aversion. Since individuals then assess uncertain events both by the mean and the dispersion, it will be necessary to model each of these influences on individual behaviour. Nevertheless, if the degree of dispersion or riskiness remains approximately constant over time, we may be able to capture the most important determinants of changes in behaviour merely by modelling changes in the mathematical expectation.

In such a world we might interpret the rather loose phrase 'expectations of the future' to mean the strict mathematical expectation of future variables, given the assessment of riskiness at the date expectations are to be formed. Of course, individuals may not make a correct assessment of the true probabilities, but then a slightly weaker concept will suffice. We could say that individuals make subjective assessments of the probabilities and use these to construct the relevant weighted average in the manner discussed above. We then say that individuals act on the basis of subjective expectations. By modelling the manner in which individuals arrive at assessments of these subjective expectations, it is then possible to construct a theory of expectations formation which relies on available information at the date expectations are to be formed.

Before embarking on this approach we should be clear about its limitations. In an uncertain world there may be no mechanism by which individuals can readily reach such an assessment, a position most forcefully advocated by Keynes. In his *Treatise on Probability*(1921), Keynes argued that probability theory was rarely an interesting way in which to describe the real world. In tossing a coin we have a reasonable idea of what is meant by the statement that the probability of obtaining a head is one half. We could certainly repeat the experiment one million times and confirm that almost half the outcomes were a head; alternatively, we could conduct laboratory tests to check that the coin was indeed fair. In contrast, what is the probability that the United States will elect a woman president before the end of the century? We might all agree that the answer lies between 0.1 and 0.9 but on what basis are we to narrow this range of possible probabilities? If we cannot define unique probabilities even subjectively we cannot describe views about an uncertain future by a single valued subjective expectation, let alone construct a theory of the way in which such expectations are revised over time.

I find this position overly pessimistic. Current decisions do depend on views about the future and macroeconomics cannot avoid this issue. It is better that we should try to model the determination of these views and undertake careful statistical analysis to evaluate the extent of our success. In later chapters I cite evidence which suggests that the problems may be less formidable than Keynes believed. Before examining the subsequent attempts of macroeconomists to make progress on this issue, I digress to consider the solution which Keynes himself adopted.

2.2 Keynes' Treatment of Expectations

In the previous section I referred to the *Treatise on Probability* in which Keynes challenged the view that single valued subjective expectations could be uniquely defined. That argument rested on the belief that individuals possessed only scanty information about uncertain future events. In the *General Theory* this argument is extended, drawing on Keynes' experience as an active investor in financial asset markets. Now the argument is not conceptual, but practical. In the famous passage about the stock market as a casino, he describes the behaviour of short-term speculators chasing immediate capital gains. Share prices depend on asset supplies and demands which depend on prospective capital gains, in turn depending on the likely assessment at a later date of further capital gains. Hence individuals are trying to guess what other individuals guess other individuals will guess about capital gains. The market may converge to any number of guesses, each of which might be self fulfilling but arbitrary, leaving the economist little hope of modelling the level of expectations or the date and amount of their revision.

This idea is fascinating because, as we shall see, it lies at the heart of the literature on Rational Expectations. The extent to which the view expressed in the *General Theory* is compatible with the hypothesis of Rational Expectations will be discussed in the concluding chapter and is a subject on which I have written elsewhere in Begg(1982). Keynes himself concluded that the modelling of endogenous expectations revision was fraught with difficulties, yet, wishing to insist on the importance of expectations, he had to find some solution. I believe he decided to adopt the device of treating expectations as exogenous in the short run. The *General*

Theory sets itself the limited task of analysing the behaviour of current endogenous variables conditional on a particular set of exogenous expectations about the future. It is then natural to analyse the comparative static properties of the model by assuming an exogenous shift in expectations as in the famous downward shift in the marginal efficiency of capital schedule. Such a device would not be appropriate if expectations were determined endogenously, for then it would also be necessary to analyse the other consequences of the shock which had induced this change in expectations.

This interpretation has one great merit. The conventional interpretation of the *General Theory* views the work as a collection of *ad hoc* relations, each of which has subsequently been 'improved' by Post-Keynesian macroeconomics. The simple consumption function has been supplanted by a version of the Permanent Income—Lifecycle model, the marginal efficiency of investment schedule has been replaced by a version of the Flexible Accelerator model, liquidity preference by more explicit analysis of the transactions cost and risk motives for money demand, and so on. In constrast, the above interpretation not only places individual relations within a modern intertemporal framework, but emphasises that they represent a coherent and internally consistent approach.

Consider the Permanent Income—Lifecycle model of consumption. Permanent income is the constant hypothetical stream whose present discounted value equals the present value of expected actual income plus any initial wealth. It is asserted that consumption will vary with permanent income, since individuals make long-run decisions subject only to long-term budget balance. However, if it is assumed that expected future incomes are exogenous and temporarily fixed, the important variation in permanent income in the short run will be induced by variation in current income. Moreover, since current income and income in the immediate future represent only a part of permanent income, variation in the former will induce smaller variation in the latter, so that we should expect a marginal propensity to consume out of current income which is positive but less than unity. In the longer run, the assumption that exogenous expected future incomes remain constant is untenable. If these shift upward over time, the short-run consumption function will also exhibit the upward drift first documented by Kuznets(1946).

When expectations of future operating profits are held exogenously constant, the most important determinant of investment decisions will be the rate at which such expected profits are discounted. In the short run, we recover Keynes' marginal efficiency of capital schedule relating desired capital stocks to rates of interest. Again, in the longer run, it will not be plausible to assume that expectations remain invariant. Shifts in expectations will shift the marginal efficiency of capital and such shifts may prove quantitatively more important as an explanation of actual investment variation than movements along the schedule for any given 'state of long-term expectation' about future operating profits. Flexible accelerator models of investment emphasise the role of current and past output changes as the determinants of investment behaviour. Provided relative factor prices and real interest rates remain fairly constant over time, future profit levels may be highly correlated with future output levels. When accelerator models appear to fit investment data reasonably well, it is possible to give the following interpretation. Individuals extrapolate past output levels to form expectations about future outputs and hence future profits to use within the conventional discounting formulation of the investment decision. Within this general framework, Keynes' theory and the accelerator model are opposite polar cases: the marginal efficiency theory adopts the simplifying assumption that the numerator of the present value formula can be treated as exogenous and emphasises variation in the denominator as the aspect which may be conveniently modelled; the accelerator neglects changes in the denominator while emphasising changes in the numerator using a simple extrapolative theory of expectations revision. In the next section, extrapolative or adaptive schemes are examined in more detail.

As a final example of the interpretation of expectations as exogeneous, consider the liquidity preference schedule which is used to explain the speculative or asset demand for money in the *General Theory*. Asset holders consider whether they wish to hold their wealth in long assets (stocks and bonds) or in short assets such as money. The current price of long assets is the stream of expected future coupon interest or corporate dividends discounted at the current long-term market interest rate. The one period yield on such an asset is not merely the current entitlement to the interest or dividend payment but also the capital gain or loss over the period. To assess the likely gain or loss, individuals must guess the market price of the asset at the end of the period, which depends on the long interest rate then being used to discount the future income stream. Expected future interest rates do not appear in Keynes' formulation of liquidity preference, even though the theory rests on speculative considerations of this kind. Once expectations are treated as given, these variables do not enter the analysis. For a given level of expectations, lower current interest rates (higher current bond prices) increase the probability of capital losses, thereby increasing the relative attractiveness of short assets such as money whose return has no capital gain dimension.

On this interpretation, the *General Theory* becomes a coherent account of the way in which expectations enter a macroeconomic model in which decisions are intertemporal. By treating expectations as exogenous, a double simplification is achieved: not only is the problem of modelling expectations formation avoided, but also the complicated intertemporal structure reduces to the more tractable case in which, conditional on a particular set of expectations, the only endogenous variables to be explained are current values of the crucial variables. On this view, the challenge which Keynes left his successors was less the elaboration of explicit models of intertemporal decision taking, than the construction of a theory of endogenous expectations revision to make such models operational. The remainder of this chapter is devoted to an analysis of the first major attempt to meet this challenge, the hypothesis of Adaptive Expectations.

2.3 Adaptive Expectations

By a theory of endogenous expectations formation I mean the specification of a rule by which individuals revise their expectations in the light of new information. The hypothesis of Adaptive Expectations, introduced by Cagan(1956), postulates that individuals use information on past forecasting errors to revise current expectations.

Let $_{t-1}x_t^e$ be the value of the variable x at time t which is expected by individuals forming expectations at the end of time $t-1$. The Adaptive Expectations hypothesis asserts that

$$_{t-1}x_t^e - {_{t-2}x_{t-1}^e} = \Phi\,(x_{t-1} - {_{t-2}x_{t-1}^e}) \qquad 0 < \Phi < 1$$

$$(2.3.1)$$

Having some forecast $_{t-2}x_{t-1}^e$ based on information available at the end of time $t-2$, individuals examine *ex post* how well that forecast predicted the actual value x_{t-1} and revise their forecast for x one period later at time t by some fraction of the forecasting error at time $t-1$. Rearranging equation (2.3.1)

$$_{t-1}x_t^e = \Phi\,x_{t-1} + (1-\Phi)_{t-2}x_{t-1}^e \qquad (2.3.2)$$

Since the same formula must hold one period earlier

$$_{t-2}x_{t-1}^e = \Phi\,x_{t-2} + (1-\Phi)_{t-3}x_{t-2}^e$$

Hence, by recursively substituting out the unobservable expectation in equation (2.3.2), we eventually obtain

$$_{t-1}x_t^e = \Phi\,x_{t-1} + \Phi(1-\Phi)\,x_{t-2} + \Phi(1-\Phi)^2\,x_{t-3}$$
$$+ \ldots + \Phi(1-\Phi)^n\,x_{t-n-1}$$
$$+ (1-\Phi)^{n+1}\,_{t-n-2}x_{t-n-1}^e \qquad (2.3.3)$$

All terms except the final term are observable. Since Φ is a positive fraction, $(1-\Phi)^{n+1}$ gets steadily smaller as n is increased. Provided only that the value of this final expectation is finite, we can shrink its influence on current expectations to an infinitesimal level by considering a sufficiently large value of n. The appeal of the Adaptive Expectations hypothesis is that it allows us to model unobservable expectations purely in terms of past observations on the relevant variable x, without the need to specify the process by which the initial level of expectations is determined.

Equation (2.3.3) also emphasises that the behavioural rule (2.3.1) is really an assertion that current expectations $_{t-1}x_t^e$ are based on an extrapolation or weighted average of past actual values of x in which the weights have the simple property of geometric decline: the coefficient on x_{t-k} in equation (2.3.3) is $(1 - \Phi)$ times the coefficient on $x_{t-(k-1)}$. For this reason, the Adaptive Expectations rule is sometimes known as the geometric distributed lag on past values of x.

Suppose the economy is in static equilibrium in which the value of x is unchanging over time. Letting all previous values of x equal the constant $\bar{x}$, equation (2.3.3) implies

$$_{t-1}x_t^e = \Phi\{ 1 + (1 - \Phi) + (1 - \Phi)^2 + (1 - \Phi)^3 + \ldots \}\, \bar{x}$$

$$= \frac{\Phi\, \bar{x}}{1 - (1 - \Phi)} = \bar{x}$$

If the economy has been in static equilibrium for a sufficient time, individuals forming Adaptive Expectations will eventually come to anticipate correctly the value which x takes on. This seems a minimal requirement for a plausible rule for modelling expectations formation. However, if the economy is not in static equilibrium, the hypothesis of Adaptive Expectations allows individuals to learn from previous forecasting errors.

Moreover, the hypothesis could be easily incorporated in empirical research. Consider the model

$$y_t = \alpha(_{t-1}x_t^e) + \beta z_t \qquad (2.3.4)$$

in which the endogenous variable y depends on an exogenous variable z and on the expectation at the end of time $t - 1$ of a second exogenous variable x. A similar equation must hold one period earlier

$$y_{t-1} = \alpha(_{t-2}x_{t-1}^e) + \beta z_{t-1} \qquad (2.3.5)$$

Subtracting equation (2.3.5) from equation (2.3.4) and using equation (2.3.1) we obtain

$$y_t - y_{t-1} = \alpha\{ _{t-1}x_t^e - _{t-2}x_{t-1}^e \} + \beta(z_t - z_{t-1})$$

$$= \alpha\Phi\{ x_{t-1} - _{t-2}x_{t-1}^e \} + \beta(z_t - z_{t-1})$$

$$= \alpha\Phi x_{t-1} + \beta(z_t - z_{t-1}) - \Phi(y_{t-1} - \beta z_{t-1})$$

which may be rearranged to yield

$$y_t = \alpha\Phi x_{t-1} + (1 - \Phi)y_{t-1} + \beta z_t - \beta(1 - \Phi)z_{t-1}$$

$$(2.3.6)$$

Fitting this equation to the data to obtain coefficient estimates, the value of Φ could be inferred from the coefficient on y_{t-1}, hence allowing the value of α to be inferred from the coefficient on x_{t-1}, while the value of β could be inferred from the coefficient on z_t. Although equation (2.3.3) makes clear that Adaptive Expectations is implicitly an extrapolation of an infinite number of previous observable x values, the trick of transforming the original equation by subtraction of the relevant multiple of y_{t-1} leads to the simple formulation (2.3.6) which is easy to implement empirically.

The hypothesis thus offered a simple solution to the needs of both theoretical and empirical macroeconomists seeking to model expectations formation; indeed, the apparently plausible behavioural assumption (2.3.1) seemed to provide a theoretical justification for the empirical practice of implicit extrapolation which was first adopted by Fisher (1930) in studying the effect of expected inflation on nominal interest rates. Nor was it necessary to confine attention to extrapolative schemes imposing a geometric decline on the weights attached to past values of the relevant variable; Almon(1965) devised an econometric technique allowing empirical economists conveniently to estimate more flexible lag shapes, the particular weights being chosen so that the implied expectations best fitted the data for the model in question.

While the hypothesis of Adaptive Expectaions, and its subsequent generalisations, represented a considerable advance, several problems remained. First, the hypothesis is entirely backward looking as equation (2.3.3) makes clear. Suppose that OPEC is meeting next week but that the outcome of their deliberations is a formality; everyone knows that they will announce a doubling of oil prices. Surely economists will be predicting higher inflation from the moment at which news of the prospective oil price increase first becomes available? Yet the hypothesis of Adaptive Expectations asserts that individuals raise inflation expectations only after higher inflation has gradually fed into the past data from which they extrapolate. Adjustment of expectations is very sluggish. Using such a rule, individuals would make systematic mistakes, underpredicting the actual inflation rate for many periods after the oil price rise. It is not plausible that individuals would take no action to amend the basis of their forecasting rule under such circumstances.

Secondly, no economic theory is offered to explain the magnitude of the adjustment parameter Φ in equations (2.3.1) and (2.3.3). The appeal of the hypothesis is its simplicity, but it is perhaps too simple. A possible generalisation is to specify a subsidiary rule for the determination of Φ as in Flemming(1976) where the size of Φ, and hence the speed of adjustment to recent events, is made to depend on the size of the most recent forecasting error. When this is large, a higher value of Φ is adopted, placing greater weight on more recent events.

Rational Expectations theorists would still raise the following objections. First, it is still imagined that the only variables which need to be considered are past values of the variable about which expectations are to be formed. Such partial equilibrium analysis does not fit comfortably within the tradition of macroeconomics in which the general equilibrium or system-wide effects are of great importance. For example, data about past rates of money growth may usefully supplement data on past inflation rates in predicting future inflation. Secondly, all mechanistic backward looking extrapolative rules allow the possibility of systematic forecasting errors for many periods in succession. The suboptimal use of available information is hard to reconcile with the idea of optimisation which is the foundation of most microeconomic analysis.

Such dissatisfaction with the Adaptive Expectations hypothesis eventually prompted economists to seek an alternative formulation. The hypothesis of Rational Expectations set out by Muth(1961) formalised the earlier work of Modigliani and Grunberg(1954) and forms the subject matter of the following chapters.

Notes on the Literature

Much of the early discussion of expectations formation is to be found not in conventional macroeconomic analysis but in the study of agricultural markets, in which the gestation period between crop planting and harvesting forced suppliers to form expectations about the likely output price at the date of harvesting. The simple hypothesis of Static Expectations $(_{t-1}x_t^e = x_{t-1})$ was frequently adopted and was shown to generate cycles in output and prices according to the famous Cobweb Theorem studied in Ezekial(1938). Static Expectations may be regarded as the special case of Adaptive Expectations in which the parameter Φ is set equal to unity. The Cobweb model was also used by Nerlove(1958) in an early discussion of Adaptive Expectations and by Muth(1961) to introduce Rational Expectations. Hicks(1939) discusses the related concept of the 'elasticity of expectations' by which is meant the extent to which a 1% increase in the current value of a variable x induces expectations of increased values of x in the future.

Keynes' views are best examined in Chapters 12 and 15 of Keynes (1936), though the less familiar Keynes(1937) also anticipates many of the arguments discussed in Section 3.4.

Begg(1982) discusses the relation between Keynes and Rational Expectations, but the reader is advised to wait until the material in Chapter 6 has been considered.

3
The Rational Expectations Hypothesis

The hypothesis of Rational Expectations pays more than lip service to the conventional tenets of economics. It is concerned with incentives to acquire information and exploit profitable opportunities for revising behaviour. It admits the notion of an equilibrium set of expectations, even when the economy is not in static equilibrium. It treats seriously the notion that bygones are bygones. It confronts the issue of when expectations formation will prove difficult even for individuals who are well informed.

In Section 3.1 I define the hypothesis of Rational Expectations. By emphasising the role of information, the hypothesis forces us to make some assumption about the degree of information individuals possess or can acquire. Different variants of the hypothesis follow from different assumptions about this degree of information. In Section 3.2 I consider the formal structure of a Rational Expectations equilibrium in the special case in which certainty is complete. The standard questions of existence, uniqueness and stability may then be analysed most easily. Although the underlying argument is mathematical, the text relies on a diagrammatic exposition since it is essential that the basic structure of the argument be mastered if the reader is to understand either the objections which have been raised against the hypothesis, or the properties exhibited by models in which the hypothesis is applied. In Section 3.3 I introduce uncertainty and study the additional complications to which this gives rise. Finally, in Section 3.4 I examine the plausibility of Rational Expectations as a model of actual behaviour.

28

3.1 The Definition of Rational Expectations

In Chapter 2 I argued that *ad hoc* rules such as Adaptive Expectations have the disturbing implication that they allow individuals to make systematic forecasting errors period after period, without requiring any amendment to the basis of the forecasting rule itself. The point of departure of Rational Expectations is that individuals should not make systematic errors. This does not imply that individuals invariably forecast accurately in a world in which some random movements are inevitable; rather, the assertion is that guesses about the future must be correct on average if individuals are to remain satisfied with their mechanism of expectations formation. The task is to make this somewhat loose statement more precise.

When uncertainty is absent and information complete, Rational Expectations reduces to the special case of Perfect Foresight. If systematic factors are much more important than random factors, this assumption may capture much of the spirit of the Rational Expectations approach, while avoiding the analytical complications which arise when one must distinguish between *ex ante* expectations and *ex post* realisations of future variables. Nevertheless, since we cannot mean Perfect Foresight to be a literal description of the uncertain world in which we live, it is important to formulate more general models in which the additional effects of uncertainty may be addressed. If present information about future variables is incomplete, what degree of information should individuals be assumed to possess? Analysis of this interesting question is still in its infancy, though I shall refer to some preliminary results in Section 3.4. For the moment, I avoid the question of how much information individuals optimally choose to acquire, adopting the simpler assumption that some particular information is available.

A simple assumption is that only past values of the variable x enter this Information Set when individuals form expectations of future values of the x variable. However, this assumption is unduly restrictive. In a simultaneous equation macroeconomic model, future values of endogenous variables are likely to depend on the values or realisations of many variables within the model. Past values of other variables are likely to convey additional information about future realisations of any particular x variable. When such information is widely available, it will be more attractive to assume that individuals know the entire structure of the model and previous values of all the relevant variables within that model, an Information Set which should allow systematically more accurate predictions than when past values of x alone are used to form expectations of its future realisations. Clearly, intermediate assumptions are possible: individuals may know some of the relevant information, but not all. Since without analysing the incentives to acquire information it would be arbitrary to suppose a particular intermediate Information Set, I shall focus on the case in which individuals are assumed to know the structure of the entire model and observe past values of all relevant variables. When the model is stochastic, reflecting the innate randomness of the world in which we live, it is assumed that individuals also know the statistical properties of these random disturbances.

In such a model, the 'true' expectation is the mathematical expectation which could be derived by writing the correct structural model of the economy including these random terms, forming mathematical expectations conditional on the information available at the date at which expectations are to be formed. The hypothesis of Rational Expectations asserts that the unobservable subjective expectations of individuals are exactly the true mathematical conditional expectations implied by the model itself. Individuals act as if they know the model and form expectations accordingly.

It is important that this should not be taken too literally. In particular, it does not require that the entire population have degrees in economics. Rather, it is claimed that an economist wishing to model expectations formation in a world in which information is widely and speedily disseminated, in which reputable forecasts are published, and in which expectations are not systematically mistaken, can most easily generate expectations meeting these requirements by proceeding 'as if' individuals undertook the above thought experiments. It is no more necessary that the expectations we wish to model are consciously based on this thought process

than it is that profit maximising firms actually evaluate
marginal cost and revenue curves. In either case, the economist is merely constructing a framework in which to model
the endogenous behaviour of smart individuals whose hunches
prove correct on average.

A simple example may now clarify the solution offered by
the Rational Expectations approach. We wish to model the
one period inflation rate expected this period. Individuals,
knowing the current price level, are assumed to guess the
price level next period, thereby inferring the expected
inflation rate. The price level next period is merely one
endogenous variable at that date. By forming their best
current guesses about the values of exogenous variables next
period, individuals may use the model to solve for the expected values of endogenous variables including the price
level. In fact, the story is usually one degree more complicated. The price level this period may depend on current
expectations of inflation, for example because these affect
current nominal wage settlements. Similarly, the price level
next period will depend on the inflation rate then expected
over the following period and so on. Thus, individuals forming Rational Expectations at the current date must form
expectations not only about the price level next period, but
in all succeeding periods. The entire future path of the economy must be assessed. In Section 3.2, I explain this solution
procedure in simple diagrammatic terms, so that the economic assumptions can then be isolated without resort to any
complicated mathematics. Initially, I ignore randomness and
assume Perfect Foresight.

3.2 The Perfect Foresight Equilibrium Path

I shall say that the economy evolves along a Perfect Foresight
equilibrium path if the evolution of the economy is consistent
with the postulated method of expectations formation. Individuals do not make forecasting errors which would induce
dissatisfaction with the forecasting rule.

Consider the simple two equation model

$$\dot{x} = ax + by + h \qquad \dot{y} = cx + dy + k \qquad (3.2.1)$$

where x and y are two variables and a, b, c, d, h, k are constants. The superscript dot denotes the rate of change of the variable over time. In this model, the rate of change of x and y depend on the levels of both variables.

Let x^* and y^* denote the steady state values of x and y, the static equilibrium in which x and y are unchanging over time. Since $\dot{x}$ and $\dot{y}$ are then zero, equation (3.2.1) implies that these steady state values are given by

$$x^* = (bk - dh)/(ad - bc) \qquad y^* = (ch - ak)/(ad - bc)$$

To study the behaviour of this dynamic model when the economy is not in the steady state, it is convenient to draw the Phase Diagrams. Let us draw the locus along which $\dot{x} = 0$. From equation (3.2.1)

$$x = (-1/a)(by + h) \tag{3.2.2}$$

Combinations of x and y satisfying equation (3.2.2) will imply $\dot{x} = 0$. If, for example, a is negative but b and h positive, this locus will slope upwards as in Figure 3.2.1. Any point on this locus, such as G, implies $\dot{x} = 0$. Hence, holding x constant but considering a larger y value — a horizontal shift to the right in Figure 3.2.1 — implies that $\dot{x}$ must now be positive since the coefficient b is assumed to be positive in

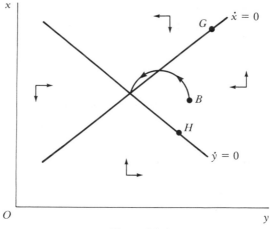

Figure 3.2.1

equation (3.2.1). Smaller y values for given x values — a horizontal shift to the left in Figure 3.2.1 — must reduce the value of by in equation (3.2.1), implying $\dot{x}$ is now negative to the left of the locus along which $\dot{x} = 0$. We can depict these results by drawing arrows of motion in Figure 3.2.1, showing x to be increasing (vertical arrow upwards in the x-direction) to the right of the locus $\dot{x} = 0$ and x to be decreasing (vertical arrow downwards in the x-direction) to the left of the locus.

By setting $\dot{y} = 0$ in equation (3.2.1), we can construct the equivalent locus for y:

$$y = (-1/d)/(cx + k)$$

If I assume that c and d are negative, this locus slopes down as in Figure 3.2.1. Beginning from a point H on the locus, points horizontally to the right, having a larger y value for a given x value, imply that $\dot{y}$ is negative, since d is negative in equation (3.2.1). To the left of H, $\dot{y}$ is positive and y increasing. Again, we may draw in the arrows of motion, this time in the y-direction.

Figure 3.2.1 is the complete Phase Diagram, given the particular assumptions about the signs of the coefficients in equation (3.2.1). The steady state is the point of intersection of two loci, at which both x and y are unchanging. When the economy is not in the steady state, the two loci divide the possible outcomes into four regions, each with an associated pair of arrows for the direction of change of x and y. Since actual changes must satisfy both sets of arrows, the evolution of the economy may be inferred. For example, in a region characterised by the pair of arrows

both x and y are increasing, so the economy must be moving to the north east as indicated by the dotted arrow above.

The important feature of Figure 3.2.1 is that the arrows in the x-direction point towards the $\dot{x} = 0$ locus and the arrows in the y-direction point towards the $\dot{y} = 0$ locus. The steady state (x^*, y^*) will then be *Globally Stable*. Begin at any point

in Figure 3.2.1 and follow the arrows of motion. The economy *always* converges to the steady state. At the point B, the
economy is moving to the north west. If the point B lies in a
particular place, movement to the north west may take the
economy directly in to the steady state without ever crossing
either of the loci $\dot{x} = 0$ or $\dot{y} = 0$. Figure 3.2.1 depicts another
possibility. Movement to the north west leads the economy
to the $\dot{x} = 0$ locus before the steady state is reached. Since x
is instantaneously unchanging along the $\dot{x} = 0$ locus, the
economy must cross the locus in an instantaneously horizontal direction. (Similarly, if the $\dot{y} = 0$ locus is ever crossed,
the direction of motion must be instantaneously vertical to
preserve constant values of y.) Having crossed the $\dot{x} = 0$ locus,
the economy moves into a region in which movement is to
the south west. Again, depending on the particular point,
this will allow either direct convergence to the steady state or
will imply that another locus, this time that along which
$\dot{y} = 0$, is reached. Repeating the argument, it is apparent that
the economy eventually converges to the steady state as in
Figure 3.2.1. An identical argument may be used to establish
convergence from any initial position.

Different phase diagrams follow from different assumptions on the constant coefficients in equation (3.2.1). When b
is negative, but a, c and d are positive, the dynamic behaviour
of the economy will be as depicted in Figure 3.2.2. Setting $\dot{x}$
and $\dot{y}$ respectively equal to zero in equation (3.2.1), we derive
the new loci. While the slopes of these loci are again positive
and negative respectively, the arrows of motion must now be
amended. Pick a point (x, y) on the locus $\dot{x} = 0$ and consider
increasing x for given y. From equation (3.2.1), the positive
constant a implies that all points vertically above points on
the $\dot{x} = 0$ locus have $\dot{x}$ positive. Above this locus, the arrows
in the x-direction now point vertically *away* from the locus,
while the arrows point vertically downwards below the locus.
It is easily checked that arrows in the y-direction also point
away from the $\dot{y} = 0$ locus in the horizontal y-direction. The
phase diagram in Figure 3.2.2 is *Globally Unstable*. The
symptom is that both sets of arrows point away from the
relevant locus. The consequence is that the economy steadily
diverges from the steady state unless it happens to begin in

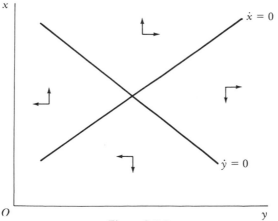

Figure 3.2.2

the steady state itself. The reader should confirm this by selecting a point in Figure 3.2.2, following the arrows of motion implied.

Having studied cases in which both arrows point towards the relevant loci and both arrows point away from the relevant loci, it remains to consider the case in which one set of arrows points towards the relevant locus and one set points away. Suppose that c and d are negative as in Figure 3.2.1, but that a is positive and b negative as in Figure 3.2.2. The phase diagram is depicted in Figure 3.2.3 overleaf.

In the x-direction the arrows point away from the $\dot{x} = 0$ locus, but in the y-direction the arrows point towards the $\dot{y} = 0$ locus. We then say that the steady state is a *Saddlepoint*. Suppose the economy begins at the point C. It will then proceed along the dotted line, crossing vertically the $\dot{y} = 0$ locus before shooting off to the north west. Similar unstable behaviour occurs along other dotted lines in Figure 3.2.3. The crucial property of a Saddlepoint is that there exists a *unique* convergent path to the steady state, a path which never crosses either of the loci. By observing the two regions in which a convergent path might conceivably lie, we can draw this path as AA' in Figure 3.2.3. Only if the economy fortuitously begins at a point on this path will convergence be possible.

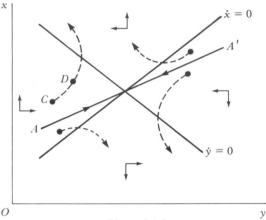

Figure 3.2.3

The Saddlepoint property is often found in macroeconomic models which include assets such as money. For a given nominal money stock, a higher price level reduces the supply of real money balances. Market clearing requires a reduction in demand for real money balances and may be achieved by a higher inflation rate. Thus, if P is the price level and $\dot{P}$ its rate of change, P and $\dot{P}$ tend to be positively correlated, generating a set of arrows which point away from the $\dot{P} = 0$ locus. If other aspects of the real economy tend to be more stable and have arrows pointing towards their loci along which real values are unchanging, a Saddlepoint will result.

This used to trouble macroeconomists: only by a fluke would the economy happen to begin at a point on the unique convergent path. The comforting belief in the underlying stability of the economic system seemed to have been challenged.

The literature on Rational Expectations stands this argument on its head. It is now argued that when the steady state is a Saddlepoint the economy will succeed in locating the unique convergent path. Moreover, if the steady state happens to be Globally Stable, it is shown that this property is no longer desirable since it now implies that expectations formation will prove extremely difficult. This reversal in the desirability of different stability properties of the model hinges on the time span individuals are assumed to consider. Under Adaptive Expectations, individuals look backwards to form expectations by extrapolation, mechanistically grinding out expectations using equations (2.3.1) and (2.3.3), but never considering the future path of the economy if such behaviour is maintained. In the fortunate event that the steady state is Globally Stable, the dynamic behaviour of the economy will nevertheless ensure convergence to the steady state, even though this is not an explicit consideration in expectations formation. In contrast, under Rational Expectations bygones are bygones and the past is of interest only in so far as it conveys information about the future path of the economy. Forward looking individuals are imagined to solve the model over all future time to arrive at current expectations. Convergence to the steady state is no longer a chance event depending on the structure of the particular dynamic model under consideration, it is intrinsic to the process of expectations formation itself.

In the preceding analysis let us interpret y as the capital stock and x as the price level. New capital is formed by investment. Since it is usual to assume a gestation lag between investment spending and the date at which the plant subsequently comes on stream, I assume that the current capital stock y is instantaneously predetermined by previous investment decisions. The price level x is an endogenous variable which is free to take on whatever value is currently necessary to satisfy equation (3.2.1), given the inherited capital y and the expected rates of change $\dot{y}$ and $\dot{x}$. These expectations are also free endogenous variables depending not on bygone behaviour of the economy, but on the future path which the economy will follow from the current date onwards.

Suppose first that the structure of the economy — here represented by the parameters a, b, c and d in equation (3.2.1) — implies that the steady state is Globally Stable as in Figure 3.2.1. Consider individuals with an inherited capital stock y currently trying to form expectations about the future path of the economy, expectations which will influence the equilibrium levels of the current endogenous variables $x, \dot{x}$ and $\dot{y}$ which must be simultaneously determined.

Because y is predetermined, the economy must begin on a line passing vertically through this value of the capital stock in Figure 3.2.1. However, because the steady state is Globally Stable, any point on this line will allow subsequent convergence to the steady state. If individuals unanimously agreed to begin at a particular point, it would be possible to follow the arrows of motion to the steady state and knowledge of the dynamics of the model would allow the entire convergent path to be calculated once the initial point had been agreed. However, the weak assumption that individuals do not readily participate in an economy which is following an explosive path is not sufficient to tie down the initial point, for there is an infinity of points which allow subsequent convergence. There is an infinity of Perfect Foresight paths corresponding to the inherited capital stock y.

Worse still, individuals in such an economy could have little confidence that their expectations would be realised. Suppose a particular initial point is somehow chosen, the dynamic equations (3.2.1) then being used to infer the subsequent convergent path to the steady state. One possibility is that these expectations are confirmed and this is what we should suppose if we mean to interpret literally the Perfect Foresight assumption. However, consider what may happen after the economy has proceeded along this path for some time, having then reached the inherited capital stock y'. Since bygones are bygones, individuals at this date are constrained only to choose an initial point on the vertical line through y' in making their forward looking assessment of the future of the economy. They might decide to begin from a new point, implying a discrete jump in x at this date. The arrows of motion would then imply a well defined convergent path from the new initial point to the steady state. Again, however, there is nothing in the structure of the model to rule out a further change of heart at some later date. Thus when the steady state is Globally Stable it is hard to argue that there exists a unique convergent path when expectations are forward looking.

Suppose next that the structural equations of the model imply that the steady state is Globally Unstable as in Figure 3.2.2. Unless the economy happens to inherit a capital stock *y* which is precisely the steady state capital stock, there exists no convergent path to the steady state. I shall then say that a Perfect Foresight equilibrium path does not exist. In such circumstances the economy might embark on a path which was known to be explosive, but individuals would realise that this path could not be followed indefinitely. At some stage the structure of the model would change, perhaps because of government intervention to avert the impending explosion, but individuals would have little basis for currently evaluating the form that this intervention would take, let alone the date at which it might be implemented.

When the steady state is a Saddlepoint the analysis is very different. Inheriting a particular capital stock *y*, individuals may now select a unique choice of the endogenous variables x, $\dot{x}$ and $\dot{y}$, namely the values implied by placing the economy on the unique convergent path AA' vertically above *y* and then inferring $\dot{x}$ and $\dot{y}$ from equation (3.2.1). Thereafter, the economy converges to the steady state along AA' in Figure 3.2.3. Suppose a certain time has elapsed and the inherited capital stock is y'. Bygones are bygones and individuals at this date are recalculating the forward solution. Reasoning as at the initial date, the only convergent forward looking solution is to place the economy on AA' vertically above y', since any other choice of *x* at this date would imply subsequent explosion. Thus, once having placed the economy on the convergent path AA' at the initial date, all subsequent decisions confirm that the path AA' will indeed be followed. There is no incentive now or in the future to depart from this path and individuals at all dates may have some confidence that the path will be subsequently followed. It is then reasonable to claim that a unique Perfect Foresight equilibrium path exists.

To reinforce this argument, imagine that individuals at the initial date contemplate the consequences of choosing some other value of the free variable *x*, say to place the economy at the point *C* in Figure 3.2.3. The economy will set off along an explosive path and the probability is high that at some future date, say when the point *D* is reached, individuals will conclude that explosive behaviour is no longer tolerable. For the then inherited level of *y*, there will be a downward jump in x to restore the economy to the convergent path. Either this development is unanticipated at the initial date, in which case we cannot describe the evolution as compatible with Perfect Foresight, or it is anticipated. In the latter case, individuals at the initial date realise that within finite time there will be a discrete jump in the value of x. Maintaining the interpretation that x is the price level of goods, it will be very desirable to hold money balances whose real value will discretely jump within finite time, and since it is assumed that such a jump may be anticipated as from the initial date, this will increase the demand for real balances at the initial date. For a given nominal money stock, market clearing at the initial date thus requires a lower initial price level x to increase the stock of real money balances. At any point C above the convergent path AA' this argument may be invoked and implies that x will have to be lower. The assumption of Perfect Foresight in a model exhibiting the Saddlepoint property not only suggests that AA' should be the anticipated evolution but also creates an incentive structure to make this the likely outcome. The knife edge path AA' from which the economy explodes if it deviates at all, far from being an unlikely freak case, provides the only sensible basis for forward looking expectations when individuals are well informed about the structure of the economy.

Before devising a simple macroeconomic model in which the preceding analysis may be applied, we should consider an important objection to this analysis. In chapter 12 of the *General Theory*, Keynes(1936) examines the consequences of differential access to information so that individuals' expectations are no longer unanimous. Suppose there are two groups of individuals, the first having a mistaken view about the true model or structure of the economy, the second knowing not only the correct model, but also the mistaken view held by the first group. Suppose the current endogenous variables place the economy on a path which the former group mistakenly believes to be convergent, but the latter group perceives to be explosive. The correctly informed individuals may find it more profitable to allow the economy to proceed for some time along the explosive path, along which asset returns will differ from those anticipated by the incorrectly informed group, switching back to the convergent path only when it is about to become evident even to the uninformed group that the explosive path is not in fact convergent. Unless the informed group have access to limitless borrowing opportunities, it may be more profitable for them to predict the crass errors of the less informed, greatly weakening the incentive to converge quickly upon the unique stable path.

Within a model of strict perfect foresight this objection does not apply: expectations are unanimous and correct. A rigorous analysis of models with differential information, while important, requires the modelling of incentives to acquire information itself, a complex subject currently the focus of much research. Since few results are yet available, I prefer to take account of Keynes' objection by arguing that the actual path which the economy follows may randomly deviate from the perfect foresight path because of short-term speculative blips of the type Keynes identified. These blips may be handled within the random models analysed in the following section. Nevertheless, since even poorly informed individuals will eventually recognise an explosive path, the convergent path emphasised by the preceding analysis remains the basis of the discussion.

(**) Mathematical Digression: The Generalised Saddlepoint Condition

The preceding discussion considered a model with only two equations. Some readers may wish to know the equivalent statement when a more general model is allowed. Consider the linear system of n first order differential equations in n variables x_{it} at time t:

$$\dot{x}_{1t} = a_{11} x_{1t} + a_{12} x_{2t} + \ldots a_{1n} x_{nt} + h_1$$
$$.$$
$$.$$
$$.$$
$$.$$
$$\dot{x}_{nt} = a_{n1} x_{1t} + a_{n2} x_{2t} + \ldots a_{nn} x_{nt} + h_n$$

which, in matrix notation, may be written

$$\dot{x}_t = A x_t + h \quad x_t \equiv \begin{bmatrix} x_{1t} \\ x_{2t} \\ . \\ . \\ . \\ x_{nt} \end{bmatrix} \quad A \equiv \begin{bmatrix} a_{11} & .. & a_{1n} \\ a_{21} & .. & a_{2n} \\ . & . & . \\ . & . & . \\ a_{n1} & .. & a_{nn} \end{bmatrix} \quad h \equiv \begin{bmatrix} h_1 \\ h_2 \\ . \\ h_n \end{bmatrix}$$

$$(3.2.3)$$

Consider the eigenvalues λ of the coefficient matrix A obtained by solving the matrix equation $|A - \lambda I| = 0$, in which I is the n by n identity matrix. These eigenvalues may be real or complex. If the real parts of all n eigenvalues are negative, the system (3.2.3) is Globally Stable, converging to the steady state from any initial position. Imagining an n-dimensional phase diagram, we could think of all the arrows of motion pointing towards the relevant loci $\dot{x}_{it} = 0$ ($i = 1, 2, .. n$).

If the real parts of all n eigenvalues are positive, the system is Globally Unstable, diverging from the steady state from all initial positions except the steady state itself.

As in the two equation model, we are interested chiefly in the case in which some eigenvalues have positive real parts and some have negative real parts. Some arrows of motion point towards the relevant loci and some point away. The crucial result we require is that the dimension of the convergent subspace is the same as the number of eigenvalues with negative real parts (arrows pointing towards the relevant loci).[1]

To illustrate this result, consider the two equation example of the text. When both arrows point towards the relevant loci, as in Figure 3.2.1, the dimension of the convergent subspace is two: all points in the (x, y) plane allow

1. When models are specified in discrete time, conditions that eigenvalues have negative real parts must be replaced by conditions that eigenvalues have absolute values of less than unity. Section 5.1 gives a formal solution of a general version of such a model.

convergence to the steady state. When no arrows point towards the relevant loci, as in Figure 3.2.2, the dimension of the convergent subspace is zero: only one point, the steady state itself, allows convergence. The Saddlepoint case depicted in Figure 3.2.3 has one set of arrows pointing towards the relevant loci and hence allows a one-dimensional convergent subspace, the line AA' (not necessarily a straight line).

Consider a system of n variables, s of which are predetermined. Suppose the dimension of the convergent subspace is s. The predetermined variables then pick off a unique point in this s-dimensional space and we may infer the unique convergent path from this date onwards by applying the differential equations of the model to this initial point. If the dimension of the convergent subspace exceeds the number of predetermined variables, the predetermined variables do not provide sufficient initial conditions to tie down a unique initial point in the convergent subspace. The Perfect Foresight path is not unique. Conversely, if the dimension of the convergent subspace is less than the number of predetermined variables, the initial conditions are overdetermined: only by chance will their s values happen to pick off a point in the convergent subspace of smaller dimension. In general, no convergent Perfect Foresight path exists.

It is also useful to derive the analytic expression for the convergent path when the Saddlepoint conditions obtain. I consider the two variable model (3.2.1), although the analysis is easily extended to the more general equation (3.2.3). As in Figure 3.2.3, I assume that the parameters of equation (3.2.1) satisfy

$$a > 0 \qquad b < 0 \qquad c < 0 \qquad d < 0$$

Writing equation (3.2.1) in matrix form

$$\begin{bmatrix} \dot{x} \\ \dot{y} \end{bmatrix} = \begin{bmatrix} a & b \\ c & d \end{bmatrix} \begin{bmatrix} x \\ y \end{bmatrix} + \begin{bmatrix} h \\ k \end{bmatrix} \tag{3.2.1b}$$

the characteristic equation for the coefficient matrix is given by

$$0 = \begin{vmatrix} a - \lambda & b \\ c & d - \lambda \end{vmatrix} = \lambda^2 - (a + d)\lambda + (ad - cb)$$

which has two solutions:

$$\lambda = \tfrac{1}{2}[(a + d) \pm \{(a + d)^2 - 4(ad - bc)\}^{\frac{1}{2}}]$$

Given the above sign restrictions on the coefficients, $(ad - bc)$ is negative and $\{(a + d)^2 - 4(ad - bc)\}^{1/2}$ is larger in absolute value than $(a + d)$, confirming that one eigenvalue λ is positive and one is negative. Choosing the negative solution

$$\lambda = \tfrac{1}{2}[(a + d) - \{(a + d)^2 - 4(ad - bc)\}^{\frac{1}{2}}]$$

the solution to equation (3.2.1b) is

$$\dot{x} = \lambda(x - x^*)$$
$$\dot{y} = \lambda(y - y^*)$$

where x^* and y^* denote the steady state values of x and y obtained when $\dot{x} = \dot{y} = 0$ in equation (3.2.1b).

$$(**)$$

With these preliminaries, we are now in a position to study a simple macroeconomic model. Suppose

$$Y = cY + \dot{K} + \delta K \qquad 0 < c < 1 \qquad \delta > 0$$
$$(3.2.4a)$$

$$Y = a_0 + a_1 K \qquad a_0 > 0 \qquad a_1 > 0 \qquad (3.2.4b)$$

$$M/P = b_1 Y - b_2 r \qquad b_1 > 0 \qquad b_2 > 0 \qquad (3.2.4c)$$

$$r = a_1 + \pi \qquad (3.2.4d)$$

Equation (3.2.4a) argues that demand for aggregate output Y depends on consumption which is simply related to income, net investment $\dot{K}$ which acts to increase the real capital stock K, and replacement investment δK which is assumed proportional to the existing capital stock through the proportional depreciation rate δ. Equation (3.2.4b) argues that the supply of real output is an increasing function of the capital stock. Equation (3.2.4c) describes the demand for real money balances, nominal money M deflated by the price level P, depending positively on real income Y and negatively on the nominal interest rate r. Equation (3.2.4d) decomposes nominal interest into perfectly expected inflation π and the real interest rate. For simplicity, I assume that the latter is merely the marginal product of capital in equation (3.2.4b).

From these equations, we infer the usual IS/LM relations. Equating the supply and demand for output, we obtain the IS equation

$$\dot{K} = a_0(1-c) + [a_1(1-c) - \delta]K \qquad (3.2.5)$$

while from equations (3.2.4b) — (3.2.4d) we obtain the LM equation for money market clearing

$$M/P = (b_1 a_0 - b_2 a_1) + b_1 a_1 K - b_2 \pi \qquad (3.2.6)$$

To complete the model, we specify government policy for supplying nominal money M. For simplicity, I assume that the nominal money supply is increased at the constant proportional rate θ. The proportional rate of change of real money balances, being the difference between the rate of change of nominal money and the rate of change of prices, is given by

$$(\dot{M/P})/(M/P) = \theta - \pi \qquad (3.2.7)$$

To analyse this model under the assumption of perfect foresight, let us construct the phase diagram, which is shown in Figure 3.2.4. Consider first the locus, along which $\dot{K} = 0$.

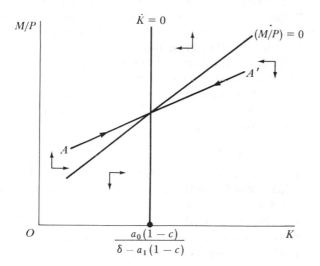

Figure 3.2.4

From equation (3.2.5) we then have

$$K = \frac{a_0(1-c)}{\delta - a_1(1-c)} \qquad (3.2.8)$$

which implies only one value of K allows $\dot{K} = 0$. Intuitively, when net investment equals zero, only one value of K ensures that replacement investment exactly matches the excess of output over consumption in a model where output and consumption depend only on K itself. I assume that δ exceeds $a_1(1-c)$ so that the implied value of K is positive. In a more realistic model, which allowed a diminishing marginal product of capital, sufficiently large outputs would ensure a value of the parameter a_1 consistent with the above assumption.

Thus in Figure 3.2.4, the $\dot{K} = 0$ locus is a vertical line through the value of K given in equation (3.2.8). To the right of this locus, $\dot{K}$ is negative and the arrows of motion point horizontally to the left in the K-direction. This follows from equation (3.2.5) which makes clear that larger values of K reduce the value of $\dot{K}$, given the assumption that δ exceeds $a_1(1-c)$. Conversely, to the left of the locus, the arrows of motion point horizontally to the right in the K-direction. Intuitively, larger stocks of capital K add more to replacement investment than to the excess of output over consumption demand, requiring a reduction in the net investment $\dot{K}$ to maintain goods market clearing.

Consider next the locus along which real money balances M/P remain constant. From equation (3.2.7) this requires that the inflation rate π equals the rate of nominal money growth θ. From equation (3.2.6), the equation for the locus $(\dot{M/P}) = 0$ is therefore given by

$$M/P = (b_1 a_0 - b_2 a_1) - b_2 \theta + b_1 a_1 K \qquad (3.2.9)$$

For a given level of θ, this locus slopes upwards in Figure 3.2.4. With $\pi = \theta$, inflation is constant, as are nominal interest rates through equation (3.2.4d). A higher capital stock is associated with higher real output and a higher demand for real money balances. Pick any point on this locus and consider moving horizontally to the right, increasing K while maintaining M/P. At all points, the demand for real

balances is given by equation (3.2.6). Since real balances are
maintained unchanged, the increase in demand for real
balances induced by higher K and hence higher real output
must be offset by a higher inflation rate π to raise nominal
interest rates. Hence, to the right of the locus along which
real balances are constant, π must exceed θ. Consequently,
real balances are falling, since nominal money growth fails to
keep pace with inflation. Thus, we draw an arrow pointing
vertically downwards in the M/P direction to the right of this
locus. Conversely, to the left of the locus, real balances are
increasing and the arrows point vertically upwards.

Figure 3.2.4 exhibits the Saddlepoint property since the
K arrows point towards the relevant locus $\dot{K} = 0$, while the
M/P arrows point away from the locus along which real
balances are constant. The unique perfect foresight convergent path is given by AA'. Assume a gestation period for
investment, so that the capital stock is instantaneously given
by previous investment decisions. Given a base level of
nominal money M and an announced growth rate θ, there
exists a unique choice of the price level P to place the economy on the convergent path with the correct level of real
money balances vertically above the predetermined stock of
real capital inherited from the past.

Within this framework, we can analyse the effects of
monetary policy. Suppose the economy is proceeding along
the path AA'. At some date there is a previously unanticipated once and for all jump in the level of nominal money,
but thereafter the rate of money growth remains θ as before.
Since the jump was unanticipated, we need not consider its
effects before the date at which it takes place. When the
jump occurs, the economy has a level of capital which is
instantaneously given. From Figure 3.2.4 we infer that the
level of real money balances required to place the economy
on the path AA' is exactly what it would have been in the
absence of the unanticipated jump, for none of the equations
from which Figure 3.2.4 was constructed has been altered
by the jump itself. Hence the jump in nominal money must
be accompanied by a contemporaneous jump in the price
level to maintain real balances at the required level. Thereafter, the economy evolves along AA' as it would have done

in the absence of the jump. Thus a once and for all increase in the money stock which is previously unanticipated but immediately recognised is neutral in the sense that it leads to an equivalent jump in the price level, leaving all real variables following the path they would otherwise have pursued.

Next, consider the consequences of changing the rate of money growth, rather than the base level of the money stock. Imagine that the economy is on the convergent path AA' with capital stock K_0 when it is confronted with a previously unanticipated decision to raise permanently the money growth rate to θ_1. Since θ does not enter equation (3.2.5) the $\dot{K} = 0$ locus is unaffected by any change in θ, but the locus $M/P = 0$ must be redrawn. From equation (3.2.9), higher rates of money growth, inflation and nominal interest rates imply a lower level of real money balances for any level of the capital stock and real output. Thus, when θ_1 becomes relevant, the locus $M/P = 0$ shifts down as in Figure 3.2.5. When the policy of faster money growth is first adopted, it requires a higher price level to deflate nominal money balances to the new lower level of real money balances which place the economy on the new convergent path BB'. Thereafter, the economy evolves along this path until the steady state is approached.

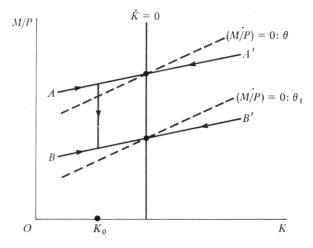

Figure 3.2.5

Both these examples of a previously unanticipated change in monetary policy illustrate a general principle which we shall encounter frequently in later chapters. While information about the structure of the economy and the nature of government policy remains unaltered, the economy proceeds smoothly along the perfect foresight convergent path. However, when new information becomes available, the immediate response is a jump to the new convergent path, after which behaviour is again continuous until further new information becomes available.

Thus far I have taken monetary policy to specify a rule for the path of the nominal money supply. Sargent and Wallace (1975) emphasised the contrast between the stable convergence which such policies allow and the unstable behaviour which might prevail under the alternative specification of monetary policy, in which it is assumed that the authorities adopt a target path for nominal interest rates, supplying whatever nominal money is required to clear the market at those interest rates. This analysis provides strong justification for the Monetarist claim that central banks should adopt money supply targets rather than interest rate targets.

To illustrate the argument, I replace the assumption of constant money growth at the rate θ by the assumption that money is supplied to enforce the constant interest rate $\bar{r}$. The IS equation (3.2.5) is unaltered by the amendment to monetary policy. The $\dot{K} = 0$ locus may be drawn as in previous diagrams and the usual argument implies that capital will be falling to the right of this locus and rising to the left of the locus. Using equation (3.2.4d), the LM equation (3.2.6) now becomes

$$M/P = b_1 a_0 + b_1 a_1 K - b_2 \bar{r} \qquad (3.2.10)$$

When interest rates are held constant the dynamic structure is greatly simplified. Figure 3.2.6 plots the LM equation on which the economy must always lie if the money market is to clear. Because we already know the arrows of motion for the capital stock K, we can infer the direction of change of real money balances to maintain the economy on the LM equation: the convergent path becomes the LM equation itself. Given a predetermined level of capital, we can infer the

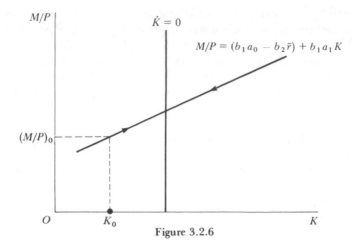

Figure 3.2.6

level of real money balances to place the economy on this path, but that is insufficient to pin down the nominal values of money and prices. Let K_0 be the predetermined level of capital and $(M/P)_0$ the corresponding level of real balances when the interest target $\bar{r}$ is adopted. If individuals believe that the initial price level will be P_0, the government may then infer the level of nominal money to supply in order to provide the correct level of real money balances. However, if individuals believe the initial price level will be $2P_0$, the government will simply provide twice the initial level of nominal money. Although Figure 3.2.6 establishes a unique level of *real* money balances, it is compatible with an infinite number of choices for the initial price level, each being matched by a corresponding supply of nominal money. A unique perfect foresight equilibrium path does not exist. Even if some price level were arbitrarily adopted at the initial date and the corresponding supply of nominal money made available, there would be little guarantee that subsequent inflation would be at the rate $(\bar{r} - a_1)$ which equation (3.2.4d) implies. That is one possibility, but the knowledge that government is committed to accommodate any subsequent jumps in the price level to maintain the path of real money balances at the target interest rate $\bar{r}$ would considerably weaken the belief that future inflation rates could be correctly anticipated. It is this insight which underlies the Monetarist policy prescription.

3.3 The Rational Expectations Equilibrium Path

In the previous section I analysed a simple macroeconomic model with perfect foresight. When uncertainty is admitted, the essential structure of the problem remains the same. Consider an equation relating two endogenous variables y and x

$$y = jx + u \qquad (3.3.1)$$

where j is constant and u is a purely random variable whose mean is zero. Let the superscript e denote individuals' subjective expectations which, under the hypothesis of Rational Expectations, are precisely the mathematical expectations formed by using the model itself conditional on information available at the date expectations are formed. For the equation above,

$$y^e = j x^e + u^e = j x^e \qquad (3.3.2)$$

where we suppose that individuals know that the mathematical expectation of u is zero. Thus $y^e = j x^e$. Individuals obtain particular values for these expectations by solving the model over all future time, as they did under perfect foresight. For example, in the previous section we studied a macroeconomic model in which the perfect foresight path assumed the continued relevance of the IS and LM relations describing goods market and money market clearing at each future date and assumed convergence to the steady state which these relations implied. When the presence of uncertainty leads to a stochastic specification of the model, we simply replace these assumptions by the assumption that individuals expect goods and money market clearing at all future dates and expect convergence to the steady state which these relations imply.

When the solution of a stochastic model differs from the solution of a deterministic or non-random model only in the trivial respect that actual values of future variables are replaced by current expectations of these future variables, we say that the random model exhibits *Certainty Equivalence*. The functional form and parameter values of the solutions to the two models are the same. Analysis of the model as if under perfect foresight will then display the essential structure of the solution to the analogous stochastic model under Rational Expectations. Since many of the models studied in this book exhibit Certainty Equivalence, it was convenient to introduce the ideas of dynamic analysis in the context of a model with perfect foresight. Admitting uncertainty leads merely to random fluctuations around the path discussed in the previous section.

Before substantiating this claim, it is important to discuss the conditions under which Certainty Equivalence is likely to obtain. Equation (3.3.1) has two key aspects: it is linear and it contains an additive random disturbance with mean zero. When both these conditions hold, Certainty Equivalence will obtain, as in Equation (3.3.2) in which the equation $y^e = jx^e$ has the same structure as would obtain under perfect foresight in a deterministic model, when we might specify the equation analogous to equation (3.3.1) as $y = jx$. A famous statistical theorem known as *Jensen's Inequality* emphasises the importance of the assumption of linearity. If y is a function of two random variables such as x and z, the mathematical expectation of any non-linear function such as $y = x/z$ is *not* the mathematical expectation of x divided by the mathematical expectation of z. Only for linear functions such as $y = j_1 x + j_2 z$ can we say that $y^e = j_1 x^e + j_2 z^e$. Because the expectation of non-linear functions is considerably more complicated, the literature on Rational Expectations typically adopts linear specifications. As will become apparent, a convenient trick which converts non-linear models into linear specifications which will allow Certainty Equivalence is to assume a particular functional form, namely that non-linear equations may be written as linear in logarithms.

These ideas may be introduced within a collapsed version of the macroeconomic model studied in the previous section, the so-called Hyperinflation model postulated by Cagan (1956). Nominal variables are changing so quickly relative to real variables that the latter may conveniently be treated as fixed. Though originally introduced to study data from countries actually experiencing very high levels of inflation, the model has become popular as an expositional device and it is for this reason that I now adopt it. In principle, the following analysis may be reworked within the context of more general models.

Let m be the logarithm of the nominal money stock M and p the logarithm of the price level P. The logarithm of real money balances M/P is thus $m - p$. Under perfect foresight, the inflation rate π is exactly $\dot{P}/P$, the proportional rate of change of prices. Mathematically this is exactly $\dot{p}$, the absolute rate of change of the logarithm of the price level. Treating capital and output as constant, we rewrite the LM equation (3.2.6) in the particular form

$$m - p = b_3 - b_2 \dot{p} \qquad b_2 > 0 \qquad b_3 > 0 \qquad (3.3.3)$$

to show the dependence of the demand for real balances on the inflation rate $\dot{p}$.

Higher inflation reduces the demand for real balances by raising nominal interest rates. Assume a constant rate of nominal money growth θ, sufficiently large to justify the hyperinflation assumption. Thus $\dot{M}/M = \dot{m} = \theta$. Hence the rate of change of real money balances is given by

$$\dot{m} - \dot{p} = \theta - \dot{p} \qquad (3.3.4)$$

The dynamic behaviour of this economy under perfect foresight is shown in Figure 3.3.1 overleaf. Given continuous clearing of the money market, the economy is always on the downward sloping line representing equation (3.3.3). In the steady state real money balances must be constant. From equation (3.3.4), the steady state inflation rate must be θ and the economy will then be at point C. If inflation $\dot{p}$ exceeds θ, real money balances are falling since nominal money growth fails to match inflation. To the right of the point C real money balances are falling, to the left of the point C they are rising. This establishes the arrows of motion along the LM equation. Since the steady state is Globally Unstable, any path which does not begin at

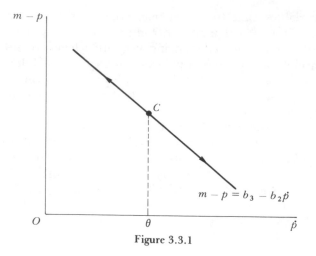

Figure 3.3.1

C will necessarily explode. Hence the unique perfect fore-sight path is to choose the price level such that

$$m - p = b_3 - b_2 \theta \tag{3.3.5}$$

taking the economy immediately to the steady state. There-after, prices rise at the rate θ, maintaining the economy in the steady state.

Having understood the hyperinflation model under perfect foresight, we may now study the analogous stochastic model under Rational Expectations. Rather than work in continuous time, it is now more convenient to work in discrete time periods since the statistical theory of continuous time stochastic processes is a little tricky. I now assume that the LM equation (3.3.3) becomes

$$m_t - p_t = b_3 - b_2({}_tp^e_{t+1} - p_t) + u_t \qquad b_2 > 0$$
$$b_3 > 0 \tag{3.3.6}$$

where the subscript t denotes the time period under study and ${}_tp^e_{t+1}$ denotes the Rational Expectation of p_{t+1} con-ditional on information available at time t. u_t is a random dis-turbance with mean zero. The demand for real money balances depends on expected inflation and on a random disturbance. Notice, crucially, that equation (3.3.6) is linear and has an additive disturbance term. *Ex ante*, we expect to derive a result which exhibits Certainty Equivalence.

In discrete time, the constant rate of money growth implies

$$m_t = m_{t-1} + \theta \tag{3.3.7}$$

We now wish to solve the model given by equations (3.3.6) and (3.3.7) under Rational Expectations. Two methods are used in the literature. The first method is known as the method of undetermined coefficients. This requires us to guess the solution and then confirm that it does indeed satisfy the above equations. After some practice at solving Rational Expectations models, readers may find this method straightforward. I prefer to describe the second method, not only because it offers a systematic approach to those less familiar with the literature, but also because it makes clear the implicit assumptions of the solution procedure and may be conveniently related to the earlier diagrammatic treatment of stability.

Rearranging equation (3.3.6)

$$p_t = \left(\frac{1}{1+b_2}\right)(m_t - b_3 - u_t) + \frac{b_2}{1+b_2}(_tp_{t+1}^e) \tag{3.3.8}$$

which again says merely that the market clears at time t. Under Rational Expectations, individuals acting as if they knew the structure of the model must expect a similar equation to hold at time $t + 1$, since they expect the money market to clear then also. Shifting all subscripts in equation (3.3.8) one period forward

$$p_{t+1} = \left(\frac{1}{1+b_2}\right)(m_{t+1} - b_3 - u_{t+1})$$
$$+ \frac{b_2}{1+b_2}(_{t+1}p_{t+2}^e) \tag{3.3.9}$$

where $_{t+1}p_{t+2}^e$ is the expectation of p_{t+2} conditional on information at time $t + 1$. Knowing the structure of this equation, individuals at time t form expectations about what is likely to happen at time $t + 1$

$$_t p_{t+1}^e = \left(\frac{1}{1+b_2}\right)\left(_t m_{t+1}^e - b_3 - {}_t u_{t+1}^e\right)$$

$$+ \frac{b_2}{1+b_2}\left[_t\left(_{t+1} p_{t+2}^e\right)^e\right]$$

$$= \frac{1}{1+b_2}\left(m_t + \theta - b_3\right) + \frac{b_2}{1+b_2}\left(_t p_{t+2}^e\right)$$

$$(3.3.10)$$

To proceed from the first line to the second line, three steps are involved. First, individuals know the money supply rule and use this at time t to guess m_{t+1}. Secondly, at time t there is no basis for forecasting deviations of u_{t+1} from its mean value of zero. Thirdly, the best guess at time t about what individuals at time $t + 1$ will expect for the price level in the following period is merely the best guess at time t for p_{t+2}.

By identical reasoning, individuals at time t expect the money market to clear at time $t + 2$ and their best guess about what will happen two periods later is given by

$$_t p_{t+2}^e = \frac{1}{1+b_2}\left(_t m_{t+2}^e - b_3 - {}_t u_{t+2}^e\right)$$

$$+ \frac{b_2}{1+b_2}\left(_t p_{t+3}^e\right) = \frac{1}{1+b_2}\left(m_t + 2\theta - b_3\right)$$

$$+ \frac{b_2}{1+b_2}\left(_t p_{t+3}^e\right) \qquad (3.3.11)$$

Equation (3.3.10) expresses $_t p_{t+1}^e$ in terms of $_t p_{t+2}^e$, while equation (3.3.11) expresses $_t p_{t+2}^e$ in terms of $_t p_{t+3}^e$. Recognising that individuals at time t expect market clearing at all future dates, we keep expressing $_t p_{t+k}^e$ in terms of $_t p_{t+k+1}^e$, substituting out the unobservable expectation by going successively forwards. Since the coefficient on the next expectation in equations like (3.3.10) and (3.3.11) is $b_2/(1+b_2)$, each substitution involves a multiple of this positive fraction. Thus, after $N - 1$ substitutions, we obtain from equation (3.3.10)

$$tp^e_{t+1} = \left(\frac{1}{1+b_2}\right)(m_t - b_3)\left[1 + \left(\frac{b_2}{1+b_2}\right)\right.$$

$$\left.+ \left(\frac{b_2}{1+b_2}\right)^2 + \ldots + \left(\frac{b_2}{1+b_2}\right)^{N-1}\right]$$

$$+ \left(\frac{\theta}{1+b_2}\right)\left[1 + 2\left(\frac{b_2}{1+b_2}\right) + 3\left(\frac{b_2}{1+b_2}\right)^2\right.$$

$$\left.+ 4\left(\frac{b_2}{1+b_2}\right)^3 + \ldots N\left(\frac{b_2}{1+b_2}\right)^{N-1}\right]$$

$$+ \left(\frac{b_2}{1+b_2}\right)^N (tp^e_{t+N+1}) \tag{3.3.12}$$

The reader might like to check that when $N = 1$ we simply recover equation (3.3.10).

This looks very messy, but it is actually very simple. Since $b_2/(1+b_2)$ is a positive fraction, $[b_2/(1+b_2)]^N$ tends to zero as we look further and further into the future. Provided tp^e_{t+N+1} is not 'too large', we can eventually ignore the unobservable final term in the above equation. The first set of terms multiplying $(m_t - b_3)$ represents a convergent geometric series. For any positive fraction α, the series

$$1 + \alpha + \alpha^2 + \alpha^3 + \alpha^4 + \alpha^5 + \ldots + \alpha^N$$

converges to $1/(1-\alpha)$ as N tends to infinity. Similarly, the second set of terms multiplying $\theta/(1 + b_2)$ converges. If S denotes the series $1 + 2\alpha + 3\alpha^2 + 4\alpha^3 + 5\alpha^4 \ldots$, then

$$S - \alpha S = 1 + \alpha + \alpha^2 + \alpha^3 + \ldots$$

Hence S converges to $[1/(1-\alpha)]^2$. Over the infinite future the expression (3.3.12) converges to

$$tp^e_{t+1} = \left(\frac{1}{1+b_2}\right)(m_t - b_3)\left[\frac{1}{1 - \dfrac{b_2}{1+b_2}}\right]$$

$$+ \left(\frac{\theta}{1+b_2}\right)\left[\frac{1}{1 - \dfrac{b_2}{1+b_2}}\right]^2$$

which simplifies to

$$_t p_{t+1}^e = m_t - b_3 + (1 + b_2)\theta \qquad (3.3.13)$$

Having obtained the Rational Expectations solution, we insert this in the LM equation (3.3.8)

$$p_t = m_t - b_3 + b_2\theta - \left(\frac{1}{1 + b_2}\right) u_t \qquad (3.3.14)$$

This expression makes clear the dependence of the endogenous current price level on the current value taken on by the random term u_t capturing non-systematic influences on money demand at time t.

Since the choice of a particular date t is arbitrary, equation (3.3.14) must describe the behaviour of the price level in all periods. At a particular time t, individuals realise that the price level at time $t + 1$ will obey

$$p_{t+1} = m_{t+1} - b_3 + b_2\theta - \left(\frac{1}{1 + b_2}\right) u_{t+1} \qquad (3.3.15)$$

Taking expectations conditional on information available at time t,

$$_t p_{t+1}^e = m_t + \theta - b_3 + b_2\theta$$

since at time t the expectation of u_{t+1} is its mean value of zero. But this expression is precisely equation (3.3.13), which confirms that we have indeed discovered the Rational Expectations solution: when the expectations are used to determine current and future behaviour, here money demand, they generate an expected path for endogenous variables, here the price level, which fulfils the expectations. Behaviour is internally consistent and knowable forecasting errors are avoided. Comparing equations (3.3.13) and (3.3.15),

$$p_{t+1} - \left(_t p_{t+1}^e\right) = - \left(\frac{1}{1 + b_2}\right) u_{t+1}$$

This *ex post* forecasting error has zero expectation at time t. Only the inevitable randomness of the model generates forecasting errors, but individuals at time t can do no better than to assume the random disturbance takes on its mean value of zero.

Having described the solution to the hyperinflation model under Rational Expectations, I now wish to relate this solution to the previous analysis of the same model under perfect foresight. If u_t happens to take on its mean value of zero, equation (3.3.14) implies

$$m_t = p_t + b_3 - b_2\theta$$

Expectations at time $t - 1$ will then have been fulfilled. Comparing this expression with equation (3.3.5) we confirm that this solution is precisely the solution derived under perfect foresight, in which it was shown that the economy would proceed immediately to the steady state level of real money balances. More generally, from equation (3.3.14) the actual level of real money balances deviates from this level only because of unavoidable forecasting errors induced by deviations of u_t from its mean value of zero. This confirms the property of Certainty Equivalence. The introduction of uncertainty has not led to a fundamentally different solution but merely to random deviations around the perfect foresight path. Because of the linear structure of the model, the simpler analysis under perfect foresight would have conveyed the essential structure of the solution path without resort to the more complicated algebra associated with the Rational Expectations solution.

It is also possible to relate the algebraic steps used in the Rational Expectations solution to the earlier analysis by phase diagrams. The messy expression (3.3.12) simplifies to the simple expression (3.3.13) only if two conditions hold. First, the series multiplying the first two terms in equation (3.3.12) must converge. This condition holds if b_2 is positive as I have assumed. Suppose b_2 was negative. The LM equation in Figure 3.3.1 would then slope upwards as in Figure 3.3.2 below.

The previous argument based on equation (3.3.4) still implies that when $\dot{p}$ exceeds the steady state rate θ, real money balances must be falling. The arrows of motion then imply that the steady state is Globally Stable with an infinite number of convergent perfect foresight paths. When a unique perfect foresight path does not exist, the algebraic symptom is the explosive behaviour of the series obtained by recursively eliminating future expectations in expressions such as

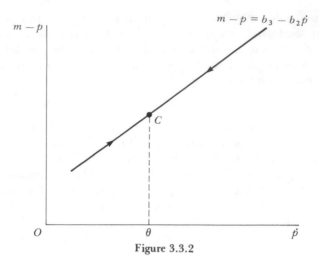

Figure 3.3.2

equation (3.1.12). Conversely, the condition that such series converge is equivalent to the stability condition discussed earlier. In the degenerate hyperinflation model, this requires that the steady state be Globally Unstable. In more general models in which certain real variables are predetermined, the corresponding condition is the Saddlepoint property.

The second condition which is required if equations such as (3.3.12) are to simplify to equations such as (3.3.13) is that the final term, the unobservable expectation at some far off date, tends to zero as we consider a sufficiently long time horizon. This will always be true if we select the particular path which converges to the steady state, but will be incorrect if we select an explosive path. I have already discussed the justification for selecting the convergent path and hence for ignoring the final term in equations such as (3.3.12). By avoiding the need for tedious algebra and allowing a more intuitive understanding of the assumptions implicitly adopted, the diagrammatic approach frequently offers a convenient method of analysis in linear stochastic models which exhibit Certainty Equivalence.

3.4 The Plausibility of Rational Expectations as a Model of Actual Behaviour

Before turning to applications of the Rational Expectations hypothesis I wish to examine whether the hypothesis offers a convincing account of the process by which individuals actually form expectations. It may be useful to begin by restating the argument of the preceding sections.

It is not attractive to assume that individuals make systematic errors in forming expectations, for such errors would eventually be discovered and would cause individuals to abandon the assumed rule of expectations formation. Macroeconomic models should recognise this, generating endogenous expectations without systematic error by imagining that individuals act as if they knew the systematic part of the model, including the government sector, and use this to form expectations. When the model is dynamic, behaviour in one period depends in part on behaviour expected in subsequent periods, so that the model must be applied to all future periods if a consistent or self-fulfilling set of expectations is to be derived. If a number of different paths converge to the steady state it will not be possible to provide a convincing description of the particular expectations adopted. While nothing in economic theory rules out this possibility, there exists a wide class of models in which only one convergent path is possible — namely when the steady state is a Saddlepoint. Incentives to speculators and fear of the consequences of explosive behaviour then combine to make likely the adoption of this set of self-fulfilling expectations. In linear models which embody random disturbance terms to reflect uncertainty, the Rational Expectations path will differ only randomly from the perfect foresight path derived in the analogous non-random model, though in principle, a Rational Expectations solution could still be derived in more complicated models not exhibiting Certainty Equivalence. The solution of a stochastic model with Rational Expectations generates expectations which are stochastically self-fulfilling: *ex post* forecasting errors cannot be predicted given the information available at the date expectations are formed. Such expectations may be described as an equilibrium set of expectations, in the sense that there is no incentive to revise the *process* by which expectations are formed, although the expected value of a particular variable will of course be revised as new information becomes available.

Stated thus, it is easy to see why many economists find Rational Expectations an appealing assumption, replacing earlier *ad hoc* treatments with an approach squarely based on incentives, information, and optimisation — the traditional themes of respectable macroeconomic foundations. Nevertheless, it is as well to look a gift-horse in the mouth. A number of economists have argued that Rational Expectations has been accepted uncricitally, not because it assumes too little, but because it assumes too much. It is convenient to organise the objections under four main headings: those which apply even when the structure of the model is correctly perceived; those which dispute that such knowledge could ever be available; those which argue that it would not be profitable ever to acquire such knowledge; and those which emphasise the diversity of expectations because individuals face different costs in acquiring the relevant information.

(a) Objections Applying Even When the Structure of the Model is Correctly Perceived

We have seen that the derivation of the Rational Expectations path requires the consideration of the economy over all future time. The first objection is simply that the computational difficulties will defeat the majority of individuals whose expectations we wish to model. This charge may be countered by two arguments. Even if we concede the literal interpretation of Rational Expectations, in which individuals perform the mental gymnastics required to evaluate the convergent forward looking path, it is not essential that all individuals perform these contortions. Governments, academics, and profit-motivated private institutions all devote considerable effort to model-based forecasting. In most economies these forecasts are widely disseminated in newspapers, on television, by word of mouth, or at a small fee. For example, many of the applications studied in subsequent chapters emphasise the expected inflation rate. In practice, sophisticated estimates of this are widely publicised, being quickly updated as new information becomes available. All that is required is that some credible body undertakes the forecasting exercise.

Alternatively, we may meet the charge of computational difficulty by adopting a more general interpretation of Rational Expectations, an interpretation I myself prefer. The crucial implication of Rational Expectations is that individuals do not make systematic, perceivable forecasting errors which could be used to improve the basis of forecasting. Although on average correct, smart individuals may reason only subconsciously, perceiving themselves to respond only to their innate hunches about what will happen. The elaborate formal solution of a model by identifying the convergent forward path is merely a device by which economists track these hunches and render them consistent with the model in which they are assumed to operate. The appeal of this interpretation is most strong when modelling markets such as financial markets, where the principle of economic Darwinism, the survival of the fittest, is most likely to operate; it is less convincing at the level of an individual household where these incentives operate less strongly. On the other hand, when discussing such disaggregated behaviour one can appeal to the *Law of Large Numbers* which argues that individual idiosyncracies are likely to cancel out in the aggregate, leaving average behaviour rather closer to the implications of the theory.

The second class of objections focuses on the non-uniqueness problems thrown up by the Phase Diagram analysis of Section 3.2. Recall that when the steady state is 'too stable' an infinite number of convergent paths, or non-explosive self-fulfilling expectations, exists. When the steady state is 'insufficiently stable', all paths will explode. Only in the knife-edge Saddlepoint case is the steady state just insufficiently stable that there exists a unique convergent path and hence a unique Rational Expectations solution. Burmeister (1980b) argues that this happy state of affairs is unlikely to apply widely, so that the practical usefulness of the Rational Expectations hypothesis is severely constrained. In one sense, the proof of this particular pudding is in the eating, for we shall discover that a wide range of models do generate the Saddlepoint property. There may also be a more fundamental reason why this objection is less worrying than it first appears. The mathematical digression in Section 3.2 discussed the Saddlepoint property in a general model with n variables, s of which were predetermined at any date. It is certainly true that one needs a particular model structure, with the correct number of variables predetermined, if there is to be a unique convergent path. It is possible to interpret this requirement as a constraint on the types of policies which the government may adopt: government policy rules are part of the economic structure and different policy choices will affect the number of predetermined variables at any date. For example, if there were insufficient predetermined variables, it might be possible for the government to adopt *both* a money supply rule and an interest rate target, leaving the price level and the level of output to clear the money market.

Let us now suppose that the Saddlepoint property occurs as in Figure 3.2.3. In Section 3.2 I argued that fear of explosion and profitable incentives to speculate would then combine to place the economy on the unique convergent path, but this argument has been challenged. Suppose, for example, we recognise that individuals have finite lives. It may then be more profitable to embark on an explosive path recognising that some subsequent generation, as yet unrepresented, will eventually have to jump back on to the convergent path rather than face indefinite explosion. Given the need to seek regular re-election, governments may also view their lives as finite, and perhaps rather short, and may connive at or positively encourage behaviour which is temporarily explosive. As Keynes emphasised, the economy must be dominated by long-sighted speculators if such pressures are to be resisted and it is at least arguable whether this is the case. The more widely understood is the model, the more likely it becomes that a return to the convergent path occurs sooner rather than later. Explosive behaviour, known in the literature as a 'speculative bubble', occurs most frequently when information is scarce. In stochastic models which allow random deviations around the perfect foresight path it may still be reasonable to emphasise the convergent path, provided such bubbles do not persist for very long.

(b) *Objections Based on the Impossibility of Discovering the Correct Model*

Another class of objections emphasises the difficulty of establishing the precise nature of the model to be used to form expectations. To the extent that such objections emphasise disagreements about the structure of the underlying model, I postpone discussion until Section (d) below. For the moment, I wish merely to examine the problems which would confront a population attempting a common research programme to determine the exact nature of the world in which they lived. The first issue is that of *Statistical Identification*, whether in principle it is possible to disentangle from the data separate estimates of all the relevant theoretical parameters of the model. This issue is not a trivial one: expectations based on an incorrect view of the model will affect behaviour and hence the data to be used in empirical work which seeks to quantify the model itself. The Identification problem is discussed in the following two chapters, in which it is shown that many models will allow the parameters to be estimated from economic data, but that it is always possible to conceive of such a sufficiently complicated dynamic structure that Identification is impossible. Although such problems are perhaps more acute in models with Rational Expectations, it should be emphasised that many conventional models raise similar problems. Indeed, the Rational Expectations assumption may sometimes aid Identification, because of the precise way in which it is asserted that expectations are formed. It is therefore impossible to draw any general conclusions; the answer will depend on the particular model under consideration.

One case has received a good deal of attention in the literature. Suppose that individuals have discovered the structure of the model, including the nature of the policy rules in operation. Such policy rules may have random disturbance terms like any other equation in the model. Government behaviour is not always predictable or systematic, even if it tends to obey certain principles. Now suppose the government adopts a different policy rule. It is argued that it will take some time for individuals to learn the new rule, since initially they will tend to regard unexpected government behaviour merely as evidence of random deviations from the original policy rule. As time elapses, it will become less and less plausible to suppose the original rule remains in operation and only gradually will individuals discover the basis of the new policy. Not only will there be a transition phase during which perception of the model is incorrect and expectations irrational in the sense that forecasting errors are systematic, but in addition the discovery of the model through empirical econometrics is frustrated both by the need to model switches in policy and by the presence of transitional periods in which expectations bear little relation to the policy then in operation.

Even committed supporters of Rational Expectations recognise that this objection has some force, but it is possible to cite two arguments in mitigation. First, it is easy to overestimate the extent of switches in policy rule. For example, it is not sufficient to note that a period of rising money supply has been followed by a period of falling money supply. The form of the monetary rule might be quite complicated, for example

$$m_t = p_{t-1} + \beta_1 (p_{t-1} - p_{t-2}) + \beta_2 y_{t-1} + \beta_3 y_{t-2}$$

where m, p and y denote the logarithms of nominal money, prices, and output. Current money supply might exhibit all kinds of behaviour over time, provided only that the past variables on which it systematically depends behave in the appropriate manner. Secondly, important changes in the nature of government policy are usually widely publicised as the government attempts to obtain political support for the policy change.

A more difficult problem is the degree of belief in the policy. For example, when a new government is elected on a manifesto of tight monetary policy, a period of suspicion may be followed by a period of credibility, followed by a period in which it is increasingly expected that the policy will be relaxed as the election approaches. Even if the same policy is pursued throughout, views about the likelihood of the policy being maintained may change quite radically.

If these remarks strike a chord, the reader should note that it is a great merit of the Rational Expectations approach that it forces us to confront such intractable yet important issues, which tend to be ignored by *ad hoc* expectations assumptions such as those which extrapolate the past. The Rational Expectations models which I discuss are still very simple models embracing single-valued expectations. In principle, it is possible to adopt more general definitions: one might define expectations to be Rational when individuals consider a whole range of possible outcomes, attaching to each a subjective probability which indeed reflects the objective mathematical probability conditional on the information available at the time. Such models are on the agenda for the second phase of the Rational Expectations revolution, but take us beyond the scope of this book.

(c) *Objections Challenging the Incentive to Acquire the Assumed Information*

Whereas the objections above challenge the possibility of obtaining the relevant amount of information, the objections I now discuss accept that it is possible to acquire this information, but argue that it may not be profitable to do so. Improving the quality of information about the structure of the economy will generally be a costly activity which will be pursued only up to the point at which marginal benefits from better information equal the marginal costs of obtaining it. Thus it is unlikely that it will ever be profitable or rational to obtain complete information. Without a more detailed examination of these costs and benefits, it is hard to decide how much information will be collected. While the assumption of any particular information is therefore arbitrary, many models implicitly assume that the relevant information set is precisely the widely available public information used by economists in empirical specifications of the model itself.

The need for further analysis of the process of information collection has recently been emphasised by Grossman and Stiglitz (1980) using the following *reductio ad absurdum*. In applying the Rational Expectations hypothesis to asset markets, the literature on Efficient Markets considered in Chapter 8 argues that all relevant information should already be reflected in asset prices for, otherwise, there would exist an incentive to buy or sell the asset until this condition was met. However, if asset prices fully reflect available information, individuals need not undertake the costly activity of information collection, they need only observe the asset price and infer the relevant information; if all individuals adopt the same line of reasoning, new information will never be profitable to collect.

It is not clear that this constitutes a decisive objection to the Rational Expectations approach which I examine in subsequent chapters. Incentives to collect and process information remain important, because they confer a temporary advantage which allows greater profit opportunities until the information is widely available and markets fully reflect this new information. If one wishes to emphasise the process of information collection, it will certainly be essential to model the sequence of trades which occur during the temporary period in which different agents have access to different information, just as the demand for money as a medium of exchange can be properly understood only if one models the sequence of trades by which individuals convert income or endowment into final expenditure. In either case, we may nevertheless be able to offer an interesting analysis of the equilibrium to which such behaviour converges, without explicit analysis of the process by which that equilibrium is reached.

(d) Objections Emphasising Differential Information

It is often argued that the Rational Expectations approach cannot hope to describe a world in which there are fundamental disagreements about the true model, as for example between Monetarist and Keynesian views about market clearing. Again, I view this not as a criticism of the approach, but as a reminder that there remains much to do. It is certainly possible to specify more general models in which there is sufficient disaggregation to allow different groups to have different information and form different expectations. Already we have simple examples of such models, for example when individuals in different industries or markets know more about the price ruling in their own market than about the price level in general. Such differences persist because information is costly to collect. By a Rational Expectations equilibrium we then mean a path along which individuals cannot improve their forecasting by using the information which they cheaply acquire. Where differential information is likely to be important, we expect disaggregation to lead to more realistic models. Until such models have been fully developed, we cannot rigorously test whether these models perform better than models which treat information as shared and expectations as unanimous. However, the latter class of models remains of interest. In subsequent chapters, I will argue that the results of these models are sufficiently promising to justify a continuing research programme along the lines set out above.

(e) Conclusion

Economic theory necessarily involves some simplification. Useful theories make powerful simplifications to yield sharp predictions which are not falsified by the data. The Rational Expectations paradigm is undoubtedly a powerful one whose striking implications will shortly be discussed. What the reader must decide is whether the above objections, taken together, amount to a conclusive refutation of the very basis of the hypothesis.

In my judgment, even the simplest versions of models with Rational Expectations produce such striking results that they deserve extensive theoretical study and empirical testing. While not literally correct, the paradigm may offer a more useful rule of thumb to working economists than any approach yet elaborated. A systematic assessment of the results to date will contribute to the information widely available to economists. These preliminary results are more than sufficient to justify a consolidation and extension of the Rational Expectations revolution. I have also argued that the real issues raised in objection to the simple hypothesis have become apparent only since economists began to think within the terms of the paradigm itself. Thus they challenge the simplicity of existing models rather than the programme of research. I have indicated the responses which are currently being pursued. For the remainder of this book, I confine my attention to the simpler models in which the key insights were first developed.

Notes on the Literature

An elementary introduction to differential equations and stability problems is Chiang(1974). Boyce and DiPrima(1977) give a clear statement of more advanced results. Explicit treatments of the phase diagram approach to the Perfect Foresight path include Begg(1980) and Burmeister(1980b). For an earlier application in a different context the reader might consult the literature on growth models with heterogeneous capital goods, for example Hahn(1966) and Shell and Stiglitz(1967).

Sargent and Wallace(1973a) provide a more detailed treatment of the hyperinflation model under Perfect Foresight. Uniqueness problems and other technical issues are also discussed in Black(1974), Gourieroux, Laffont and Monfort(1979), McCallum(1981), Blanchard(1979), Blanchard and Kahn(1980), Taylor(1977) and Wallace(1980). Keynes (1936) Chapter 12 and Keynes(1937) should also be re-read.

The important survey article by Shiller(1978) includes a forceful statement of many of the objections to the Rational Expectations hypothesis. Fellner(1980) and Haberler(1980) succinctly summarise some widely held misgivings. The problem of how individuals first learn the information assumed by the hypothesis is studied in Taylor(1975), Blanchard(1976) and DeCanio(1979). Friedman, B.M.(1979) is also criticial of the information assumed by simple Rational Expectations models.

Stochastic differential equation models are widely analysed in other disciplines, of which the most relevant is perhaps the literature on optimal control theory. Chow(1975) provides an excellent introduction to issues such as Certainty Equivalence, forward solutions, and learning about the structure of the model.

4
Rational Expectations and Empirical Research

In the last chapter I set out the hypothesis of Rational Expectations and developed the tools we require for theoretical analysis. The purpose of this chapter is to develop the equivalent tools for empirical analysis. I do not assume that the reader has any prior knowledge of econometric theory; technical issues will be discussed in the next chapter. Rather, I aim to provide a simple introduction to the issues which arise in empirical research on Rational Expectations models, a self-contained discussion which will allow the reader to assess the evidence cited in subsequent chapters.

In Section 4.1 I summarise the statistical properties which follow from the analysis of Chapter 3, since much of the empirical work attempts to establish whether these properties are satisfied by the data. Section 4.2 discusses the problem of Statistical Identification, by which we mean the question of whether separate estimates of the unknown parameters can be disentangled from the data relevant to a particular model. In Section 4.3 I consider the possibility of testing hypotheses about either the process of expectations formation, or the economic structure of the model in which these expectations are embedded. Finally, Section 4.4 points out the devastating criticism of conventional policy analysis made by Lucas (1976) and examines whether a satisfactory response can be offered.

4.1 Statistical Properties of Rational Expectations Models

Rational Expectations are the true mathematical expectations implied by the model, conditional on the information assumed available at the time expectations must be formed. Let I_t denote the information set available at time t. This information set has three components: knowledge of the structure of the model; knowledge of government policies in operation; and knowledge of the past values of economic variables. In Chapter 3, I used the notation $_t y_{t+k}^e$ to denote the Rational Expectation at time t of the variable y at time $t + k$. In more detail, we might write this as $E(y_{t+k} | I_t)$ to emphasise that it is conditional on the information I_t available at time t. I now state four properties of Rational Expectations models which follow from the analysis of Chapter 3.

Property I: $E\{[E(y_{t+i+j} \mid I_{t+i})] \mid I_t\} = E(y_{t+i+j} \mid I_t)$ (4.1.1)

The right hand side is the best guess of individuals at time t about the value of y at time $t + i + j$. The left hand side is the best guess of individuals at time t about what they will expect for the same value y_{t+i+j} at some intermediate date $t + i$. If individuals at time t knew they would have changed their minds by time $t + i$, they would be knowably mistaken at time t. Property I asserts that individuals have no basis for predicting how they will change their expectations about future variables such as y_{t+i+j}.

Property II: $E\{[y_{t+i} - E(y_{t+i} \mid I_t)] \mid S_t\} = 0$ (4.1.2)

Let S_t be some subset at time t of the full information set I_t actually used by individuals at that date. *Ex post,* actual forecasting errors are given by $y_{t+i} - E(y_{t+i} \mid I_t)$. Property II states that this forecasting error is uncorrelated with each and every component S_t of the information set I_t. This property has obvious empirical applications, since we can attempt to check whether forecasting errors are correlated with particular pieces of information clearly available at the date expectations were formed. Property II assures us that it is unnecessary to collect data on all the information used to form expectations and allows simpler tests of the Rational Expectations hypothesis. Examples of such tests are presented in Chapters 6–8.

Property II asserts that no information available at the date expectations are formed may be used systematically to improve forecasting errors if expectations are Rational. Since one kind of information available is data on previous forecasting errors, a special case of Property II is

Property III: $\{y_{t+1} - E(y_{t+1} \mid I_t)\}$ is serially uncorrelated
with mean zero   (4.1.3)

A random variable u_{t+1} is serially uncorrelated if previous values of this variable contain no information about how u_{t+1} will deviate from its mean value. It is important to note that Property III applies only when we consider the sequence of forecasting errors relating expectations at time t to outcomes one period later. Suppose instead that individuals at time t form expectations $_{t}y^e_{t+2}$ about the value of y two periods ahead. By Property II the expectation of the the forecasting error $(y_{t+2} - _{t}y^e_{t+2})$, given information available at time t, is zero. However, this forecasting error, which I denote ϵ_{t+2}, embodies new information which becomes available at time $t + 1$ and even more new information available at time $t + 2$. We might decompose the forecasting error ϵ_{t+2} as follows

$$\epsilon_{t+2} = \eta_{t+1} + \eta_{t+2}$$

where η_{t+1} and η_{t+2} are random variables reflecting new information about y_{t+2} first available at $t + 1$ and $t + 2$ respectively. By the definition of *new* information, these random variables must be serially uncorrelated with mean zero. Similarly, ϵ_{t+3}, the forecasting error $(y_{t+3} - _{t+1}y^e_{t+3})$, may be composed into $(\eta_{t+2} + \eta_{t+3})$ where η_{t+3} reflects new information at $t + 3$. Even though new information η_t is uncorrelated with new information at any other date (Property III), the two period forecasting errors ϵ_{t+2} and ϵ_{t+3} will be serially correlated because they overlap. Unanticipatable shocks at time $t + 2$ will affect both forecasting errors. An interesting application of this principle is Brown and Maital (1981) who analyse multiperiod overlapping forecasts elicited from economists by survey questionnaires.

Most of the models we shall study are linear. In such models, Rational Expectations satisfy the *Chain Rule of Forecasting*. The simplest way to describe this is by means of an example. Suppose it is known that

$$y_t = ay_{t-1} + u_t$$

where the constant parameter a is a positive fraction and u_t is a random disturbance which is serially uncorrelated with mean zero. I_t comprises past values of u_t and of y_t, but the former are of no use in predicting current and future values of u_t. At the beginning of time t, before u_t is known, the Rational Expectation of y_t is given by

$$E(y_t \mid I_t) = E(ay_{t-1} + u_t \mid I_t) = ay_{t-1}$$

At the same date, the Rational Expectation of y_{t+1} may be formed thus:

$$E(y_{t+1} \mid I_t) = E(ay_t + u_{t+1} \mid I_t) = aE(y_t \mid I_t) = a^2 y_{t-1}$$

Similarly, to form $E(y_{t+2} \mid I_t)$, we first express y_{t+2} in terms of y_{t+1} and u_{t+2}. The current expectation of the latter is certainly zero. The expectation of the former can be evaluated by expressing y_{t+1} in terms of y_t and u_{t+1}. Again, the expectation of the latter is zero given I_t. Proceeding through one more step we eventually obtain $a^3 y_{t-1}$ as the solution. Thus we use the Chain Rule of Forecasting to build up expressions for expectations at time t of all future values of y. In every case, the solutions must be expressed only in terms of variables already known at time t.

4.2 Statistical Identification and Observational Equivalence

A macroeconomic model is a set of simultaneous structural equations. By a structural equation we mean an equation modelling a particular aspect of behaviour such as consumption demand or labour supply. Each structural equation will be characterised by certain unknown parameters or co-efficients multiplying the relevant variables suggested by economic theory. For example, we studied earlier the consumption function

$$C = c_0 + c_1 Y + c_2 W$$

where C, Y and W denote consumption, income and wealth and c_0, c_1 and c_2 denote constant parameters. The actual value of consumption will depend on the values of the endogenous variables Y and W, which are determined within the set of simultaneous equations of which the consumption function is merely one component. Exogenous variables are not determined within the model, but are given from outside. Different paths for exogenous variables will clearly generate different paths for endogenous variables. By characterising an equation as structural, we mean that its parameters should remain constant over a wide range of possible paths for the exogenous variables: induced variation in consumption should arise from variation in the equilibrium level of the endogenous variables Y and W, but not from changes in the parameters c_0, c_1 and c_2.

If in principle separate estimates of each of these structural parameters can be disentangled from the corresponding economic data, we say that the model is statistically identified. When this is not possible, a given data sample is consistent with an infinity of different structural models which are said to be observationally equivalent, since it is impossible to distinguish between them. Identification is a serious issue in all genuinely simultaneous equation models, whether or not they encompass Rational Expectations. Econometrics textbooks typically begin a discussion of simultaneous equation models by demonstrating that it will *never* be possible to identify structural parameters by the data alone. Some *a priori* assumptions are required. For example, if wealth enters the consumption function but is assumed not to enter the investment function, it may be possible to identify the marginal propensity to consume out of wealth by studying the data correlation between consumption and wealth. However, when wealth also enters the investment function, a change in wealth will not only increase consumption directly, but will also affect consumption indirectly by changing investment and hence income; it is then much harder to disentangle the parameters c_1 and c_2 in the above equation.

While identification problems are not confined to Rational Expectations models, they are often particularly acute in these models and it is easy to illustrate why this should be so. Consider the following simple model

$$y_t = b_1 \left(_{t-1} y_t^e \right) + b_2 z_t + b_3 z_{t-1} + u_{1t} \tag{4.2.1}$$

$$z_t = \phi z_{t-1} + u_{2t} \tag{4.2.2}$$

The structural equation for the endogenous variable y_t suggests that y_t depends on its Rational Expectation at the end of time $t - 1$ and on current and lagged values of some other variable z_t. z_t depends only on its own past value. The random disturbances u_{1t} and u_{2t} are assumed to have mean zero and be serially uncorrelated.

Individuals know both equations and use them to form Rational Expectations. From equation (4.2.1), taking expectations conditional on information available at the end of time $t - 1$

$$_{t-1} y_t^e = b_1 \left(_{t-1} y_t^e \right) + b_2 \left(_{t-1} z_t^e \right) + b_3 z_{t-1}$$

so that

$$_{t-1} y_t^e = \left(\frac{1}{1 - b_1} \right) \left[b_2 \left(_{t-1} z_t^e \right) + b_3 z_{t-1} \right] \tag{4.2.3}$$

However, from equation (4.2.2), $_{t-1} z_t^e = \phi z_{t-1}$ and substituting into equation (4.2.3)

$$_{t-1} y_t^e = \left(\frac{1}{1 - b_1} \right) (b_2 \phi + b_3) z_{t-1}$$

Finally, from equation (4.2.1) we obtain the observable equation

$$y_t = b_2 z_t + \left(\frac{1}{1 - b_1} \right) (b_2 b_1 \phi + b_3) z_{t-1} + u_{1t} \tag{4.2.4}$$

Given data on the path of the variables y and z, we can estimate the coefficients on the variables z_t and z_{t-1} in the above equation. Moreover, using only data on z, we can estimate the parameter ϕ directly from equation (4.2.2). This parameter is immediately identified, as is b_2 which will be estimated as the coefficient on z_t when fitting equation (4.2.4) to the data. However, the single estimated coefficient on z_{t-1} in equation (4.2.4) cannot be uniquely decomposed into estimates of b_1 and b_3, even given the prior estimate of ϕ from equation (4.2.2). The parameters b_1 and b_3 are not identified.

This problem occurs frequently in Rational Expectations models. The lagged exogenous variable z_{t-1} enters the observable equation (4.2.4) for two distinct reasons: it occurred in the original structural equation (4.2.1) capturing the idea that the endogenous variable y_t responds only sluggishly to changes in z, so that past values of z are relevant to the current determination of y; it also enters because past values of z help to predict current values of z and hence enter the Rational Expectations $_{t-1}z_t^e$ and $_{t-1}y_t^e$. Because lagged variables fulfil this dual role in Rational Expectations models, it is sometimes impossible to disentangle the separate effects from the data. Only when the relevant economic theory suggests that the lag patterns in equations such as (4.2.1) and (4.2.2) are very different will it be possible to identify separately the two sets of parameters. Whether such assumptions seem unduly restrictive can be judged only in the context of a particular model.

Suppose for example the relevant economic theory suggests that b_3 equals zero in equation (4.2.1), because y_t is a variable which plausibly adjusts immediately to changes in z_t. Equation (4.2.4) may then be written as

$$y_t = b_2 z_t + \left(\frac{b_1}{1-b_1}\right)b_2 \phi z_{t-1} + u_{1t} \qquad (4.2.5)$$

As before, an estimate of ϕ may be obtained by fitting equation (4.2.2) directly to the data. Fitting equation (4.2.5) yields an estimate of b_2 as the coefficient on z_t. Hence the estimated coefficient of z_{t-1} may now be used to infer an estimate of the remaining unknown parameter b_1. The model is now identified. Intuitively this is possible because z_{t-1} enters equation (4.2.5) only through its role as a predictor of z_t.

4.3 Hypothesis Testing under Rational Expectations

A Rational Expectations model embodies both a particular expectations assumption and an assumption about the structure of the economic model in which that expectations assumption is embedded. Together these imply an observable equation such as (4.2.4) which may be fitted to the data. If we conclude that such an equation does not provide an adequate explanation of the data, it is hard to infer whether this is due to a failure of the expectations assumption, or the assumption about the structure of the model, or both. However, if we are confident about the validity of one of the assumptions, we may choose to regard the adequacy of the final observable equation as a test of the validity of the other assumption. The empirical literature is concerned with both types of test: testing that expectations are Rational rather than Adaptive, conditional on the belief that the underlying model has been correctly specified; and testing the assumption about the underlying model, for example market clearing rather than disequilibrium behaviour, conditional on the validity of Rational Expectations.

Consider first how we might test Rational Expectations against an alternative hypothesis of extrapolative expectations conditional on a particular underlying model. To be specific, suppose the underlying model is given by equations (4.2.1) and (4.2.2) under the assumption that b_3 equals zero. Under Rational Expectations, the observable equation is (4.2.5). Suppose we decide to model the alternative hypothesis of extrapolative expectations as

$$_{t-1}y_t^e = \gamma_1 z_{t-1} + \gamma_2 z_{t-2} + \gamma_3 z_{t-3} \qquad (4.3.1)$$

Substituting into the version of equation (4.2.1) in which b_3 equals zero, we obtain

$$y_t = b_2 z_t + b_1\gamma_1 z_{t-1} + b_1\gamma_2 z_{t-2} + b_1\gamma_3 z_{t-3} + u_{1t} \quad (4.3.2)$$

We are now in a position to test the assumption of Rational Expectations conditional on the validity of the underlying economic model. Suppose we fit the general equation

$$y_t = \delta_1 z_t + \delta_2 z_{t-1} + \delta_3 z_{t-2} + \delta_4 z_{t-3} + u_{1t}$$

choosing estimates of the delta parameters which best fit the data. Under the assumption of Rational Expectations, equation (4.2.5) implies that the coefficients on z_{t-2} and z_{t-3} should be zero, whereas under extrapolative expectations these coefficients will not be zero. By establishing whether the estimated coefficients are sufficiently close to zero we may derive a test of the assumption of Rational Expectations.

It is important to note that such tests may be possible even when the model is not completely identified. In Section 4.2, we saw that when b_3 is not restricted to be zero in equation (4.2.1) the parameters b_1 and b_3 could not be separately identified in the observable Rational Expectations equation (4.2.4). Nevertheless, this equation omits, or imposes zero coefficients on, the variables z_{t-2} and z_{t-3}. Under the extrapolative scheme (4.3.1), the full equation (4.2.1) now becomes

$$y_t = b_2 z_t + (b_1 \gamma_1 + b_3) z_{t-1} + b_1 \gamma_2 z_{t-2} + b_1 \gamma_3 z_{t-3} + u_{1t}$$

so the previous test procedure based on the estimated coefficients on z_{t-2} and z_{t-3} remain appropriate.

Identification problems may prove more intractable when the object is not to test the expectations assumption but rather to test the assumption about the underlying economic structure, for a statistical test on the value of a parameter becomes impossible if the parameter is not identified. For example, if one economic theory implies a non-zero value for b_3 in the Rational Expectations model (4.2.4), while another economic theory implies a zero value, estimation of this equation provides no basis for a test since the coefficient on z_{t-1} cannot be unscrambled into estimates of b_1 and b_3. Specific examples of this general argument will be found in subsequent chapters.

One caveat should be borne in mind. Suppose the competing economic theories predict different values for the parameter b_1 in equation (4.2.1), but neither theory suggests that z_{t-1} should have much influence on the value of y_t. Imposing this assumption that b_3 equals zero, we find that equation (4.2.4) is identified so that tests on the value of b_1 may be conducted conditional on a belief in the validity of Rational Expectations. A researcher conducts such a test and concludes that the data is incompatible with one of the competing economic theories. Nevertheless, this result is disputed by the proponents of the discredited theory who argue as follows. Although there is not much to suggest that z_{t-1} affects y_t in equation (4.2.1), equally it would be surprising if changes in z_t fed through to y_t instantaneously. We should therefore treat the coefficient b_3 on z_{t-1} as small but not literally zero, but then the parameters b_1 and b_3 cannot be separately identified in equation (4.2.4) and so the test is invalid and the apparently discredited theory has not been definitively rejected. Readers will recognise that this type of reasoning may be applied to any piece of empirical work; what they must decide is whether, in the context of a particular model, the argument carries very much weight. All models are simplifications and it is always possible to quibble that the model is not exactly correct. Without *a priori* assumptions, neither theoretical nor empirical results can be derived.

I began this section by emphasising that observable equations such as (4.2.4) embody joint hypotheses about the structure of the model and the expectations assumption. The test procedures discussed above are rigorous in the sense that they specify which hypothesis is to be taken as given and what are the competing variants of the other hypothesis, carefully deriving the implications for the observable equations to be estimated. Much of the empirical literature does not follow this route, but adopts the short cut of examining whether or not some of the fundamental properties listed in Section 4.1 are satisfied by the data. While this may seem appealing, it evades rather than solves many of the problems cited above. Only by clearly specifying what the alternative hypothesis is taken to be, can we infer how the properties of the observable equations should differ from the null or maintained hypotheses, that the model has been correctly specified and that expectations are Rational. Without such detailed analysis *a priori*, it is impossible to infer what we should conclude if a fundamental property is not satisfied by the data, or indeed how likely it is that alternative hypotheses will yield results which are very similar to the maintained hypotheses. Thus, while much of the empirical literature finds that the data display the fundamental properties implied by Rational Expectations, the reader should probably conclude that at best this represents only weak evidence in favour of the hypothesis.

4.4 Econometric Policy Evaluation and the Lucas Critique

Macroeconomists participate in the debate about which economic policies ought to be pursued. In part, this reflects their differing views about positive economics — how the economy actually works — but in part it also reflects differing normative positions or subjective value judgments. For example, even if economists were all to agree that higher unemployment would reduce inflation, some might prefer high unemployment and low inflation, others high inflation and low unemployment. Although such judgments are inherently political, if the discussion of economic policy is to be an informed one, the positive consequences of pursuing different policies should be investigated as thoroughly as possible. This exercise in positive economics is a legitimate concern of macroeconomics and I shall refer to it as Policy Evaluation. It is unlikely that such evaluation can be confined to theoretical macroeconomic analysis for two reasons. First, in a simultaneous system of relations, the indirect effects of a policy may frustrate the direct obvious effects and it will be necessary to quantify the different effects to reach an overall judgment. Secondly, unless one makes extreme value judgments such as that only inflation matters, it will be necessary to investigate how much one objective can be traded off against another to reach a subjective judgment about the preferred combination. For these reasons, empirical analysis is essential.

In practice, Policy Evaluation usually proceeds as follows. First, empirical macroeconomists estimate a large model of the economy using past data. Many countries have such models, each comprising several hundred equations. Using the estimated coefficients, the model is simulated under current policies to produce a forecast of what would happen if current policies were maintained unchanged. A hypothetical alternative policy is then specified and a new simulation is undertaken, the differential behaviour of the paths of the economy being taken as a measure of the consequences of altering government policy. As macroeconometric models have become more sophisticated, increasing emphasis has been placed on formal econometric policy evaluation. Some governments not only conduct such experiments in their Treasury Departments, but they also have computer terminals close to their debating chambers so that the consequences of any proposal can be evaluated very quickly.

Lucas (1976) first drew attention to the fact that such

evaluations may be seriously misleading if expectations are Rational. Individuals model government behaviour and use this information in forming expectations. If the estimated coefficients of observable equations implicitly contain policy parameters which have entered through their role as predictors of the future, these parameters will change when a new policy is adopted. Changing the policy rule affects not merely the parameters of the equation describing policy itself, but also parameters in other equations. Hence, parameter estimates derived under old policies are inappropriate in simulating new policies.

A simple example may clarify this argument. Consider the model

$$m_t = m_{t-1} + \theta \tag{4.4.1}$$

$$m_t = p_t + \alpha_1 - \alpha_2\theta + \epsilon_{1t} \quad \alpha_1 > 0 \quad \alpha_2 > 0 \tag{4.4.2}$$

$$e_t = p^* - p_t \tag{4.4.3}$$

where m_t denotes the logarithm of the nominal money stock. Equation (4.4.1) describes the money supply rule in which money grows at the constant rate θ which, as in Section 3.3, I assume to be sufficiently large that the simple hyperinflation model may be invoked. Equation (4.4.2) rewrites equation (3.3.14) and is the corresponding expression for money demand under Rational Expectations, where α_1 and α_2 are positive and ϵ_{1t} denotes the random disturbance with mean zero and no serial correlation. The model is extended to include an equation determining the floating exchange rate. In this hyperinflation model all real variables are constant, including the real exchange rate or level of real competitiveness, and nominal exchange rates adjust to offset exactly differential inflation across countries. Let P and P^* denote the domestic and foreign price level and let E denote the exchange rate measured as the number of units of foreign currency which exchange for one unit of the domestic currency. Thus $P^* = PE$. In the literature on exchange rate determination, this result is sometimes known as the Law of One Price or Purchasing Power Parity. Let p^*, p and e denote the logarithms of P^*, P, and E. Thus at any date t,

$$p_t^* = p_t + e_t$$

I assume for simplicity that there is no inflation in the foreign country, so that p_t^* is constant at the value p^*. Hence we obtain equation (4.4.3).

Eliminating p_t between equations (4.4.2) and (4.4.3) we obtain

$$e_t = (p^* + \alpha_1 - \alpha_2 \theta) - m_t + \epsilon_{1t} \qquad (4.4.4)$$

Equation (4.4.4) is the Rational Expectations solution for the nominal exchange rate e_t in this hyperinflation model. For a given rate of money growth θ, a higher level of nominal money must be matched by higher domestic prices to maintain real money balances at the level implied by equation (4.4.2). Higher domestic prices require a currency depreciation to maintain real competitiveness as the hyperinflation model requires. Given data from a sample period in which the rate of money growth had been maintained at the constant level θ and in which foreign prices p^* had indeed been constant, it would in fact be adequate to model the determination of the exchange rate by the equation

$$e_t = \alpha_3 - m_t + \epsilon_{1t} \qquad (4.4.5)$$

We may now consider the Lucas critique. Suppose conventional macroeconometric models contain equations such as (4.4.5) which have been estimated over past sample periods in which particular policies have been in force. Such equations may be useful in predicting the future, provided that existing policy rules are maintained. They *cannot* be used for policy evaluation, although this is the usual practice. Suppose we wish to evaluate a policy change which involves a lower rate of money growth; to be specific, let us consider the extreme case in which the value $\theta = 0$ is contemplated, so that nominal money would then be constant for evermore. Conventional policy evaluation using equation (4.4.5) would conclude that, under a policy of zero money growth, the exchange rate would gradually appreciate relative to the path it would have followed under monetary expansion, as the tighter monetary policy successively holds down the nominal money stock m_t by ever increasing amounts relative to the previous policy.

Reverting to equation (4.4.4) we can see the error in this line of reasoning. Under Rational Expectations individuals are assumed to understand the policy in force and use this information in forming expectations. The rate of money growth θ enters equation (4.4.4) precisely because it represents the Rational Expectation of inflation on which nominal interest rates and hence the demand for money depend in the hyperinflation model. To simulate the new policy of zero money growth using an estimated value of α_3 derived from a sample period of fast money growth and high inflation is to assert that individuals continue to expect inflation at the rate θ, even when the new policy has been adopted. Such expectations would be systematically mistaken and are not compatible with the assumption of Rational Expectations. Rather, if a hypothetical policy is to be evaluated, it should be assumed that individuals would understand the nature of the policy, recompute the new Rational Expectations solution, and use these expectations of inflation in assessing their demand for money, hence influencing prices and the exchange rate.

Indeed, equation (4.4.4) indicates the ideal manner in which to proceed. Suppose we have separate estimates of p^*, α_1, α_2 and θ derived from past sample data. We now consider adopting the policy of setting θ equal to zero. All we need do is set θ equal to zero in equation (4.4.4), thereby calculating *a priori* how much to adjust the parameter α_3 in equation (4.4.5). Simulating the hypothetical policy in this amended model will be internally consistent, in the sense that it assumes a set of expectations which are consistent with the hypothetical policy, were it in operation. Not only does the Rational Expectations approach draw attention to the inconsistency of conventional policy evaluation, it also provides a solution to the problem. Suppose that the switch to zero money growth is immediately perceived and that expectations are adjusted accordingly. Setting θ equal to zero in equation (4.4.4) implies an immediate upward *jump* in the exchange rate due purely to expectations revision, even before the tighter monetary policy starts to take effect via the term m_t. This jump is analogous to the jump depicted in Figure 3.2.5 and again represents a move to a new convergent path under Rational Expectations. The force of Lucas' criticism is thus twofold. A change in policy will alter the behaviour of the economy by changing the structural equation describing policy itself. Under Rational Expectations, this will alter the convergent path to the steady state and will usually alter both the slope and the height of this path. Not only must extrapolative coefficients be amended to reflect the change in slope, but the initial jump to the new path must also be modelled.

If the structural model is identified, past sample data will yield estimates of the structural parameters such as α_2, the interest elasticity of money demand. Because these are structural parameters, they may be assumed invariant with respect to the exogenous change in policy. By imposing the parameters of the hypothetical policy rule (here $\theta = 0$) we may mathematically recompute the new Rational Expectations solution using the methods of Chapter 3, thus modelling both the initial jump when the new policy is announced and the subsequent dynamic behaviour along the convergent path now implied.

Two issues remain and serve to remind us that this solution to the Lucas problem is only tentative. First, it is not always possible to decompose estimated coefficients into separate estimates of the relevant structural parameters, without which it is impossible to recompute the new Rational Expectations solution once the policy parameters are adjusted. Secondly, we must be confident that the policy change will not affect the true values of structural parameters, so that estimates from previous sample periods remain reliable even under different proposed policies. This question is also discussed in Lucas (1976). Suppose the government switches from a relatively certain policy to a relatively random policy. It is then plausible that elasticities of response to current variables in supposedly structural equations will be altered as individuals perceive that current events become random and transient. Given a sufficiently well developed set of microeconomic foundations for macroeconomic relations, it might then be possible to model the relation between response elasticity and the degree of randomness in the model, allowing previously estimated structural parameters to be amended when hypothetical policy changes are undertaken. Such models are the focus of continuing research, but are considerably more sophisticated than the somewhat *ad hoc* macroeconomic models with which we typically deal both in macroeconomic theory and in macroeconometric model building. My own guess would be that some progress will be made on this front, but that a more pressing task in the short run is to try to meet Lucas' first objection within existing *ad hoc* macroeconometric models by seeking to model the discrete revisions of expectations discussed earlier in this section.

4.5 Conclusion

In this chapter, I have introduced the themes which recur in empirical research on particular applications of the Rational Expectations hypothesis in macroeconomics. Section 4.1 set out four key implications of the hypothesis which are sufficiently striking that they have become the focus of much research. Provided that we are confident that the underlying structure of the model has been correctly specified, these implications offer a quick check list of properties which should be examined. In Section 4.3 I discussed additional evidence which might be brought to bear in seeking to establish whether expectations are indeed Rational.

Section 4.3 also discussed the more difficult question of trying to distinguish between views of the underlying economic structure conditional on the assumption of Rational Expectations. Section 4.4 discussed the Lucas critique of conventional econometric policy evaluation, a critique of great significance for those who actually operate large macroeconometric models and make policy pronouncements. In studying applications of the Rational Expectations hypothesis in subsequent chapters, I do not attempt anything as ambitious as a discussion of how to construct a complete model of the economy under Rational Expectations. Nevertheless, Lucas' central point remains relevant: if expectations are Rational, any change in policy, whether actual or hypothetical, should be assumed to be quickly understood by individuals, providing a discrete piece of new information which requires a complete reassessment of the Rational Expectations equilibrium path. Typically, there will be a jump in endogenous variables at the date the information is first available.

Running through the discussion of this chapter has been the issue of identification. If parameters cannot be separately identified from the data and the *a priori* restrictions implied by economic theory, hypothesis testing is impossible and the proposed solution to the Lucas problem of policy evaluation cannot be made operational. I have dwelt on the issue of identification at some length, because it is an idea which may be unfamiliar to readers who have never studied the econometric theory of simultaneous equations. This lengthy discussion should not be taken to imply that identification problems inevitably arise. Many interesting empirical studies will be considered in subsequent chapters.

In this chapter I have introduced the key implications of the Rational Expectations hypothesis for empirical research in macroeconomics. Since some readers will require a more rigorous treatment of these issues, the following chapter examines the extension of conventional econometric theory to models with Rational Expectations. This starred chapter assumes that the reader is familiar with the textbook treatment of the econometric theory of simultaneous equations and with simple dynamic representations of stochastic processes. Readers who do not wish to pursue this level of rigour may proceed directly to Chapter 6, in which I begin the discussion of specific applications of Rational Expectations in macroeconomics. The present chapter will provide sufficient background for the subsequent discussion of empirical research. In the Notes on the Literature below, I give references for the econometric theory assumed in the following chapter. These may be of assistance to readers who wish to check the material which is assumed, readers who wish to refresh their memories, and readers currently unfamiliar with econometric theory who wish to pusue the subject at some future date.

Notes on the Literature

Stewart (1976) provides an excellent introduction to econometrics for those who wish to understand the main ideas without becoming embroiled in technical detail. It is highly recommended. Johnston (1972) and Theil (1971) are standard econometrics texts, though readers with some knowledge of statistics and matrix algebra might go straight to Schmidt (1976) which gives an excellent treatment of static models. Harvey (1981) is slightly less rigorous, but has a much wider coverage. Its sections on hypothesis testing and dynamic models are especially useful. The sometimes difficult survey article by Shiller (1978) not only discusses identification, but contains a fuller account of the statistical properties discussed in Section 4.1. More advanced material on these topics is given in the next chapter.

The seminal paper by Lucas (1976) on policy evaluation is not very technical and contains many interesting variants on the basic theme.

Although empirical economists have considered the application of Rational Expectations to individual equations, the task of respecifying and re-estimating a complete macroeconometric model under Rational Expectations is altogether more formidable. Minford (1980) describes a brave attempt to implement this strategy.

5
Econometric Implications of the Rational Expectations Hypothesis**

This chapter is organised as follows. In Section 5.1 I discuss the structure of simultaneous equation models with Rational Expectations, drawing on the analysis of Section 3.2. Section 5.2 examines more rigorously the question of statistical identification introduced in Section 4.2. Estimation of Rational Expectations models is discussed in Section 5.3. In Section 5.4 I address the problem of testing Rational Expectations against the alternative hypothesis that expectations are extrapolative, emphasising that the data are generated jointly by a process of expectations formation and the structure of the underlying economic model in which these expectations are formed. Thus it is possible to test the expectations assumption conditional on the validity of the assumed model of the underlying structure, but unconditional tests of the expectations hypothesis are not possible. Similarly, in Section 5.5 I examine tests of the underlying model conditional on the validity of the Rational Expectations approach to modelling expectations formation. The Lucas problem is reconsidered in Section 5.6.

5.1 The Structure of Rational Expectations Models

The purpose of this section is to show how the usual econometric discussion of simultaneous equation models must be amended when the model recognises that behaviour depends on expectations which are Rational. Since standard econometrics texts focus chiefly on static models, it is simplest to begin with such a framework. Thus the structural specification at time t contains expectation variables of the form $_{t-1}x_t^e$, but not of the form $_{t-k}x_t^e$ or $_{t-1}x_{t-1+k}^e$, $(k > 1)$. As will become apparent, this assumption removes the dynamic structure which requires consideration of the whole future path of the economy and was discussed in Section 3.2. Having analysed the simpler case, I then restore the dynamic structure. Finally, I complicate this structure still further by supposing that current structural equations include not only current values of exogenous variables, but also a distributed lag on past values of exogenous variables.

Consider the familiar simultaneous equation model with m equations for m endogenous variables whose values at time t are described by the column m-vector y_t. Some subset of these endogenous variables also enters the structure because its expectations directly affect behaviour at time t. Suppose that there are m_1 such variables $(m_1 < m)$ and write the system, and hence the y_t vector, so that the *ex post* values of these variables about which expectations are formed happen to be the first m_1 components of the vector y_t. I assume that there are k exogenous variables whose values at time t are described by the column k-vector z_t. By exogenous we mean that the process determining the values of z_t does not depend on the process determining the endogenous variables y_t. In the current jargon, y must not Granger-cause z, by which we mean that past values of y_t do not enter the process determining z_t. Nor must contemporaneous random disturbances in the z_t process be correlated with disturbances in the structural model for y_t. Thus I assume that the exogenous vector z_t obeys the vector autoregressive process of order p

$$z_t = \phi_1 z_{t-1} + \phi_2 z_{t-2} + \ldots + \phi_p z_{t-p} + \epsilon_t \qquad (5.1.1)$$

where the vector ϵ_t has mean zero and is serially uncorrelated.

For the moment, we do not need to specify its contemporaneous covariance matrix, nor its distribution. The $(k \times k)$ matrices ϕ_i describe the parameters of the autoregressive process determining z_t.

I assume that the structural equations for the endogenous variables y_t are given by

$$By_t + \Gamma_1(_{t-1}y^e_{1,t}) + \Gamma_2 z_t = u_t \qquad (5.1.2)$$

where $y_{1,t}$ denotes the column m_1-vector, the first m_1 components of y_t, and $_{t-1}y^e_{1,t}$ denotes the Rational Expectation of this vector given information available at $t-1$. The parameter matrices B, Γ_1, and Γ_2, are of dimension $(m \times m)$, $(m \times m_1)$ and $(m \times k)$ respectively. The column m-vector of contemporaneous disturbances u_t is assumed to have mean zero, be serially uncorrelated, and be uncorrelated with all current, past and future values of ϵ_t, the disturbance vector in equation (5.1.1). For the moment, we do not need to specify either the contemporaneous covariance matrix of u_t, or its distribution.

As in the usual econometric discussion, I assume that the matrix B is of full rank: given particular values for $_{t-1}y^e_{1,t}$, z_t, and u_t, the above m equations uniquely determine y_t. Premultiplying equations (5.1.2) by B^{-1}

$$y_t = -B^{-1}\Gamma_1(_{t-1}y^e_{1,t}) - B^{-1}\Gamma_2 z_t + B^{-1}u_t$$

which I redefine as

$$y_t = \Pi_1(_{t-1}y^e_{1,t}) + \Pi_2 z_t + v_t \qquad \begin{aligned}\Pi_1 &\equiv -B^{-1}\Gamma_1 \quad (5.1.3)\\ \Pi_2 &\equiv -B^{-1}\Gamma_2\\ v_t &\equiv B^{-1}u_t\end{aligned}$$

Since the Rational Expectations variables are predetermined at time t, having been formed at $t-1$ before current disturbances were known, equation (5.1.3) is analogous to the conventional reduced form. In particular, the vector v_t, being linear combinations of the components of u_t, has mean zero, is serially uncorrelated, and is uncorrelated with all values of ϵ_t. Since the Rational Expectations are not directly observable, I shall refer to equation (5.1.3) as the unobservable reduced form. Partitioning this equation into the first m_1 equations and the last $m-m_1$ equations, and denoting the latter by the subscript 2, we may write the unobservable reduced form as

$$y_{1,t} = \Pi_{11}(_{t-1}y^e_{1,t}) + \Pi_{12}\, z_t + v_{1,t} \tag{5.1.4a}$$

$$y_{2,t} = \Pi_{21}(_{t-1}y^e_{1,t}) + \Pi_{22}\, z_t + v_{2,t} \tag{5.1.4b}$$

where

$$v_t = \begin{pmatrix} v_{1,t} \\ v_{2,t} \end{pmatrix} \quad \Pi_1 = \begin{pmatrix} \Pi_{11} \\ \Pi_{21} \end{pmatrix} \quad \Pi_2 = \begin{pmatrix} \Pi_{12} \\ \Pi_{22} \end{pmatrix}$$

Thus the dimensions of $\Pi_{11}, \Pi_{12}, \Pi_{21}$, and Π_{22} are respectively $(m_1 \times m_1)$, $(m_1 \times k)$, $[(m-m_1) \times m_1]$ and $[(m-m_1) \times k]$.

Assume that individuals forming expectations at the end of time $t-1$ know the parameters of the model and know the history of all variables in the model up to and including time $t-1$. Taking mathematical expectations through equation (5.1.4a) conditional on this information, we obtain

$$_{t-1}y^e_{1,t} = \Pi_{11}(_{t-1}y^e_{1,t}) + \Pi_{12}(_{t-1}z^e_t) + 0$$

Hence the Rational Expectations solution in this static model is given by

$$_{t-1}y^e_{1,t} = (I - \Pi_{11})^{-1}\, \Pi_{12}(_{t-1}z^e_t) \tag{5.1.5}$$

I assume that the matrix $(I - \Pi_{11})$ is of full rank and hence has an inverse. The justification for this assumption will be given shortly. Substituting from equation (5.1.5) into equations (5.1.3)

$$y_{1,t} = \Pi_{11}(I-\Pi_{11})^{-1}\, \Pi_{12}\,(_{t-1}z^e_t) + \Pi_{12}\, z_t + v_{1,t} \tag{5.1.6a}$$

$$y_{2,t} = \Pi_{21}(I-\Pi_{11})^{-1}\, \Pi_{12}\,(_{t-1}z^e_t) + \Pi_{22}\, z_t + v_{2,t} \tag{5.1.6b}$$

From equation (5.1.1) the Rational Expectation $_{t-1}z^e_t$ is given by

$$_{t-1}z^e_t = \phi_1 z_{t-1} + \phi_2 z_{t-2} + \ldots + \phi_p z_{t-p} \tag{5.1.7}$$

By substituting this expression into equations (5.1.6) we may obtain an observable reduced form relating current values of endogenous variables to current and lagged values of the exogenous variables. Since the only reason lagged values of z_t enter is because they help individuals at time $t-1$ to predict z_t, values of z before time $t-p$ do not enter the observable reduced form, given the assumption (5.1.1) about the nature of the process generating the exogenous variables.

It is also useful to examine the forecasting error for two reasons: to confirm Properties II and III of Section 4.1 and to emphasise a feature of which I shall make use when discussing estimation. Taking expectations through equation (5.1.6) conditional on information available at the end of time $t-1$

$$_{t-1}y_{1,t}^e = \Pi_{11}(I-\Pi_{11})^{-1}\Pi_{12}(_{t-1}z_t^e) + \Pi_{12}(_{t-1}z_t^e)$$
$$(5.1.8)$$

It is simple algebra to check that this expression is identical to equation (5.1.5). Subtracting equation (5.1.8) from equation (5.1.6a)

$$y_{1,t} -_{t-1}y_{1,t}^e = \Pi_{12}(z_t -_{t-1}z_t^e) + v_{1,t} = \Pi_{12}\epsilon_t + v_{1,t}$$
$$(5.1.9)$$

Individuals at time $t-1$ fail to forecast $y_{1,t}$ for two distinct reasons: failure to forecast the stochastic component of z_t in equation (5.1.1) and failure to forecast the disturbances $v_{1,t}$ in the reduced form equation (5.1.6a). Equation (5.1.9) confirms that one period ahead forecasting errors not only have conditional expectation zero as of time $t-1$, but are also serially uncorrelated. Properties II and III of Section 4.1 are satisfied. Hence actual values of $y_{1,t}$ deviate from their Rational Expectations one period earlier only by a serially uncorrelated random term with mean zero.

Finally, I justify the assumption that $(I-\Pi_{11})$ is non-singular in equations (5.1.5)–(5.1.8). This condition is analogous to the usual requirement that B is non-singular and says merely that we have specified a model which in principle allows a unique solution. The condition has nothing to do with the stability analysis of Section 3.2 in which uniqueness is a non-trivial issue, for the model we are currently studying is static. To take a specific example, suppose that the model was entirely deterministic, with all the random terms identically zero. Consider the steady state in which any plausible expectations formation process would correctly anticipate $y_{1,t}$ and z_t. Denoting steady state values by the bar superscript, a deterministic version of equation (5.1.4a) implies

$$\bar{y}_1 = \Pi_{11}\bar{y}_1 + \Pi_{12}\bar{z}$$

Hence if $(I-\Pi_{11})$ is singular, there are an infinite number of steady state solutions $\bar{y}$ corresponding to the value $\bar{z}$. The requirement that this matrix be non-singular is thus a weak requirement that the model is sensibly specified, and is no more restrictive than the usual assumption that B is non-singular.

I turn now to a model in which the intertemporal structure is restored, so that the Rational Expectations solution requires the evaluation of the entire future path of the economy. I amend equation (5.1.2) to

$$By_t + \Gamma_1({}_{t-1}y^e_{1,t+1}) + \Gamma_2 z_t = u_t \qquad (5.1.10)$$

where all previous assumptions hold, except that $y_{1,t+1}$ now denotes the first m_1 components of y_{t+1}. It is easy to motivate such a specification. Consider the example discussed in Section 3.3 in which individuals at the end of time $t-1$ had to forecast the inflation rate $(p_{t+1} - p_t)$ relevant during period t. Thus, the expectation of an endogenous variable at time $t+1$ enters the structural equations at time t. Equation (5.1.10) simplifies by assuming that the only expectational variables are ${}_{t-1}y^e_{1,t+1}$. Wallis (1980) considers the more general case in which both ${}_{t-1}y^e_{1,t}$ and ${}_{t-1}y^e_{1,t+1}$ enter the structural equations. Although the algebra is more complicated, the principles of the solution procedure remain the same.

Proceeding as in the static case, we obtain the unobservable reduced form equations for $y_{1,t}$

$$y_{1,t} = \Pi_{11}({}_{t-1}y^e_{1,t+1}) + \Pi_{12} z_t + v_{1,t} \qquad (5.1.11)$$

Taking expectations conditional on information available at time $t-1$

$$_{t-1}y^e_{1,t} = \Pi_{11}({}_{t-1}y^e_{1,t+1}) + \Pi_{12}({}_{t-1}z^e_t) \qquad (5.1.12)$$

This is a linear first order difference equation system in conditional expectation, which may be solved forwards by recursive substitution in the manner of equations (3.3.9)–(3.3.13). In that hyperinflation model, the steady state was globally unstable, but since the relevant variables were not predetermined it was possible to jump immediately to this steady state by choosing the initial price level appropriately. The model we are now studying includes predetermined z variables which preclude this possibility in general. If a

Rational Expectations equilibrium is to exist, it must be based on the Saddlepoint analysis of Section 3.2, treating the k variables $_{t-1}z_t^e$ as predetermined.

Equation (5.1.12) differs from equation (3.2.3) in the Mathematical Digression in Section 3.2 in only two respects: it is specified in discrete time rather than continuous time and the variables $_{t-1}z_t^e$ will not be constant over time. Because the equation is in discrete time, the Saddlepoint condition now requires that the m_1 eigenvalues of the $(m_1 \times m_1)$ matrix, Π_{11}, be less than unity in absolute value. This condition is analogous to the requirement that the matrix A has m_1 negative eigenvalues in equation (3.2.3) when the equation is specified in continuous time and m_1 variables are not predetermined. Secondly, although $_{t-1}z_t^e$ is no longer constant over time, this vector will not introduce any additional difficulties in the forward solution, provided z_{t+T} is expected to converge to a steady state vector as T tends to infinity. Formally, we require that the vector autoregressive process (5.1.1) is stationary. This implies that the parameters ϕ_i must lie in certain ranges, the precise conditions for which are given in Box and Jenkins (1970). A simple example will illustrate the general idea.

Consider the first order autoregressive process for a single variable z_t

$$z_t = \rho_0 + \rho_1 z_{t-1} + \epsilon_t \tag{5.1.13}$$

where the random disturbance has mean zero and is serially uncorrelated. Thus $_{t-1}z_t^e = \rho_0 + \rho_1 z_{t-1}$. By the Chain Rule of Forecasting

$$_{t-1}z_{t+1}^e = \rho_0 + \rho_1(\rho_0 + \rho_1 z_{t-1}) = (1 + \rho_1)\rho_0 + \rho_1^2 z_{t-1}$$

$$_{t-1}z_{t+2}^e = \rho_0 + \rho_1[(1 + \rho_1)\rho_0 + \rho_1^2 z_{t-1}] =$$
$$(1 + \rho_1 + \rho_1^2)\rho_0 + \rho_1^3 z_{t-1}$$

$$_{t-1}z_{t+T}^e = (1 + \rho_1 + \rho_1^2 + \rho_1^3 + \ldots + \rho_1^T)\rho_0 +$$
$$\rho_1^{T+1} z_{t-1}$$

Hence in this simple example, if the absolute value of ρ_1 is less than unity in equation (5.1.13), z_t is a stationary process which is expected at time $t-1$ to converge to the value $[\rho_0/(1-\rho_1)]$.

Assume that individuals at time $t-1$ expect the stationary autoregressive process (5.1.1) to converge to the vector $\bar{z}$. Reasoning as in the static model, a well defined set of values $\bar{y}_{1,t}$ exists only if the rank of $(I-\Pi_{11})$ is m_1, so that this $(m_1 \times m_1)$ matrix is non-singular. Thus the condition.

$$\text{Rank } (I-\Pi_{11}) = m_1$$

may now be given the interpretation that it ensures that individuals forming Rational Expectations can identify a unique steady state set of values $\bar{y}_{1,t}$ to which they expect the model to converge. As we saw in Section 3.2, it is essential that individuals can locate this steady state if they are to solve for the Rational Expectations equilibrium path.

Under these assumptions, we can now solve equation (5.1.12) by recursively substituting out the term $_{t-1}y^e_{1,t+1}$ from the right hand side, using the Chain Rule of Forecasting to determine the associated expectations of z variables. This forward recursion yields

$$_{t-1}y^e_{1,t} = \sum_{s=0}^{\infty} \Pi^s_{11} \, \Pi_{12}(_{t-1}z^e_{t+s}) \qquad (5.1.14)$$

for which the relevant expectations $_{t-1}z^e_{t+s}$ can be calculated from equation (5.1.1). Notice that the assumptions that z_t follows a stationary process and that the eigenvalues of the matrix Π_{11} are less than unity in absolute value guarantee the convergence of the above expression, confirming that the Saddlepoint assumptions deliver a unique Rational Expectations equilibrium path.

Shifting equation (5.1.14) forward one period

$$_{t}y^e_{1,t+1} = \sum_{s=0}^{\infty} \Pi^s_{11} \, \Pi_{12}(_{t}z^e_{t+s+1})$$

By Property I of Section 4.1, the Rational Expectation at time $t-1$ of what this Rational Expectation will be at time t is simply

$$_{t-1}y^e_{1,t+1} = \sum_{s=0}^{\infty} \Pi^s_{11} \, \Pi_{12} \, (_{t-1}z^e_{t+s+1}) \qquad (5.1.15)$$

which describes the Rational Expectations solution we are seeking. Moreover, it is easy to see how this expression may be rewritten in an observable form. Consider again the simpler example (5.1.13) and the subsequent examples of the use of the Chain Rule of Forecasting to evaluate particular values of

$_{t-1}z^e_{t+s}$. Each expectation of a future z value depends only on z_{t-1}, the relevant information available at time $t-1$, but as we consider different s values the weights on z_{t-1} change, though in each case they are simply functions of powers of the ρ parameters in equation (5.1.13). In this simple case, the convergent series (5.1.15) would thus be a linear function of z_{t-1}, with the coefficient depending on $(\Pi_{11}, \Pi_{12}, \rho_0, \text{and } \rho_1)$ after the convergent series had been evaluated. In the more general model given by equations (5.1.1) and (5.1.15), the solution for $_{t-1}y^e_{1,t+1}$ will be a linear combination of the variables $z_{t-1} \ldots z_{t-p}$, all of which convey information at time $t-1$ about future values of z_t. The coefficients will be different non-linear functions of the parameter matrices $(\Pi_{11}, \Pi_{12}, \phi_1, \ldots \phi_p)$ which enter the convergent series.

Hence we may express equation (5.1.15) in observable or final form

$$_{t-1}y^e_{1,t+1} = F_1 z_{t-1} + F_2 z_{t-2} + \ldots + F_p z_{t-p} \quad (5.1.16)$$

where the $(m_1 \times k)$ matrices F_i may be calculated in the manner just described. Substitution of equation (5.1.16) into equation (5.1.11) then generates an observable reduced form.

Again it is useful to examine the forecasting error $(y_{1,t+1} - {}_{t-1}y^e_{1,t+1})$. Shifting equation (5.1.11) forward one period

$$y_{1,t+1} = \Pi_{11}({}_t y^e_{1,t+2}) + \Pi_{12} z_{t+1} + v_{1,t+1}$$

Taking expectations conditional on information available at time $t-1$ and subtracting from the above equation

$$y_{1,t+1} - {}_{t-1}y^e_{1,t+1} = \Pi_{11}({}_t y^e_{1,t+2} - {}_{t-1}y^e_{1,t+2})$$
$$+ \Pi_{12}\,\phi_1\,\epsilon_t + \Pi_{12}\epsilon_{t+1} + v_{1,t+1} \quad (5.1.17)$$

The revision in forecasts at time t about $y_{1,t+2}$ arises because it is then possible to observe ϵ_t, the component of z_t which could not be anticipated at time $t-1$. Rational Expectations of y_{t+2} are thus based on more recent information about z from which future values of z may be estimated. As pointed out in Section 4.1, while the forecasting error given in equation (5.1.17) has conditional expectation zero given information at time $t-1$, it is not serially uncorrelated, because the two period lag between the date expectations are formed and the date variables are actually realised implies that two sets of new information become available. The forecasting error may thus be described by the general form

$$y_{1,t+1} - {}_{t-1}y^e_{1,t+1} = \eta_{t+1} + \theta\eta_t \qquad (5.1.18)$$

where η_t is a serially uncorrelated random variable with mean zero which reflects new information at time t. This property will become important when I consider the estimation of such models.

Finally, I consider models which also allow lagged exogenous variables directly in the structural equations to reflect sluggish adjustment of current behaviour to current exogenous variables. I rewrite the static model (5.1.2) as

$$By_t + \Gamma_1({}_{t-1}y^e_{1,t}) + \Gamma_{20}z_t + \Gamma_{21}z_{t-1} + \ldots$$
$$+ \Gamma_{2q}z_{t-q} = u_t \qquad (5.1.19)$$

Proceeding as before, we now find that the lagged vectors $z_{t-1} \ldots z_{t-q}$ enter the reduced form directly, because of their presence in the structural equations. Recalling that the lagged vectors $z_{t-1} \ldots z_{t-p}$ enter the observable reduced form in all Rational Expectations models because of the information they convey about future z values, this clearly leads to the possibility that we may be unable to disentangle the two sources of coefficients on lagged values of exogenous variables. It is to such identification problems that I now turn.

In this section we have studied a particular set of structural equations which include unobservable Rational Expectations, established the conditions for the existence of a unique Rational Expectations solution and derived specifications in which all the systematic variables are observable. This approach may be extended to other specifications. The case in which lagged endogenous variables enter the structural equations is briefly examined in Wallis (1980). Another case of considerable interest is that in which some elements of z_t are knowable at time $t-1$ and may be forecast exactly. Seasonal dummy variables are one example.

5.2 Statistical Identification in Rational Expectations Models

By the statistical identification of parameters we mean the property that they may be inferred uniquely, and hence estimated consistently, from the parameters of the observable reduced form which contains all the information embodied in a particular data sample. In this section, I am interested only in the additional complications which arise from the assumption of Rational Expectations. A convenient device, first exploited by Wallis (1980), is to assume that there are sufficient *a priori* assumptions on the structural equations to identify the structural parameters (B, Γ) once consistent estimates of the parameters Π of the unobservable reduced form have been obtained. Thus I focus on the problem which arises because the Rational Expectations in this reduced form are statistically predetermined but unobservable, preventing direct estimation of this reduced form as in the usual simultaneous model.

Consider first the static model (5.1.2), together with the description (5.1.1) of the process determining the exogenous variables. We wish to know when we can retrieve consistent estimates of the Π parameters from estimates of the parameters of the observable reduced form (5.1.6). For convenience, I rewrite the latter in matrix notation

$$\begin{bmatrix} y_{1,t} \\ y_{2,t} \end{bmatrix} = \begin{bmatrix} \Pi_{11}(I - \Pi_{11})^{-1}\,\Pi_{12}\,\Pi_{12} \\ \Pi_{21}(I - \Pi_{11})^{-1}\,\Pi_{12}\,\Pi_{22} \end{bmatrix} \begin{bmatrix} {}_{t-1}z_t^e \\ z_t \end{bmatrix} + \begin{bmatrix} v_{1,t} \\ v_{2,t} \end{bmatrix}$$

$$(5.2.1)$$

Equation (5.1.1) may be consistently estimated by OLS. Let the parameters $\hat{\phi}_i$ be these OLS estimates, form ${}_{t-1}\hat{z}_t \equiv \hat{\phi}_1 z_{t-1} + \ldots + \hat{\phi}_p z_{t-p}$, and replace the unobservable Rational Expectations ${}_{t-1}z_t^e$ by this estimate ${}_{t-1}\hat{z}_t$ in equation (5.2.1). Since the $\hat{\phi}_i$ are consistent estimates of the true parameters ϕ_i, given a sufficiently large sample from which to estimate these parameters we can drive our estimate ${}_{t-1}\hat{z}_t$ as close as we please to the unobservable Rational Expectation in equation (5.1.7). In discussing consistent estimation of the model, we may thus treat ${}_{t-1}z_t^e$ as observable. Putting the matter differently, by this prior regression on equation (5.1.1) we can effectively impose on equation (5.2.1) the Rational Expectations restrictions that ${}_{t-1}z_t^e$ is a particular linear combination of past values of z_t.

After making this substitution, we can then estimate equation (5.2.1) by OLS to obtain consistent estimates of the parameter matrices multiplying these variables. What we wish to know is whether separate estimates of the individual matrices Π_{ij} can be recovered from these estimates. Using standard theorems from the literature on non-linear identification, Wallis (1980) shows that the *Rank Condition* for identification of the Π_{ij} matrices is

$$\text{Rank} \, (\Pi_{12}) = m_1 \qquad\qquad (5.2.2)$$

Since this matrix is of dimension $(m_1 \times k)$, the associated *Order Condition* is

$$m_1 \leqslant k$$

Thus there must be at least as many exogenous variables as there are expectational variables. Provided these conditions hold, we may retrieve first the Π parameters and then the structural parameters (B, Γ) from consistent estimates of equation (5.2.1).

We may use the discussion of the previous section to interpret the Wallis condition (5.2.2). Consider again equation (5.1.5)

$$_{t-1}y^e_{1,t} = (I - \Pi_{11})^{-1} \, \Pi_{12} (_{t-1}z^e_t)$$

We have already seen that $(I - \Pi_{11})$ must be non-singular if the specification is to be sensible. If condition (5.2.2) does not hold, the m_1 elements of $_{t-1}y^e_{1,t}$ must be linearly dependent, since equation (5.1.5) must hold for all conceivable values of $_{t-1}z^e_t$. Thus we can express one element of $_{t-1}y^e_{1,t}$ as a linear combination of other elements of this vector and eliminate this expectation from the structure, changing the definition of the Π_{ij} matrices. Since we can arbitrarily drop any element of $_{t-1}y^e_{1,t}$ we can alter any element of the Π matrices. Hence these matrices cannot be inferred from the data, unless condition (5.2.2) holds and the elements of $_{t-1}y^e_{1,t}$ are linearly independent.

Consider next the model with forward expectations given by equations (5.1.1) and (5.1.10). From the discussion of the previous section, a unique Rational Expectations equilibrium is possible only if $(I - \Pi_{11})$ is non-singular and if the eigenvalues of Π_{11} are all less than unity in absolute value. These conditions must be necessary for the identification of the Π

parameters. Again we shall require that the m_1 elements of the expectations vector $_{t-1}y^e_{1,t+1}$ are linearly independent if we are to rule out the possibility that different models are observationally equivalent. Let F be the matrix

$$F = [F_1 \ F_2 \ \dots \ F_p]$$

where F_i denotes the $(m_1 \times k)$ matrices given in equation (5.1.16). Thus the partitioned matrix F has dimension $(m_1 \times pk)$. From equation (5.1.16) the m_1 elements of the vector $_{t-1}y^e_{1,t+1}$ will be linearly dependent only if

$$\text{Rank} \ (F) = m_1 \tag{5.2.3}$$

Since we saw that F depends in part on the ϕ parameters of the stochastic process determining z_t, this introduces the idea that the identification of the Π parameters may depend on the nature of the process which the exogenous variables obey. Given assumption (5.2.3), the model is identified and its parameters may be consistently estimated by methods discussed in the following section.

It is useful to consider one method of estimation immediately, because it allows us to see why identification is more difficult when the model is generalised to allow lagged values of z_t to enter the structure directly as in equation (5.1.19). The estimation method may be illustrated in the simpler model I have just discussed. The unobservable reduced form is given by equation (5.1.11) and its counterpart for $y_{2,t}$

$$\begin{bmatrix} y_{1,t} \\ y_{2,t} \end{bmatrix} = \begin{bmatrix} \Pi_{11} & \Pi_{22} \\ \Pi_{21} & \Pi_{22} \end{bmatrix} \begin{bmatrix} _{t-1}y^e_{1,t+1} \\ z_t \end{bmatrix} + \begin{bmatrix} v_{1,t} \\ v_{2,t} \end{bmatrix} \tag{5.2.4}$$

Consider equation (5.1.16), the final form for the unobservable Rational Expectation $_{t-1}y^e_{1,t+1}$. Equation (5.1.18) shows how observable *ex post* values of $y_{1,t+1}$ differ from the Rational Expectations formed at time $t-1$. Hence equation (5.1.16) may be written in observable form

$$y_{1,t+1} = F_1 z_{t-1} + F_2 z_{t-2} + \dots F_p z_{t-p} + \eta_{t+1} + \theta \eta_t \tag{5.2.5}$$

In discussing equation (5.2.1) I suggested the use of a prior regression to form $_{t-1}\hat{z}_t$ which might be used in place of the unobservable expectations $_{t-1}z_t^e$. I now adopt the same strategy for the unobservable expectations $_{t-1}y_{1,t+1}^e$ in equation (5.2.4), making use of the observable equation (5.2.5). From the discussion of equation (5.1.18), the random disturbances η_t and η_{t+1} are uncorrelated with all information available at time $t-1$ and in particular are uncorrelated with $(z_{t-1}, \ldots z_{t-p})$. Because the disturbances in equation (5.2.5) follow a first order moving average process, estimation of this equation by OLS will yield inefficient estimates of the F matrices; nevertheless these estimates will be consistent and will suffice for our purpose, even though more sophisticated estimation methods are possible. Letting $\hat{F}_i$ denote the OLS parameter estimates, form $_t\hat{y}_{1,t+1} \equiv \hat{F}_1 z_{t-1} + \hat{F}_2 z_{t-2} + \ldots + \hat{F}_p z_{t-p}$ and replace $_{t-1}y_{1,t+1}^e$ by this estimate in equation (5.2.4). One further OLS regression on this amended form of equation (5.2.4) will then yield consistent estimates of the Π parameters directly, provided two conditions are met: first, there must not be perfect collinearity within the $_{t-1}y_{1,t+1}^e$ vector, which is precisely the condition ensured by equation (5.2.3), and secondly $_{t-1}y_{1,t+1}^e$ and z_t must not be perfectly collinear, a condition ensured by the stochastic specification (5.1.1) which guarantees that realisations of the current disturbance ϵ_t will prevent z_t being an exact linear combination of its p previous values. This analysis illustrates a method for the consistent estimation of the Π parameters and stresses the role which the Rank Condition (5.2.3) plays.

I now consider the model (5.1.19) which also allows q lagged values of z_t to enter the structure directly. The unobservable reduced form for $y_{1,t}$ is now given by

$$y_{1,t} = \Pi_{11}(_{t-1}y_{1,t}^e) + \Pi_{12,0}z_t + \Pi_{12,1}z_{t-1} + \ldots$$
$$+ \Pi_{12,q}z_{t-q} + v_{1,t} \qquad (5.2.6)$$

with an analogous equation for $y_{2,t}$. The Rational Expectation $_{t-1}y_{1,t}^e$ is therefore

$$_{t-1}y_{1,t}^e = (I - \Pi_{11})^{-1} [\Pi_{12,0}(_{t-1}z_t^e) + \Pi_{12,1}z_{t-1} + \ldots$$
$$+ \Pi_{12,q}z_{t-q}] \qquad (5.2.7)$$

Since, in matrix notation,

$$t_{-1}z_t^e = [\phi_1 \; \phi_2 \; \ldots \; \phi_p] \begin{bmatrix} z_{t-1} \\ z_{t-2} \\ \cdot \\ \cdot \\ z_{t-p} \end{bmatrix}$$

equation (5.2.7) may be written

$$_{t-1}y_{1,t}^e = H\tilde{z}_t \tag{5.2.8}$$

where $\tilde{z}_t$ is a partitioned column vector with the columns z_{t-1}, z_{t-2}, etc. stacked vertically one above the other with the last entry being z_{t-p} or z_{t-q} according as p is larger or smaller than q. The partitioned H matrix has m_1 rows and the maximum of pk or qk columns. Thus the m_1 elements of $_{t-1}y_{1,t}^e$ are linearly independent only if

$$\text{Rank } (H) = m_1 \tag{5.2.9}$$

In previous models, a condition of this kind was sufficient to identify the Π parameters, but this is no longer the case. Suppose we implement the estimation strategy described above, regressing $y_{1,t}$ on $\tilde{z}_t$ to form consistent estimates of the H parameters in equation (5.2.8), then substituting this estimate $_{t-1}\hat{y}_{1,t}$ for the unobservable Rational Expectations in equation (5.2.6) and the counterpart equation for $y_{2,t}$. Consider a final regression on these amended equations which it is hoped will yield consistent estimates of the Π parameters. If $q \geqslant p$, the number of lagged exogenous variables directly entering the structure and the reduced form are at least as great as the number of lagged exogenous variables required at time $t-1$ to forecast z_t and hence $y_{1,t}$. Even though condition (5.2.9) ensures that the elements of $_{t-1}y_{1,t}^e$ are themselves linearly independent, $_{t-1}y_{1,t}^e$ is an exact linear combination of $(z_{t-1} \ldots z_{t-q})$, since no other variables enter the $\tilde{z}_t$ vector in equation (5.2.8). Hence the final regression will break down and the Π parameters are no longer identified. When the model includes lagged exogenous variables directly in the structure, we require not only equation (5.2.9) but also the condition

$$q < p \tag{5.2.10}$$

By ensuring that some lagged exogenous variables enter the observable reduced form purely through their usefulness in forecasting future values of z_t and hence $y_{1,t}$, this condition allows us to disentangle the two sets of parameters on other lagged exogenous variables, provided that the process (5.1.1) can be directly estimated.

It may be helpful to give a simple example in which condition (5.2.10) fails. Suppose there is one endogenous variable $y_{1,t}$ and one exogenous variable z_t such that

$$y_{1,t} = \Pi_{11}({}_{t-1}y^e_{1,t}) + \Pi_{12,0}z_t + \Pi_{12,1}z_{t-1} + v_{1,t} \tag{5.2.11}$$

$$z_t = \phi z_{t-1} + \epsilon_t \tag{5.2.12}$$

Thus, in our earlier notation, $p = q = m = m_1 = k = 1$. The Rational Expectation ${}_{t-1}z^e_t$ is simply ϕz_{t-1} and the Rational Expectation ${}_{t-1}y^e_{1,t}$ is given by

$$_{t-1}y^e_{1,t} = \frac{\phi\,\Pi_{12,0} + \Pi_{12,1}}{1 - \Pi_{11}}\,z_{t-1}$$

As before, I assume that $(1 - \Pi_{11})$ is non-zero and that the numerator is non-zero. Hence condition (5.2.9) holds. Substituting into equation (5.2.11)

$$y_{1,t} = \Pi_{12,0}\,z_t + \frac{\Pi_{12,1} + \phi\,\Pi_{11}\,\Pi_{12,0}}{1 - \Pi_{11}}\,z_{t-1} + v_{1,t} \tag{5.2.13}$$

Thus, even beginning with a prior estimate of ϕ from equation (5.2.12), only the parameter $\Pi_{12,0}$ is identified. It is impossible to decompose the coefficient of z_{t-1} into separate estimates of the remaining two unknown parameters Π_{11} and $\Pi_{12,1}$. Once we drop the lagged exogenous variable by imposing the condition $\Pi_{12,1} = 0$, equation (5.2.13) satisfies condition (5.2.10), since q is zero and p is unity. Estimation of equation (5.2.13) by OLS then allows Π_{11} to be inferred from the coefficient on z_{t-1}, given the estimated coefficient on z_t and the estimate of ϕ from a prior regression using equation (5.2.12).

Thus, the relative size of p and q is central to the identification of all parameters in Rational Expectations models, though the above example makes clear that some parameters may be identified even when condition (5.2.10) fails. It is possible that hypothesis testing may still be carried out, even when the model is not completely identified. Moreover, it should be recognised that the above analysis assumes the vector autoregressive representation of order p for the exogenous variables. Other assumptions on the process z_t are possible and may mitigate the identification problem discussed above. For example, if z_t has a moving average component which is invertible, it will be possible to represent z_t by an infinite autoregressive process. To be specific, if z_t obeys the first order moving average process

$$z_t = \epsilon_t - \theta \, \epsilon_{t-1} \tag{5.2.14}$$

where ϵ_t is a serially uncorrelated random variable with mean zero and the parameter θ is less than unity in absolute value, we may rewrite this equation as

$$z_t = \epsilon_t - \theta z_{t-1} - \theta^2 z_{t-2} - \theta^3 z_{t-3} \ldots - \theta^p z_{t-p} - \cdots$$

If the structural equations contain only a finite number of lagged exogenous variables, it will thus be possible to satisfy condition (5.2.10) when z_t has a moving average component. Conversely, if the structural equations contain infinite distributed lags so that exogenous variables have effects which only gradually die away, complete identification may be impossible. Some authors such as Sargent (1976b) have pointed out that there is nothing in economic theory to preclude such a specification. It should also be noted that the type of restriction which should be imposed *a priori* on lag lengths is an issue which holds in all dynamic models, not merely those with Rational Expectations. Interested readers may refer to Hatanaka (1975).

In this section, I have examined the identification of models with Rational Expectations. The analysis has aimed to establish the conditions under which the Π parameters of the unobservable reduced form will be identified; retrieving the structural parameters (B, Γ) from these reduced form parameters will then be possible under the usual identification conditions. Two points should be noted. First, the identification conditions discussed in this section bear little resemblance to the conventional identification conditions in standard texts, which usually rely heavily on exclusion restrictions to identify structural parameters. In Rational Expectations models, non-linear cross equation restrictions play a key role, since the solution procedure imposes a particular set of restrictions about the way lagged exogenous variables determine the Rational Expectations of current or future endogenous variables. Also, since models are usually dynamic, assumptions about lag lengths play a role which is not possible in entirely static models. The second point to note is that it is not necessary to identify structural parameters by the two step method considered in this section. Rather than determining whether the parameters of the unobservable reduced form are identified and then working back to the structural parameters, it may be possible to proceed directly to the structural parameters themselves. This problem is currently the focus of much research, though the possibility was noted by Wallis (1980) whose two step strategy I have followed in this section. If, given Π, the structural parameters (B, Γ) are overidentified by restrictions on the structural equations themselves, it is well known that these overidentifying restrictions will impose non-linear cross equation restrictions on the Π parameters. By using these additional restrictions we may be able to identify the Π parameters, even when the identification conditions of this section are not met; equivalently, we may be able to identify the structural parameters directly, even though the parameters of the unobservable reduced form cannot be identified without imposing the additional restrictions implied by the overidentified structure. Thus, the conditions of this section are exact when the original structure is just identified by the Π parameters but are only sufficient conditions when the original structure is overidentified.

5.3 Estimation of Rational Expectations Models

When structural equations are overidentified, *Full Information* estimation methods such as *Three Stage Least Squares* (3SLS) will be more efficient than *Limited Information* estimation methods such as *Two Stage Least Squares* (2SLS). Moreover, since many of the Rational Expectations restrictions are cross equation, it might seem natural to use Full Information methods in which these restrictions can be imposed *a priori*. Nevertheless, there are two reasons why Limited Information estimation may still be attractive, provided equations can be identified within this framework: it is much simpler to implement and it is more robust. When incorrect restrictions are imposed in any equation, Full Information methods spread this misspecification throughout the system, leading to inconsistent estimates in all equations, but Limited Information methods *may* confine the inconsistent estimates to the equation in which the incorrect restrictions are imposed. These advantages have led many authors to use Limited Information estimation and I begin with a discussion of such procedures.

Consider first the static model given by equations (5.1.1) and (5.1.2) in which the ith structural equation may be written

$$y_i = Y_i\beta_i + Y_{1i}^e\gamma_{1i} + Z_i\gamma_{2i} + u_i \qquad (5.3.1)$$

where y_i and u_i are column T-vectors of the T observations on the endogenous variable y_{it} and the disturbance u_{it} in the ith equation. Y_i is the $(T \times m_i)$ matrix of observations of the m_i included right hand side endogenous variables and Z_i the $(T \times k_i)$ matrix of observations on the k_i included exogenous variables in this equation, after the exclusion restrictions have been imposed. Y_{1i}^e is the $(T \times h_i)$ matrix of observations on the h_i included Rational Expectations variables, the typical row of which is the $(1 \times h_i)$ vector $(_{t-1}y_{1it}^e)'$, the included elements of the full Rational Expectations vector $(_{t-1}y_{1,t}^e)'$ in equation (5.1.2). Thus the vectors β_i, γ_{1i} and γ_{2i} have dimensions $(m_i \times 1)$, $(h_i \times 1)$ and $(k_i \times 1)$ respectively, and are the transposes of the ith rows of the matrices B, Γ_1, and Γ_2 in equation (5.1.2) after the known zero elements have been omitted, as in the usual discussion of 2SLS under exclusion restrictions on the structural equations.

The first estimation strategy, proposed by Sargent (1973) (1976a) and Wallis (1980), is the method I adopted in the previous section when illustrating identification problems.

Equations (5.1.5), (5.1.7) and (5.1.9) imply

$$y_{1,t} = G_1 z_{t-1} + G_2 z_{t-2} + \ldots$$
$$+ G_p z_{t-p} + (\Pi_{12} \epsilon_t + v_{1,t}) \qquad (5.3.2)$$

where the matrices G_i may be inferred from the parameters of the model. The disturbance term is uncorrelated with the right hand side variables, since it is the pure Rational Expectations forecasting error and lagged values of z_t are known at the date expectations are formed. Hence an OLS regression leads to consistent estimates of the G_i matrices, from which we may form $_{t-1}\hat{y}_{1,t}$, select the appropriate elements $_{t-1}\hat{y}_{1i,t}$, and thus construct the matrix $_{t-1}\hat{Y}_{1i}$ with which to replace the unobservable matrix Y_{1i}^e in equation (5.3.1). Although the argument is straightforward, proceeding by analogy with 2SLS, it may be helpful to work through the matrix algebra at least once. Transposing equation (5.3.2) and stacking the T observations vertically, we obtain

$$Y_1 = Z_0 G + \Lambda$$

where Y_1 is $(T \times m_1)$, as is the matrix of pure forecasting errors Λ, while Z_0 is the $(T \times pk)$ partitioned matrix of observations on the p lagged k-vectors z_{t-i} and G is the transpose of the partitioned matrix $\{G_1\ G_2 \ldots G_p\}$. Running OLS

$$\hat{G} = G + (Z_0' Z_0)^{-1} Z_0' \Lambda$$

whence

$$\hat{Y}_1 = Z_0 \hat{G} = Z_0 G + Z_0 (Z_0' Z_0)^{-1} Z_0' \Lambda$$
$$= Y_1^e + Z_0 (Z_0' Z_0)^{-1} Z_0' \Lambda$$

For convenience, I suppose that all m_1 expectational variables enter equation (5.3.1), though the reasoning is identical when only a subset m_{1i} of these variables appears. Equation (5.3.1) may now be written

$$y_i = Y_i \beta_i + \hat{Y}_1 \gamma_{1i} + Z_i \gamma_{2i} + [u_i - Z_0 (Z_0' Z_0)^{-1} Z_0' \Lambda \gamma_{1i}]$$

$$= [Y_i\ \hat{Y}_1\ Z_i] \begin{bmatrix} \beta_i \\ \gamma_{1i} \\ \gamma_{2i} \end{bmatrix} + [u_i - Z_0 (Z_0' Z_0)^{-1} Z_0' \Lambda \gamma_{1i}]$$

Defining X_i and δ_i appropriately, this may be written

$$y_i \equiv X_i\delta_i + \{ u_i - Z_0(Z_0'Z_0)^{-1}Z_0' \Lambda \gamma_{1i}\} \qquad (5.3.3)$$

As in the usual discussion of 2SLS, consistent estimates of the parameters δ_i may now be obtained by selecting a matrix of instruments W_i and forming the instrumental variable estimator

$$\hat{\delta}_i = (W_i'X_i)^{-1} W_i'y_i \qquad (5.3.4)$$

where the instrument matrix W_i should include Z_i and $\hat{Y}_1$ (or $\hat{Y}_{1i}$ if only m_{1i} of the expectational variables enter equations (5.3.1) and (5.3.3)) and other linear combinations of current and lagged exogenous variables. Since this argument differs from the usual 2SLS reasoning only in asserting that $\hat{Y}_1$ is asymptotically uncorrelated with the disturbance in equation (5.3.3), it will be sufficient to check this assertion.

$$\text{plim} \frac{1}{T} \hat{Y}_1' [u_i - Z_0(Z_0'Z_0)^{-1}Z_0'\Lambda\gamma_{1i}] =$$

$$\text{plim } \hat{G}' \left(\frac{Z_0'u_i}{T}\right) - \text{plim } \hat{G}' \left(\frac{Z_0'Z_0}{T}\right)\left(\frac{Z_0'Z_0}{T}\right)^{-1} \left(\frac{Z_0'\Lambda}{T}\right) \gamma_{1i} = 0$$

$$\text{since} \quad \text{plim } \hat{G}' = G' \quad \text{plim } \left(\frac{Z_0'u_i}{T}\right) = 0 \quad \text{plim } \left(\frac{Z_0'\Lambda}{T}\right) = 0$$

Thus the instrumental variable estimator given in equation (5.3.4) will be consistent, provided additional elements of W_i are uncorrelated with the disturbance in equation (5.3.3), but correlated with Y_i.

McCallum (1976a) proposes an alternative estimation strategy. Recall that the actual values Y_1 differ from their Rational Expectations only by the pure forecasting errors Λ. McCallum suggests replacing the unobservable Rational Expectations Y_{1i}^e in equation (5.3.1) by the *ex post* values of the relevant variables Y_{1i}, so that the equation may be written

$$y_i = Y_i\beta_i + Y_{1i}\gamma_{1i} + Z_i\gamma_{2i} + \{u_i - \Lambda_i\gamma_{1i}\} \qquad (5.3.5)$$

where Λ_i is the relevant submatrix of Λ, corresponding to the forecasting errors on the h_i included expectational variables. The McCallum substitution induces an 'errors in variables' problem, since Y_{1i} is now correlated with the augmented disturbance term, but the usual solution to this problem must be carefully applied. Equation (5.1.9) indicates that the Rational Expectations forecasting errors Λ_i occur partly because of unanticipatable shocks ϵ_t to exogenous variables at time t. Although by definition these shocks are uncorrelated with the structural disturbances u_{it}, they are contemporaneously correlated with Λ_i. Thus the McCallum substitution not only induces correlation between Y_{1i} and the disturbance term, it also induces contemporaneous correlation between Z_i and Λ_i, so that Z_i can no longer be treated as stochastically predetermined. McCallum proposes that we estimate equation (5.3.5) by instrumental variables, finding instruments not only for the variables Y_i and Y_{1i}, but also for the variables Z_i. The usual considerations suggest the choice of instruments for Y_i and Y_{1i} and instruments for Z_i follow immediately from equation (5.1.1): lagged exogenous variables will be appropriate.

The McCallum substitution has two disadvantages, but one advantage over the estimation method proposed earlier. The first disadvantage is that it cannot be used when the ith equation includes on the right hand side both a current endogenous variable and its own Rational Expectation from one period earlier, for once the substitution has been made, the current value of the endogenous variable enters twice and it is impossible to identify separately the relevant elements of β_i and γ_{1i}. The second disadvantage is that current exogenous variables can no longer be used as instruments, so that the identification condition is now more stringent: it is easy to devise examples in which there are sufficient instruments to obtain consistent estimates of equation (5.3.4), but insufficient instruments to use in equation (5.3.5); see Wallis (1980). The corresponding advantage occurs when the process (5.1.1) determining the exogenous variables involves a large number of lags. In practice, it is possible that the number of observations will not be sufficiently large to allow the estimation of this process, since at least pk observations are required. If the number of lags is artificially truncated, the resulting estimate $\hat{Y}_{1i}$ will not in fact reflect the unobservable Rational Expectations and the second stage estimates will be inconsistent if equations (5.3.3) and (5.3.4) form the basis of the estimation. In contrast, the McCallum procedure, being a single application of the method of instrumental variables, will still obtain consistent estimates, even if the instruments do not include the full set of lagged exogenous variables relevant to the Rational Expectations solution. This follows from the fact that forecasting errors are uncorrelated with any of these lagged variables, whilst current values of y and z are at least partly correlated with any subset of the relevant lagged variables. Thus, it is not possible to offer a definitive recommendation as to which estimation method should be adopted; the answer will depend on the nature of the model to be estimated.

Limited Information estimation of the dynamic model (5.1.1) (5.1.10) may be treated in similar fashion. The matrix Y_{1i}^e in equation (5.3.1) is now taken to refer to the T observations on the Rational Expectations formed at time $t-1$ about the values of endogenous variables at time $t + 1$. One additional complication is introduced as equation (5.1.18) makes clear: the matrix of forecasting errors Λ_i now comprises individual forecasting errors which are no longer serially uncorrelated. Rather, forecasting errors follow a first order moving average process, reflecting both new information at time $t + 1$ and new information at time t. However, because forecasting errors must be uncorrelated with information available at time $t-1$ when the expectations are formed, consistent estimates will still be obtained provided some care is taken when specifying forecasting rules and matrices of instrumental variables.

Consider the first estimation method proposed above and discussed also in the previous section. OLS estimates from equation (5.2.5) will be consistent and may be used to form $\hat{Y}_{1i}$ to be used in equation (5.3.1). Similarly, in the McCallum substitution the *ex post* value $Y_{1i, t+1}$ may be used, provided instruments before time t are used in the subsequent estimation. While consistent estimates may be obtained, the fact that the disturbance now includes a moving average component implies that estimates will not be efficient even in a Limited Information context, just as OLS is inefficient when the standard regression model has a non-scalar covariance matrix. Moreover, extending the parallel, the reported covariance matrix when the computer uses formulae treating the covariance matrix as scalar will be incorrect, though it is straightforward to correct the estimated covariance matrix of the estimates once the problem has been recognised. For a simple application of this procedure, the reader is referred to Brown and Maital (1981).

Such estimates remain inefficient because the disturbance covariance matrix is non-scalar and it is tempting to apply in addition the usual GLS transformation to obtain more efficient estimates. To be specific, suppose Ω is the covariance matrix of the augmented disturbances in equation (5.3.5), after making the McCallum substitution in the dynamic version of equation (5.3.1). For compactness, write equation (5.3.5) as

$$y_i = X_i \delta_i + \xi_i \qquad X_i \equiv \{ Y_i \ Y_{1i} \ Z_i \} \qquad \delta \equiv \begin{bmatrix} \beta_i \\ \gamma_{1i} \\ \gamma_{2i} \end{bmatrix}$$

$$\xi_i \equiv [u_i - \Lambda_i \gamma_{1i}] \qquad (5.3.6)$$

Let W_i be the matrix of all candidates for instruments, for which the tth observation is the set of exogenous variables valued between dates $t-1$ and $t-p$ inclusive, which are uncorrelated with ξ_{it} but correlated with X_{it}. Thus the usual 2SLS estimator is

$$\hat{\delta}_i = (X_i'W_i(W_i'W_i)^{-1}W_i'X_i)^{-1}X_i'W_i(W_i'W_i)^{-1}W_i'y_i \quad (5.3.7)$$

whilst a GLS type correction may be applied by forming δ_i^* given by

$$\delta_i^* = (X_i'\Omega^{-1}W_i(W_i'\Omega^{-1}W_i)^{-1}W_i'\Omega^{-1}X_i)^{-1}$$
$$X_i'\Omega^{-1}W_i(W_i'\Omega^{-1}W_i)^{-1}W_i'\Omega^{-1}y_i \qquad (5.3.8)$$

After substituting from (5.3.6) into (5.3.8) we obtain on the right hand side δ, plus a product of matrices the last of which is

$$W_i'\Omega^{-1}\xi_i \qquad (5.3.9)$$

The consistency proof must rest on the plim of $(1/T)$ times this matrix equalling zero. In the usual simultaneous equation model this condition is fulfilled, since the matrix of instruments W_i comprises variables which are strongly exogenous, being uncorrelated with all past, present and future values of the structural disturbances. This assumption does not hold in Rational Expectations models as has now been noted by many authors — Bernanke (1977), Hansen (1980), Flood and Garber (1980b), Hayashi (1980), Hayashi and Sims (1980), Hansen and Hodrick (1980), Hakkio (1980) and Obstfeld, Cumby and Huizinga (1981).

In Rational Expectations models of the type (5.3.6), the appropriate elements of W_i are lagged observations on exogenous variables, whilst ξ_i includes observations on Rational Expectations forecasting errors, one component of which is failure to predict disturbances in exogenous variables. When the covariance matrix Ω of observations on these disturbances is non-scalar, its inverse is not diagonal. Hence when expression (5.3.8) is evaluated, terms such as ξ_{it} do not merely pick off past disturbances in the exogenous variables, but also pick off contemporaneous disturbances. Thus the GLS transformation is inconsistent. Notice that this problem does not arise in equation (5.3.7), when no attempt is made to undertake a GLS correction: corresponding to the term in (5.3.8) we now have $W_i' \xi_i$, in which each disturbance ξ_{it} picks off only previous values of exogenous variables with which it is uncorrelated, confirming the earlier assertion that such estimates will be consistent, provided sufficient instruments exist to implement equation (5.3.7). Although conventional GLS corrections are no longer appropriate in Rational Expectations models, more sophisticated corrections are possible and do allow consistent and more efficient estimation than the methods proposed earlier. The interested reader is referred to Hayashi (1980), Hayashi and Sims (1980) and Obstfeld, Cumby and Huizinga (1981). The general treatment offered in the last of these papers is also applicable when the structural disturbances u_i are serially correlated.

This completes my discussion of Limited Information estimation. Full Information estimation is obviously more complex, but in one sense is conceptually simple: given a distributional assumption of normality, or invoking the relevant asymptotic distribution theory to claim normality, the most efficient estimation is *Full Information Maximum Likelihood* imposing all the known *a priori* restrictions. Interested readers are referred to Taylor (1979a), Wallis

(1980), Hayashi (1980), Hansen and Sargent (1980a and b) and Sargent (1981). I shall confine my remarks to several brief comments.

First, Sections 5.1 and 5.2 make clear that many of the Rational Expectations restrictions take the form of highly non-linear cross equation restrictions which make the implementation of FIML computationally complicated. Feasible iterative procedures have been suggested by Wallis (1980), Fair (1979b) and Fair and Taylor (1980). Secondly, since the parameters ϕ of the exogenous process (5.1.1) enter the Rational Expectations restrictions on structural equations when the latter are written in observable form, it is more efficient to estimate jointly the two sets of equations. Thirdly, Full Information methods exploit not only the contemporaneous covariance across structural disturbances, but also the contemporaneous covariance of Rational Expectations forecasting errors if the observable form is derived by the McCallum substitution. Fourthly, although much of the early empirical literature uses Limited Information estimation methods and frequently estimates reduced form rather than structural parameters, future empirical research will undoubtedly pay more attention to Full Information estimation of structural parameters. By utilising the richness of the cross equation restrictions implied by the Rational Expectations hypothesis, Full Information methods take advantage of identifying information which is not utilised in Limited Information estimation; by focusing directly on structural coefficients, not only is additional information brought to bear when the structure is overidentified, but also we obtain estimates which are more robust with respect to the changes in policy rules or exogenous processes to which Lucas first drew attention.

5.4 Testing the Rational Expectations Hypothesis

In this section I consider testing the Rational Expectations hypothesis conditional on the validity of the specification of the structural equations. Beginning once more with the static model (5.1.1) (5.1.2), equation (5.1.5) implies

$$Y_1^e = Z^e \Pi_{12}'(I - \Pi_{11}')^{-1} \tag{5.4.1}$$

where Y_1^e is the $(T \times m_1)$ matrix of observations on $(_{t-1}y_{1,t}^e)'$ and Z^e the $(T \times k)$ matrix of observations on $(_{t-1}z_t^e)'$. From equation (5.1.7)

$$Z^e = \{ Z_{-1} \ Z_{-2} \ldots Z_{-p} \} \begin{bmatrix} \phi_1' \\ \cdot \\ \cdot \\ \cdot \\ \phi_p' \end{bmatrix} \equiv Z_0 \phi' \tag{5.4.2}$$

where Z_{-i} is the $(T \times k)$ matrix of observations on $(z_{t-i})'$, and Z_0 and ϕ' are the appropriate partitioned matrices satisfying the above definition. From the unobservable reduced form (5.1.4a)

$$Y_1 = Y_1^e \Pi_{11}' + Z\Pi_{12}' + V_1 \tag{5.4.3}$$

where Z is the $(T \times k)$ matrix of observations on $(z_t)'$ and V_1 the $(T \times k)$ matrix of observations on $(v_{1,t})'$. Combining equations (5.4.1)–(5.4.3), under Rational Expectations

$$Y_1 = Z_0 \phi' \Pi_{12}'(I - \Pi_{11}')^{-1} \Pi_{11}' + Z\Pi_{12}' + V_1 \tag{5.4.4}$$

It is now necessary to specify the alternative hypothesis about expectations formation. It may seem natural to treat this hypothesis as an extrapolation of past values of Y_1 and I shall return to this shortly. For the moment, I adopt the simpler route of supposing that the alternative hypothesis takes the form

$$Y_1^e = Z_1 D' \quad Z_1 = \{ Z_{-1} \ Z_{-2} \ldots Z_{-p} \ldots Z_{-q} \}$$
$$D = \{ D_1 \ D_2 \ldots D_q \} \tag{5.4.5}$$

where D_i is an $(m_1 \times k)$ matrix and the partitioned matrix D' has dimension $(qk \times m_1)$ where q is at least as great as p. Hence the matrix Z_1 includes all the elements of Z_0, plus possibly some additional lagged exogenous variables. Substituting equation (5.4.5) into equation (5.4.3)

$$Y_1 = Z_1 D' \Pi_{11}' + Z\Pi_{12}' + V_1 \tag{5.4.6}$$

Where Z_1 includes more lagged exogenous variables than Z_0, it is convenient to define these additional variables by Z_* and partition Z_1 according to

$$Z_1 \equiv \{Z_0 \, Z_*\} \qquad Z_* \equiv \{Z_{-p-1} \, \ldots \, . \, Z_{-q}\}$$

Partitioning D conformably into D_0 and D^*, equation (5.4.6) may be rewritten

$$Y_1 = Z_0 D_0' \Pi_{11}' + Z_* D_*' \Pi_{11}' + Z \Pi_{12}' + V_1 \qquad (5.4.7)$$

Thus the Rational Expectations restrictions may be written as

$$D_0' = \phi' \Pi_{12}' (I - \Pi_{11}')^{-1} \qquad D_* = 0 \qquad (5.4.8)$$

Before discussing how these restrictions may be tested, we must reconsider the question of identification. Under the conditions given in the previous section, the parameters of equation (5.4.4) are separately identified. However, in equation (5.4.7) only the parameters Π_{12}' are identified under the alternative hypothesis. Consider any square non-singular matrix Q of dimension $(m_1 \times m_1)$ and define $\tilde{D}'$ and $\tilde{\Pi}_{11}'$ by

$$\tilde{D}' \equiv D'Q \qquad \tilde{\Pi}_{11}' \equiv Q^{-1} \Pi_{11}'$$

These new matrices also satisfy equation (5.4.7) for any choice of Q. There is no unique way to split the matrix product $D' \Pi_{11}'$ into separate matrices D' and Π_{11}'.

This of course is a standard problem with extrapolative expectations and has a standard solution in the literature. Consider the simple model

$$y_t = x_t^e \gamma + u_t \qquad x_t^e = x_{t-1} \delta_1 + x_{t-2} \delta_2 + \ldots + x_{t-q} \delta_q$$

When the expression for x_t^e is substituted into the structural equation for y_t, there are $(q+1)$ parameters to be inferred from the q coefficients on x_{t-i}. The literature on Adaptive Expectations typically imposes the identifying condition

$$\delta_1 + \delta_2 + \ldots + \delta_q = 1 \text{ or } \delta_1 = 1 - \delta_2 - \delta_3 - \ldots - \delta_q$$

which then allows the remaining q parameters $(\delta_2, \delta_3, \ldots, \delta_q, \gamma)$ to be inferred once the model is rewritten as

$$y_t = x_{t-1} \gamma + (x_{t-2} - x_{t-1}) \gamma \delta_2 + \ldots$$
$$+ (x_{t-q} - x_{t-1}) \gamma \delta q + u_t$$

While any such identifying restriction is arbitrary, the above restriction is sometimes defended by the claim that it ensures that expectations are unbiased when the model reaches a steady state in which $x_{t-1} = x_{t-2} = x_{t-3} = \ldots = x_{t-q} = \bar{x}$.

Thus one solution to the underidentification of D' and Π'_{11} in equation (5.4.7) is to specify additional restrictions on these matrices, and since the restrictions are arbitrary they may as well be chosen to simplify the algebra as much as possible. Revankar (1980) proposes one set of possible constraints which identify the parameter matrices under the alternative hypothesis. It is then simplest to conduct a Wald test of the restrictions (5.4.8). Readers who wish to refresh their memories about Statistical Inference should consult Harvey (1981). To implement the Revankar procedure, run OLS on equation (5.4.7) obtaining estimates of $(D'\Pi'_{11})$ and Π'_{12}, then impose the constraints *ex post* to infer separate estimates of D' and Π'_{11}. There is no efficiency gain compared with imposing the constraints *ex ante*, since they are chosen to just identify the relevant matrices and the estimation is more complicated. A regression of Z on its p lagged values yields OLS estimates of the ϕ parameters. We may thus check how closely these estimates derived under the alternative hypothesis satisfy the Rational Expectations constraints by considering the test statistic

$$\{[D'_0 - \phi'\Pi'_{12}(I - \Pi'_{11})^{-1}] \qquad D'_*\}$$

Evaluated under the estimates described above, this partitioned matrix should have every element close to zero. By stacking its elements in a column vector and evaluating the variance covariance matrix of this vector, we can derive a Wald test statistic whose asymptotic distribution is chi-squared with degrees of freedom equal to the number of overidentifying restrictions implied by equation (5.4.8).

Since this test takes account of the cross equation restrictions (5.4.8) it will be more powerful than simpler test procedures which do not make full use of these restrictions. For expositional clarity, the above discussion focused only on the set of unobservable reduced form equations for Y_1. However, Y_1^e also enters the reduced form for the other endogenous variables Y_2. A more powerful test may be constructed by applying the argument above to the full set of reduced form equations.

Less powerful tests are more straightforward to construct and are frequently used in the empirical literature. The simplest example is to estimate equation (5.4.7) by OLS and test whether all coefficients on Z_* are zero, which may be conducted using a standard F test. More generally, using estimation methods previously described in Sections 5.2 and 5.3, we might form $\hat{Z}$ by a prior regression on equation (5.1.1) and consider the formulation

$$Y_1 = \hat{Z}A_1' + Z\Pi_{12}' + (Z_{-2}\ Z_{-3}\ \ldots\ Z_{-q}) \begin{bmatrix} D_2' \\ D_3' \\ . \\ . \\ D_q' \end{bmatrix} + V_1 \qquad (5.4.9)$$

without imposing the known restrictions

$$A_1' = \Pi_{12}'(I - \Pi_{11}')^{-1}\Pi_{11}'$$

from equation (5.4.4). OLS estimation of equation (5.4.9) yields consistent estimates of the parameter matrices and allows the simple test that

$$D_2' = D_3' = \ldots = D_q' = 0$$

Notice that we cannot additionally include all the elements of Z_0 in equation (5.4.9), for then $\hat{Z}$ will be an exact linear combination of these extra variables. I have arbitrarily dropped Z_{-1}, though other choices are possible. Because such tests throw away knowable restrictions on the coefficient matrix A_1' and because lagged exogenous variables may be highly serially correlated and hence nearly collinear, it is not likely that such tests will be very powerful, a consideration which should be borne in mind when assessing the empirical evidence on Rational Expectations.

The foregoing analysis carries over to dynamic expectation models such as equation (5.1.10). Equations (5.1.15) and (5.1.16) indicate the Rational Expectations constraints which then apply in equation (5.4.4). While these are even more non-linear than in the model we have just considered, the same principles apply.

I conclude this section with a caution. I have been careful to specify the alternative hypothesis about expectations formation as an extrapolation of past exogenous variables, for this leads most straightforwardly to a nested test of the standard type. How should the preceding analysis be amended when the alternative expectations hypothesis is taken to be an extrapolation of the past values of the relevant endogenous variables?

Wallis (1980) shows that it will generally be possible to express each endogenous variable $y_{i,t}$ as a univariate autoregressive moving average (ARMA) model of the form

$$y_{i,t} - \rho_1 y_{i,t-1} - \rho_2 y_{i,t-2} - \ldots =$$
$$\omega_t + \theta_1 \omega_{t-1} + \theta_2 \omega_{t-2} + \ldots \qquad (5.4.10)$$

where ω_t is a serially uncorrelated random variable with mean zero. This will certainly be possible in linear Rational Expectations models in which the exogenous variables follow a stationary autoregressive process, as I have assumed. We can rearrange the above equation as an expression for ω_t and by considering the same equation at earlier dates we can obtain expressions for previous values of ω_t which may then be substituted into equation (5.4.10). After such recursive elimination we obtain an expression for $y_{i,t}$ as an extrapolation of all its own lagged values, plus the current disturbance ω_t. The crucial point of this exercise is that it is possible to rewrite linear Rational Expectations models in extrapolative form, using only past values of the relevant endogenous variable itself. Naturally, the coefficients ρ and θ bear an explicit relation to the parameters of equations (5.1.1) and (5.1.4) although this relation is rather complicated. Similarly, the random disturbances ω_t are functions of the new information made available at time t when the disturbances in equations (5.1.1) and (5.1.4) become known.

Two points must be made about such extrapolative specifications of Rational Expectations models. First, since they are legitimate ways of describing the model, individuals using such specifications must form unbiased forecasts: given the past history of $y_{i,t}$ up to time $t-1$, the conditional expectation of ω_t is zero and expectations of $y_{i,t}$ will on average be correct. However, Wallis proves that the variance of the Rational Expectations forecasting error around its zero mean will be larger than when Rational Expectations are based directly on the full structural equations as I have hitherto supposed. Essentially, the above extrapolative procedure is inferior because it collapses separate information about different disturbances into the single random variable ω_t, thus throwing away usable information.

Secondly, and of direct relevance to testing the Rational Expectations hypothesis, the mere fact that an extrapolative predictor of $y_{i,t}$ from its own lagged values works reasonably well does not constitute evidence against the Rational Expectations hypothesis. Rigorous tests using the extrapolative formula can be derived by analogy with equation (5.4.9). The question is not whether extrapolation works, but whether the extrapolative formula satisfies the Rational Expectations restrictions implicit in the structure of the model. However, such tests are harder to implement than the tests considered earlier, because the extrapolative formula itself is more complex.

5.5 Testing the Structural Equations Conditional on Rational Expectations

I now examine the other half of the problem of statistical inference in Rational Expectations models, testing hypotheses about the underlying economic structure conditional on the hypothesis of Rational Expectations. Since that assumption is maintained in Sections 5.1–5.3, the discussion draws heavily on the analysis of those sections. The general principle follows the usual treatment of hypothesis testing found in textbooks such as Harvey (1981). It is assumed that the economic hypothesis under consideration can be nested within a more general specification which is still identified according to the criteria of Section 5.2. The null hypothesis represents an additional set of restrictions within the more general model. These restrictions may then be tested using a Likelihood Ratio test, Lagrange Multiplier test, or Wald test.

It is hard to go beyond this brief and abstract summary of hypothesis testing without specifying a particular model; specific applications will be discussed in the following three chapters. Here, I merely wish to emphasise again the special considerations which have been established in the preceding sections of this chapter. A central issue remains the identification problem studied in Section 5.2, for we have seen that identification conditions in Rational Expectations models depart considerably from the standard textbook discussion of identification in simultaneous equation models. For example, when lagged exogenous variables directly enter the structural equations we have seen that parameters can be identified only if the length of this structural lag is less than the length of the lag in the stochastic process generating the exogenous variables on which Rational Expectations of current and future variables directly depend. When this condition fails, different models of the structural equations are observationally equivalent if expectations are Rational. Thus, whenever an empirical test rejects a particular economic hypothesis, it is always open to those whose hypothesis has been discredited to claim that the economic structure embodies longer lags than the empirical researchers allowed, making competing models observationally equivalent and weakening the force of any evidence against the particular hypothesis. The reader might think that lag lengths themselves could be subject to empirical test, but two difficulties emerge. First, while it is possible in principle to estimate the process determining the exogenous variables, in practice tests for different lag lengths are not powerful. Economic time series tend to exhibit strong serial correlation which makes successive observations quite collinear and makes it difficult to determine any particular coefficient with great precision. Secondly, even if the nature of the exogenous process can be confidently established, there remains the problem of determining the length of the distributed lag in the structural equations with whose length that of the exogenous process must be compared. If parameters are not identified they cannot be consistently estimated. Thus we cannot estimate, let alone test, structural lags whose length exceeds that of the exogenous process. Identification conditions are necessarily *a priori* acts of faith. Nevertheless, as I argued in Chapter 4, merely because different logical possibilities exist does not mean that the reader or other economists should suspend all judgment. All simultaneous equation models require identifying assumptions about which we may quibble; what matters is the plausibility of the assertions being made. An example of such a debate is provided in the next chapter.

5.6 The Lucas Problem Reconsidered

In Chapter 4, I introduced the Lucas critique of conventional policy evaluation. We may now study this critique more formally. Suppose first that we consider policy rules in which there is no feedback from information about current endogenous variables to future levels of policy variables. A simple example of such a policy rule is a permanent commitment to maintain a 5% rate of nominal money growth, regardless of the paths it generates for inflation and unemployment. However, more complicated rules may be considered and all rules meeting the assumption stated above can be treated as falling within equation (5.1.1). Thus I now interpret some of the z_t variables as policy variables set without reference to the evolution of endogenous variables. The policy choice has two aspects, determining the relevant ϕ parameters which influence the systematic evolution of these policy variables over time and choosing the random deviations ϵ_t around this systematic path. The assumption that feedback is absent rules out choices of these deviations which reflect the past realisations of systematic or random components of endogenous variables, the assumption that ϵ_t is serially uncorrelated rules out feedback from past exogenous variables or policy variables, and the assumption that ϵ_t is uncorrelated with contemporaneous disturbances rules out contemporaneous feedback.

Thus when policy is truly exogenous, it may be modelled within equation (5.1.1). The coefficients in observable reduced form equations such as (5.4.4) thus depend on the systematic ϕ parameters of the policy rule. If, as in equations (5.4.7) and (5.4.9), these policy parameters and the Π parameters derivable from the structural equations are lumped together in a single matrix of coefficients, any change in the policy rule as reflected in the ϕ parameters will change these collapsed together coefficient matrices. In particular, if econometric models use equations such as (5.4.7), treating expectations as following an invariant set of extrapolative weights, rather than the optimal policy-dependent set of weights implied by Rational Expectations, any change in policy, whether actual or hypothetical, should be expected to change the matrix of coefficients in the extrapolation.

Viewed in this way, the Lucas problem may be reconsidered using the discussion of the preceding sections. If the model is identified, it is possible separately to identify and estimate the parameters both of the Z process and of the structure or reduced form. The definition of structural parameters requires them to be invariant with respect to the process the exogenous variables actually follow. If a policy change is to be considered, and if it is supposed that individuals catch on almost immediately to the parameters of the new policy, the coefficients of the observable reduced form can be appropriately amended and this new equation will serve as the basis for a simulation of the economy under the new policy rule.

Moreover, it is clear that the above analysis may be extended to the case in which policy rules admit a feedback. We need only re-interpret the relevant Y variables as policy variables and the structural parameters in their equations as the characteristics of the systematic components of the policy rule. If policy reacts only to lagged information about exogenous variables the model will then be of the form given in equation (5.1.19), but if current policy variables also react to lagged endogenous variables these too must be entered in the structural equations. Although I have not explicitly treated this case in this chapter, the same general principles apply and are studied in more detail in Wallis (1980). Having estimated the parameters of the model from past sample data, the Lucas problem of policy evaluation now requires that we recalculate the relevant reduced form parameters Π when a policy rule is changed. Since these parameters may be derived from the structural parameters (B, Γ) provided the latter are identified, it is now necessary to have estimates of these parameters if the new values of Π are to be recomputed from the new policy components of (B, Γ) and the original private sector components which are assumed invariant. With this small amendment, the earlier solution to the Lucas problem may be extended to the case in which policy rules include feedback components.

Once the Lucas problem has been recognised, only the following problems prevent the complete implementation of the above solution. First, the model may not be identified so that it is impossible to disentangle the complete set of structural or reduced form coefficients which are to be assumed invariant. Secondly, the past sample period over which the parameters were originally estimated may itself have seen several switches either in the policy rules in force or in the stochastic process driving the exogenous variables. Even if participants in the economy are clever enough to recognise these changes and alter forecasting rules accordingly, econometricians must be careful to discover any such switches, for the incorrect imposition of a single process (5.1.1) will lead to inconsistent estimates of all parameters. Thirdly, while it may be desirable to base long-run policy evaluation on the proposition that all individuals cannot be systematically mistaken all of the time, it must be a simplification to assume that policy switches are instantaneously recognised and acted upon. Given the other identification problems which arise, the possibility of generalising existing Rational Expectations models to model such transitional learning seems relatively remote, unless structural equations can be devised which embody much sharper restrictions. This observation is closely related to the final point which I wish to make.

The structural equations which I have examined extend the conventional textbook treatment of simultaneous equation econometric models. In practice, the microeconomic foundations of many empirical macroeconomic models are at best dubious. If the equations we typically think of as structural are really partly reduced form, we cannot necessarily place much weight on the requirement that structural coefficients will remain invariant under policy changes which significantly affect expectations of the future. This point was made in Lucas (1976) and is illustrated in Chapter 2, in which I argued that consumption may seem to bear a reasonably stable relation to current income while expectations of future incomes remain roughly constant, but may change dramatically when expectations of future income change. If the justification for inclusion of Rational Expectations variables is that individuals make intertemporal decisions, the equations which we term structural must be compatible with intertemporal optimisation.

Recently, a number of authors — Abel (1979), Kennan (1979), Hansen and Sargent (1980a and b), Sargent (1981), Blanchard (1980) (1981) — have begun to emphasise explicit modelling of intertemporal optimisation in an attempt to derive genuinely structural equations which remain invariant with respect to changes in policy or exogenous variables. It is too early to claim that the problems which Lucas stated so clearly have been solved, but the way forward seems apparent.

5.7 Conclusion

In this chapter I have examined the implications of the Rational Expectations hypothesis for econometric methodology, maintaining where possible the usual notation of the discussion of simultaneous equations in econometric theory. In Section 5.1 I discussed the structure of stochastic simultaneous equation models with Rational Expectations, establishing the parameter restrictions which allow a unique Rational Expectations solution and then deriving the restrictions which are placed on observable equations.

In Section 5.2 I assumed that conventional exclusion restrictions on structural equations were sufficient to identify the structural parameters, given consistent estimates of the reduced form parameters, so that the only remaining identification problem arises because stochastically predetermined expectations are not directly observable. I should point out that the implication of the recent work on decision rules obtained from explicit intertemporal optimisation is that exclusion restrictions may be rather scarce, since all past exogenous variables may be used to forecast the future variables on which these intertemporal decisions are based; in such a framework, cross equation restrictions play a more important role than is normal. In the simpler framework pursued in Section 5.2 it was shown that identification of the Π parameters, and hence the underlying structural parameters, could not be taken for granted even where a unique Rational Expectations solution exists. In particular, the presence of lagged exogenous variables in the structural equations might pose identification problems.

In Section 5.3 it was shown that identified parameters could be consistently estimated by Limited Information methods, either by constructing a suitable proxy for the unobservable Rational Expectation, or by making the McCallum substitution and treating the resulting model as an example of errors in variables. Both procedures make use of the fact that *ex post* values differ from their Rational Expectations only by random variables which are uncorrelated with all information available at the date expectations are formed. The Rational Expectations structure offers extremely precise information about which instrumental variables are appropriate. When Rational Expectations are formed for variables more than one period forward, the overlapping nature of these expectations implies that forecasting errors will follow moving average processes reflecting new information accruing in each of the intervening periods. Because of the dynamic structure of these models and because one component of errors in forecasting future endogenous variables arises from the failure to forecast exogenous variables, some care is required in attempting to correct for non-scalar disturbance covariance matrices. The principles of Full Information estimation were briefly discussed.

Section 5.4 analysed how the Rational Expectations hypothesis might be tested against alternative expectations hypotheses, provided it was assumed that the underlying structural equations had been correctly specified. Identification under the alternative hypothesis necessarily required additional arbitrary restrictions. Within this framework, the null hypothesis of Rational Expectations then implied overidentifying cross equations restrictions which could be tested. Simpler but less powerful tests which did not exploit cross equation restrictions were also considered.

Section 5.5 examined the analogous problem of testing hypotheses about the economic structure conditional on the validity of the Rational Expectations hypothesis. Although standard principles of statistical inference apply if the model is identified, we have seen that identification may not always be straightforward.

Finally, in Section 5.6 I reconsidered the problem of policy evaluation. Given a period in which a single set of policy rules was in operation for a length of time sufficient to collect a reasonable number of sample observations, the structural parameters and the parameters of the policy rules can be consistently estimated, provided the model is identified. It is then straightforward to amend the observable reduced forms to reflect any change in these policy rules. The amended reduced forms may then be used for forecasting or policy analysis. However, it is crucial that the other parameters of structural equations are genuinely invariant with respect to changes in the path of exogenous variables or policy variables. This invariance is more likely to be the case the more attention is paid to the microeconomic foundations of the structural equations. In Rational Expectations models there is some presumption that this requires consideration of intertemporal optimisation.

Notes on the Literature

General surveys of econometric issues in Rational Expectations models include Wallis (1980), Shiller (1978) and Hayashi (1980). The discussion of this chapter draws most heavily on the first of these. Many issues are also discussed in the macroeconomics textbook by Sargent (1979a). Blanchard and Khan (1980) analyse the Rational Expectations solution procedure in detail.

Full Information estimation was first proposed by Wickens (1977) and is discussed in Wallis (1980), Taylor (1979a), Fair (1979b), Fair and Taylor (1980) and Hayashi (1980). Limited Information estimation has been studied by Sargent (1973) (1976a), Wallis (1980), Hayashi (1980) and McCallum (1976a and b) (1979a). The possible inconsistency of GLS corrections in dynamic models has been recognised since Durbin (1970), but in the Rational Expectations literature is due to Bernanke (1977), Hansen (1980), Flood and Garber (1980a and b), Hayashi (1980), Hayashi and Sims (1980), Hansen and Hodrick (1980), Hakkio (1980), and Obstfeld, Cumby and Huizinga (1981).

Tests of the Rational Expectations hypothesis are discussed briefly in Wallis (1980) and at greater length in Revankar (1980) and Hoffman and Schmidt (1981) who present several simple examples of testable restrictions and also report the results of Monte Carlo studies comparing different test procedures. Readers who have not encountered Hendry (1980) are strongly advised to consult this more general discussion of econometric methodology.

For an example of the difficulties which emerge in trying to test competing models of the economic structure under Rational Expectations, the reader should consult the debate over the testing of the Natural Rate hypothesis contained in the sequence of papers by Sargent (1976b), McCallum '(1979c), Sargent (1979c) and Buiter (1980b).

As indicated in Chapter 4, the seminal paper on econometric policy evaluation is Lucas (1976). For papers critical of the conventional approach to structural equations, see Sims (1979), Hansen and Sargent (1980a and b) and Sargent (1981). Other papers treating intertemporal optimisation explicitly include Abel (1979), Hall (1978), Sargent (1978a) and Kennan (1979).

(**)

6
Rational Expectations, the Natural Rate Hypothesis, and the Stabilisation Policy Debate

In this chapter, I examine the use of monetary and fiscal policy for stabilising the level of aggregate output and employment in macroeconomic models with Rational Expectations. In the textbook IS/LM analysis these policies may be used in the short run to shift either the IS curve describing goods market clearing or the LM curve describing money market clearing, or both. Unless the economy is at full employment, an appropriate combination of monetary and fiscal policy will secure an increase in output and employment.

In the two decades following 1945 this theme was elaborated at some length. Tinbergen (1956) extended the theory of economic policy by noting that if one policy instrument could secure the desired level of one goal variable, an appropriate mix of two policy instruments could simultaneously secure the desired level of two distinct goal variables. Indeed, under certain conditions, an arbitrary number of targets could be simultaneously achieved provided the government had at least that number of independent policy instruments at its disposal. This idea was extended to stochastic models in which random shocks cause variables to deviate *ex post* from the path which the government had envisaged in its policy choices. Recognising the inherent dynamic structure of the economy, techniques of mathematical optimal control theory were applied to devise feedback rules to 'fine tune' the economy as information about new shocks became available, and such techniques were extended even to the case in which the government was less than certain about the true structure of the economy. With these developments the macroeconomic theory of demand management had advanced far beyond the simple discussion of introductory textbooks.

The development of large scale macroeconomic models allowed this body of theory to be made operational. Forecasting and Policy Evaluation became standard. In many Western economies, the government accepted the commitment to maintain full and stable employment, and whether or not their macroeconomic policies were always framed with fine tuning in mind, economic commentators of the day often assessed these policies by this criterion.

In most of these economies, the last decade has seen an important change in macroeconomic policy. In Begg (1982) I argue that the reduction in emphasis on demand management may be attributed to two distinct factors. The first was the view that the above framework did not pay sufficient attention to inflation. As inflation rose, governments typically made the normative value judgment that the control of inflation was more important than the preservation of full employment, and increasingly adopted the positive judgment that a necessary condition for this was strict control of the money supply. Following the pioneering work of Christ (1968), economists began to take account of the obvious fact that monetary and fiscal policies are not independent in the way that the Tinbergen-based analysis assumed: they are related by the budget constraint of the government. If there is any restriction on the supply of bonds which may be issued, such as the political unpopularity of high mortgage interest rates for house purchase, then the money supply can be strictly controlled only if fiscal spending is also controlled. Thus an increasing preoccupation with the rate of inflation tended to weaken the attraction of demand management policies, especially when these would have implied higher deficit spending.

However, it is the second factor with which I am concerned in this chapter. Two developments in the positive theory of macroeconomics undoubtedly contributed to the weakening of the Keynesian influence on which the case for demand management rested. The increasing emphasis on the microeconomic foundations of macroeconomics questioned the compatibility of some of the Keynesian assumptions with individual optimisation at the microeconomic level and the literature on Rational Expectations demonstrated that models embodying optimising assumptions could be pushed to the point at which demand management has no real effect even in the short run. Moreover, as inflation and unemployment grew in most countries, these theoretical doubts were reinforced by the practical feeling that the old policies were no longer working.

One contribution of the Monetarist school has been the insistence that models should not contain arbitrary *ad hoc* assumptions. At the simplest level, even if the textbook IS/LM model allows a short-run role for demand management, it cannot allow output to be increased without bound. Eventually a position of full capacity must be reached at which supply constraints become binding, so that increases in some components of aggregate demand such as government spending merely crowd out other components such as private investment. However, the main thrust of the Monetarist criticism concerns the specification of wages and prices. Simple IS/LM models treat wages and prices as given, but at best this assumption can be valid only in the short run; at issue is the question of what happens to wages and prices over some longer period. The Monetarist analysis rests on two fundamental assumptions: first, that individuals have no money illusion; second, that all markets in disequilibrium quickly initiate adjustments which restore market clearing. In the Monetarist jargon, wages and prices adjust to restore the Natural Rate of output and employment. Given the absence of money illusion, these Natural Rates refer to real rather than nominal variables and, while not literally constant over time, can change only rather slowly through demographic changes, productivity growth and so on. Hence the eventual consequence of an increase in the nominal quantity of money will be to induce a broadly equivalent increase in nominal wages and prices to leave real money balances and real wages at their full employment or Natural Rates. The Quantity Theory of Money can be given a more sophisticated representation than $MV = PT$.

Many, but not all, economists would now accept the above reasoning as a description of what happens in the long run and modern introductions to macroeconomic theory usually treat this issue. Such economists would accept that demand management policies may not have permanent effects, since the economy eventually returns to the constraints imposed by full employment aggregate supply. Economists who would describe themselves as Keynesian contend that the return to full employment is at best protracted, so that short-run scope for demand management remains important. Monetarists would typically claim that this process works much more quickly, so that the effect of demand management is correspondingly reduced. If one believes either that the difficulty of fine tuning leads to a large risk that attempts will be positively counterproductive in a world of some uncertainty, or that the inflationary consequences of such attempts are undesirable, one may offer the policy prescription that attempts at fine tuning should be abandoned.

The above discussion is probably a fair summary of the debate immediately prior to the introduction of the Rational Expectations hypothesis. It is clear that such a debate could never have been resolved decisively. Differences rested first on value judgments about the relative importance of inflation and temporary unemployment and secondly on the length of the time it required to restore full employment in the absence of intervention by the government. Positive economic theory can contribute little to either disagreement and empirical macroeconomics finds it hard to disentangle from the data the precise lags involved in the economy.

In this context, the significance of the Rational Expectations hypothesis was that it appeared to offer a clear-cut answer. Lucas (1972b), Sargent (1973), Sargent and Wallace (1975) and Barro (1976) develop Rational Expectations models with striking conclusions. Systematic, and therefore anticipatable, monetary policy would have no real effects even in the short run; systematic fiscal policy would not affect current real output or employment, and would affect these variables in the long run only to the extent that, by manipulating the composition of the given output level, it could affect investment and hence future aggregate supply. Moreover, random or non-systematic components of monetary and fiscal policies would typically only increase the uncertainty and fluctuations in the economy. Thus the introduction of the Rational Expectations hypothesis seemed to remove the ambiguity about how soon the Monetarist long-run analysis became relevant: it applied immediately. This analysis also appeared to formalise the intuitive prescription advanced by Friedman (1959) that the monetary authority ought to adopt a steady and predictable rate of money growth rather than attempt any fine tuning; to provide a theoretical underpinning for Friedman's (1968) Presidential Address to the American Economic Association in which he disputed the power of monetary policy to affect real variables; to explain the vertical Phillips Curve in which unemployment is independent of expected inflation rates, yet exhibits some *ex post* correlation with actual inflation; and to justify the earlier assertion of Irving Fisher (1930) that a rise in the expected inflation rate will raise nominal interest rates by the same amount, leaving expected real interest rates unaltered. Any economist familiar with recent controversies in macroeconomics will recognise immediately the significance of these claims.

The purpose of this chapter is to offer an assessment of these developments. In Section 6.1 I set out a simple macroeconomic model in which the impotence of systematic demand management policy may be established. These results are not the inevitable consequence of the assumption of Rational Expectations. It is important to distinguish between the expectations assumption and the structure of the model in which this assumption is embedded. In the model of Section 6.1, it is instructive to rework the analysis under the alternative hypothesis of Adaptive Expectations. The sense in which Rational Expectations frustrates the power of stabilisation policy then becomes apparent. However, the model of Section 6.1 is very restrictive. More general models, still within the Monetarist tradition of full market clearing, are considered in Sections 6.2 and 6.3. These models do allow a role for active stabilisation policy under Rational Expectations, though this role remains limited.

The textbook representation of Keynesian macroeconomics specifically assumes that some markets do not clear. Such models have a fundamentally different economic structure from those of Sections 6.1—6.3 and the difference in results cannot be attributed solely to differences in expectations assumptions. In Section 6.4 I reconsider whether it is possible to develop plausible microeconomic foundations for models which do not exhibit continuous clearing of all markets. I present some recent work on the harder question of applying the Rational Expectations hypothesis to disequilibrium models in which continuous market clearing is not always present. In such models, a full role for conventional demand management may be re-established, even though expectations are Rational.

I argue that the disagreement between the Monetarists and the Keynesians continues to rest on differing views about the speed with which markets clear. The answer to this question must depend on transactions costs, uncertainty, the nature and cost of information available, and the institutional structure of the economy as well as the process of expectations formation. From the discussion of the following sections it will become clear that, while the Rational Expectations hypothesis does shed important light on the debate over demand management, it cannot of itself resolve all the outstanding issues. Section 6.5 discusses empirical research designed to shed light on the issues raised in this chapter.

6.1 The Natural Rate and the Ineffectiveness of Stabilisation Policy

Since my point of departure is the textbook IS/LM model, it is important to be clear what this simple model assumes and what it does not. The markets for output and money are clear, for it is these conditions which the IS and LM relations separately describe. While the demand for output is modelled explicitly, the supply of output is usually given less attention, being taken to be passive or demand determined. In a Keynesian world with surplus capacity, it may be reasonable to assume that the supply of output is perfectly elastic in the short run; in the Monetarist world which this section assumes, such an assumption is not appropriate. The IS/LM model also holds the labour market in the background. Labour demand is related to output produced and if this falls below full employment output, involuntary unemployment results. Somehow, wage adjustments fail to clear the labour market, but the IS/LM model is not a suitable vehicle for examining this issue because it emphasises the two markets, for output and money, which are assumed to clear.

A more complete macroeconomic model must address both these deficiencies: it must model planned supply of goods and it must treat the labour market explicitly. The model of this section cuts through these difficulties by assuming that the labour market clears in a particular way. Imagine that all workers participate in a bargain to determine the nominal wage contract for a single period at a time. At the beginning of each period, workers and firms agree a nominal wage for the period. Since firms and workers care about *real* wages, this requires that they form expectations about the price level which will prevail over the duration of the nominal wage contract. If prices are higher than expected, firms can obtain labour at a lower real wage than had been anticipated when the nominal wage was negotiated. Firms will temporarily expand output and take on extra labour to take advantage of the temporarily low real wages. At the end of the period, there is an opportunity to renegotiate the nominal wage contract. If the underlying real factors which determine the market power of workers and firms remain constant over time, the expected real wage determined by the negotiation will remain constant over successive periods. Thus, at the end of the period the effects of any unforeseen change in prices may be absorbed into the nominal wage, explaining why a particular shock has only temporary effects on the real wage. This analysis suggests the following aggregate supply equation for goods

$$y_t = y_n + \alpha_1 (p_t - {}_{t-1}p_t^e) + \epsilon_{1t} \quad \alpha_1 > 0 \qquad (6.1.1)$$

where y_t and p_t are the natural logarithms of real output and the price level at time t; y_n is the logarithm of the Natural Rate of output; ϵ_{1t} is a serially uncorrelated random disturbance with mean zero, and $_{t-1}p_t^e$ is the Rational Expectation of p_t, conditional on information available at the end of the previous period when the nominal wage bargain for period t was determined. Since $_{t-1}\epsilon_{1t}^e$ is zero, equation (6.1.1) implies that actual output will equal the Natural Rate y_n when all expectations are fulfilled, i.e. when $\epsilon_{1t} = 0$ and $p_t = {}_{t-1}p_t^e$. Equation (6.1.1) argues that when p_t exceeds its Rational Expectation, and hence real wages (whose logarithm at time t is $(w_t - p_t)$ where w_t is the logarithm of nominal wages) are lower than their expectation $(w_t - {}_{t-1}p_t^e)$ when the known nominal wage was agreed, output will be increased relative to the Natural Rate by an amount $\alpha_1 (p_t - {}_{t-1}p_t^e)$. In the simple model of this section, I assume that y_n is constant. In a growing economy, it might be preferable to model this full employment output as growing at an exogenous rate. None of the analysis of this section would be affected by such an assumption.

Assume that the demand for labour depends on the level of output and the real wage rate, and that the supply of labour depends on the real wage rate. Thus the equilibrium expected real wage at the date the nominal wage bargain is made is assumed to be set in the expectation of clearing the labour market. Because the economy in practice is dynamic, with individuals entering the labour force, changing job in midstream as employment opportunities alter, and leaving the labour force on retirement, this labour turnover will imply that there are always some individuals registered as unemployed at any date t. When we say that the labour market clears, we do not mean that measured unemployment is literally zero. Rather we mean that no individuals are involuntarily unemployed in the sense that they are prepared to work at the going real wage, but cannot find employment. Friedman has termed this full employment rate of measured unemployment the *Natural Rate of Unemployment*. Thus I assume that nominal wages are set each period to produce an expected real wage which is expected to generate measured unemployment at the Natural Rate. Corresponding to equation

(6.1.1) we have

$$U_t = U_n - \beta(p_t - {}_{t-1}p_t^e) + \epsilon_{2t} \quad \beta > 0 \qquad (6.1.2)$$

where U_t is the actual level of unemployment at time t, U_n is the Natural Rate of Unemployment and ϵ_{2t} is a random disturbance with mean zero and no serial correlation. When p_t exceeds ${}_{t-1}p_t^e$, real wages are unexpectedly low. Firms temporarily increase their demand for labour while labour supply temporarily falls off; together, these reduce unemployment below the Natural Rate until nominal wage contracts can be renegotiated at the end of the period.

Equations (6.1.1) and (6.1.2) represent different ways of describing the same phenomenon. For the moment, I base my analysis on equation (6.1.1) which is sometimes called the Lucas–Sargent aggregate supply equation. To complete the specification of a stochastic macroeconomic model, we add an equation for aggregate goods demand, an LM equation for money market clearing, and equations describing the policy rules determining the evolution over time of the variables which the government is assumed to set. Since equation (6.1.1) is log-linear, these other equations are usually written in log-linear form in order to make the solution procedure as simple as possible. An example of a complete model is presented in the next section.

The question which I wish to consider is this: how is the actual Rational Expectations path for this model altered if fiscal or monetary policy rules are changed. Under Rational Expectations, the remarkable implication of equation (6.1.1) is that, no matter how we define the rest of the model and no matter which systematic parts of policy rules are altered, the effect on the path of real output will be nil. Suppose we write down a particular model, including the equations which describe policy. By Property II of Section 4.1, if a unique Rational Expectations solution exists, it must have the property

$$p_t = {}_{t-1}p_t^e + \eta_t \qquad (6.1.3)$$

where η_t has mean zero and is uncorrelated with all information available at $t - 1$, including ${}_{t-1}p_t^e$. The Rational Expectations forecasting errors η_t arise because of unforeseeable deviations of random disturbances at t from their mean values of zero. These disturbances come from structural equations, such as (6.1.1), and from any non-systematic components of policy equations. Equation (6.1.3) asserts that individuals do not make mistakes which are knowable at $t - 1$ when expectations are formed.

Substitute equation (6.1.3) into equation (6.1.1). This yields

$$y_t = y_n + \alpha_1 \eta_t + \epsilon_{1t} \qquad (6.1.4)$$

Under Rational Expectations, output deviates from the Natural Rate only because of random shocks which are not foreseeable at the date expectations are formed. Consider now the consequences of a change in government policy. Suppose for example that monetary policy takes the form

$$m_t = \gamma_1 m_{t-1} + \epsilon_{3t} \qquad (6.1.5)$$

where m_t describes the logarithm of nominal money supply at time t and ϵ_{3t} is a random disturbance with mean zero and no serial correlation, describing the extent to which actual money supply deviates unpredictably from its systematic component $\gamma_1 m_{t-1}$. I consider first the consequence of a change in the systematic part of the policy rule. This might take the form of changing the value of γ_1, or of making the policy rule depend on different variables such as

$$m_t = \gamma_1 m_{t-1} + \gamma_2 m_{t-2} + \gamma_3 y_{t-1} + \epsilon_{3t}$$

Inclusion of terms like lagged output is compatible with the idea that policy is used to attempt fine tuning by reacting to previous changes in output as this information becomes available. Assume that any change in the systematic component of government policy is immediately recognised by individuals in the economy. They know the new policy rule and immediately use it to obtain a new Rational Expectations solution to the model. Thus, if policy is changed at the end of time $t - 1$, the consequence of the policy change will be to alter $_{t-1}p_t^e$ from the value it would have attained under the former policy. p_t will also be affected by the policy change. Provided it is assumed that individuals immediately recognise the policy change, equation (6.1.3) must continue to hold. Individuals still avoid knowable forecasting errors. If only the systematic components of policy have been altered, ϵ_{3t} is unaffected in equation (6.1.5). Since all the other disturbances in the model are the result of exogenous random shocks, it follows that the Rational Expectations forecasting error η_t in equations (6.1.3) and (6.1.4) is also unaffected by the change in systematic policy. Hence the evolution of y_t is independent of the systematic policy. Systematic attempts at demand management will have no effect in this model.

This result depends crucially on the Lucas–Sargent aggregate supply equation in which only forecasting errors for the price level matter. Under Rational Expectations, the consequences of a policy change for p_t are completely discounted in $_{t-1}p^e_t$ and so forecasting errors are unaffected. To the extent that a policy change is not immediately recognised by individuals in the economy, expectations may not immediately discount the full effects on p_t. A systematic policy change will then be able to affect y_t until individuals have fully recognised the change in policy. While it would be difficult to maintain that all systematic policy changes are immediately understood by the private sector, the spirit of this analysis is that demand management at best can have only very temporary effects. Individuals observing data on government behaviour and taking account of government statements of its policy intentions quickly infer the policy rule in operation.

Next consider the consequences of purely stochastic changes in policy. Suppose the government increases the variability of ϵ_{3t} in equation (6.1.5) by making policy less predictable. Thus the mean of ϵ_{3t} remains zero, but deviations from this mean, in both positive and negative directions, are on average larger. Since this has no effect on the mean of η_t, nor on its Rational Expectation $_{t-1}\eta^e_t$, the form of equations (6.1.3) and (6.1.4) remains the same, but the forecasting error η_t, which includes the inability of the private sector to forecast government policy, may now deviate more in both directions from its mean of zero. Thus more random policies may increase the *ex post* variation of output y_t around its mean level, the Natural Rate of Output. Authors such as Sargent and Wallace (1975) have used this analysis to argue that policy rules should be as predictable as possible. Since systematic policy has no real effects on real output and random policies may increase the variability of output, this analysis can be used to justify the prescription of Friedman (1959) that the monetary authority should adopt a constant rate of money growth. Attempts at fine tuning should be abandoned.

In order to isolate the role of Rational Expectations in the argument above, consider what would happen if this hypothesis were replaced by the hypothesis of Adaptive Expectations. From equation (2.4.3) expectations then follow

$$_{t-1}p_t^e = \lambda p_{t-1} + \lambda(1-\lambda)p_{t-2} + \lambda(1-\lambda)^2 p_{t-3} + \ldots \quad (6.1.6)$$

$$0 < \lambda < 1$$

Given any past history of an economy we can construct $_{t-1}p_t^e$. In such a model it is easily seen that government policy may have real effects, provided the price level is an endogenous variable. Consider an increase in the money supply m_t which is knowable at time $t - 1$. Since p_t is endogenous, its value will depend in part on m_t. For any expectation $_{t-1}p_t^e$ which depends only on the past history of prices with weights λ which are fixed, we can always increase m_t, and hence p_t, sufficiently to make $(p_t - _{t-1}p_t^e)$ positive. By accelerating the rate of money growth sufficiently we can keep $(p_t - _{t-1}p_t^e)$ positive for many successive periods, and possibly for ever. Given the Lucas—Sargent aggregate supply equation, this implies that systematic policy can be used to manipulate the level of output relative to its Natural Rate. Under Adaptive Expectations, a role for demand management is re-established.

While the above analysis is based on equation (6.1.1), it is possible to restate the argument in terms of equation (6.1.2). This version may look even more familiar if we note that equation (6.1.2) implies

$$U_t = U_n - \beta\{(p_t - p_{t-1}) - (_{t-1}p_t^e - p_{t-1})\} + \epsilon_{2t}$$

However, $p_t - p_{t-1}$ is simply the actual inflation rate π_t between $i - 1$ and t, and $(_{t-1}p_t^e - p_{t-1})$ is simply the expected inflation rate $_{t-1}\pi_t^e$. These mathematical formulae follow from the fact that p_t is defined in logarithms. Thus we may write equation (6.1.2) as

$$U_t = U_n - \beta(\pi_t - _{t-1}\pi_t^e) + \epsilon_{2t} \quad (6.1.7)$$

which is a simple Phillips Curve. Under Rational Expectations, the government cannot systematically manipulate the forecasting error $(\pi_t - {}_{t-1}\pi_t^e)$ and actual unemployment U_t deviates only randomly from its Natural Rate U_n. The Phillips Curve is vertical even in the short run: policies to change π_t will change ${}_{t-1}\pi_t^e$ by the equivalent amount. Nevertheless, equation (6.1.7) will exhibit the statistical Phillips properties in some circumstances. For example, over a period in which ${}_{t-1}\pi_t^e$ is roughly constant, *ex post* fluctuations in π_t which by hypothesis are chiefly due to unanticipated random shocks will be negatively correlated with *ex post* fluctuations in measured unemployment.

Under Adaptive Expectations we recover the argument of Friedman (1968). This version of the expectations-augmented Phillips Curve is depicted in Figure 6.1.1. Suppose at time 0 expected inflation π_0^e is zero and that unemployment attained its Natural Rate in the previous period. Maintaining nominal wages at their previous level will be expected to preserve real wages at the level which again secures the Natural Rate. If inflation at time 0 exceeds its zero expectation, real wages will be lower than expected, leading to an increase in output

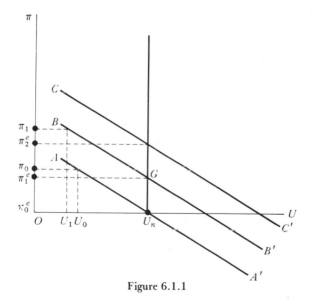

Figure 6.1.1

and labour demand. In the short run there is a trade-off AA' between inflation and unemployment. Higher inflation π_0 is associated with lower unemployment U_0. At the beginning of the next period, wage bargainers use Adaptive Expectations to guess the inflation rate at time 1, reacting to the unexpected inflation at time 0 by raising their previous expectations π_0^e to some higher level, say π_1^e. The agreed nominal wage increase is expected to place the economy at the point G at which the Natural Rate of unemployment will occur if inflation expectations are fulfilled. Again, equation (6.1.7) implies that if actual inflation π_1 exceeds this expectation, there will be a trade-off — now BB' — between inflation and unemployment. Thus an actual outcome π_1 above π_1^e leads to an unemployment level U_1, but inflation expectations for the following period will be revised upwards to imply a short-run trade-off CC'. While demand management policies can hold unemployment below the Natural Rate, this can be achieved only at the expense of accelerating inflation. If inflation is not to be explosive, eventually the authorities must accept the Natural Rate of Unemployment: the long-run Phillips Curve is vertical.

Thus under Adaptive Expectations interventionist demand management policies may affect real output and employment for a considerable time. If these are to be held above their Natural Rates, inflation will accelerate: if initially high inflationary expectations are to be dragged down, this can be achieved only by a period of increasing deflation which shifts down the short-run trade-offs in Figure 4.1.1. In contrast, under Rational Expectations even the short-run role for demand management vanishes. Output and employment deviate only randomly from their Natural Rates. While monetary and fiscal policy may have no systematic effect on the forecasting error $(p_t - {}_{t-1}p_t^e)$, they do affect both p_t and ${}_{t-1}p_t^e$. Hence these policies should be chosen to achieve the desired inflation rate and this should be the major consideration in choosing these policies. In the longer run, policies may affect the Natural Rates U_n and y_n themselves. For example, it may be thought that tax incentives affect labour supply and hence the voluntary unemployment which the Natural Rate describes. However, these supply side implications of monetary and fiscal policies are a far cry from the textbook treatment of demand management by monetary and fiscal means.

The content of the above analysis is that governments cannot affect $(p_t - {}_{t-1}p_t^e)$ when expectations are Rational. I shall call this the *Weak Neutrality Theorem*. Some economists, notably Sargent and Wallace (1975), have asserted a *Strong Neutrality Theorem*. I shall focus on the Lucas–Sargent aggregate supply equation (6.1.1). The Strong Theorem asserts not only that the government cannot manipulate the forecasting error under Rational Expectations, but also that conventional demand management cannot be used to affect y_n, the Natural Rate of Output. Thus demand management is completely impotent under Rational Expectations. The remainder of this section is devoted to an examination of the Strong Neutrality Theorem. Equation (6.1.1) cannot provide a basis for this discussion, since it *assumes* that y_n is exogenous: the Strong Neutrality Theorem seeks to *prove* that this is the case even when a more general specification is allowed. Since the distinction between the Weak and Strong Theorems has nothing to do with $(p_t - {}_{t-1}p_t^e)$, which will always be independent of systematic policy under Rational Expectations, it will simplify the discussion to ignore uncertainty. I assume for the rest of this section that all random disturbances are identically zero, in which case Rational Expectations reduces to the simpler case of Perfect Foresight.

I assume that the labour force is constant. The most important determinant of the Natural Rate of Output y_n is the capital stock available. Since investment is a component of aggregate demand, a complete macroeconomic model must recognise that capital is changing over time and that this process is endogenous to the model. In the Keynesian short run it may be legitimate to pretend that investment is small relative to existing capital stocks, so that this relation between aggregate demand and aggregate supply can be ignored; since a Rational Expectations or Perfect Foresight equilibrium requires us to solve forwards over all future time, the contribution of present investment to future aggregate supply cannot be ignored. Rewriting equation (6.1.1) to eliminate uncertainty but allow the dependence of y_n on the current capital stock, the goods supply equation becomes

$$y_t = \alpha_0 + \alpha_2 k_t \quad \alpha_2 > 0$$

where k_t is the logarithm of the capital stock. I assume a log-linear aggregate demand equation similar to equation (3.2.5)

$$y_t = cy_t + (k_{t+1} - k_t) + \phi k_t \quad c > 0 \quad \phi > 0$$

Aggregate demand comprises consumption depending on output through the marginal propensity to consume, net investment which adds to the capital stock, and replacement investment related to the capital stock through the constant depreciation rate ϕ. The IS equation for goods market clearing is therefore

$$\alpha_0 + \alpha_2 k_t = c(\alpha_0 + \alpha_2 k_t) + (k_{t+1} - k_t) + \phi k_t \quad (6.1.8)$$

which may be rewritten as

$$k_{t+1} = \alpha_0 (1 - c) + \{\alpha_2 (1 - c) + 1 - \phi\} k_t \qquad (6.1.9)$$

There is a one period gestation for investment — today's investment does not come on stream until tomorrow — so the economy has a predetermined current capital stock at whichever date we choose to begin the analysis, say at time t. Given this initial value k_t, equation (6.1.9) uniquely describes the evolution of future capital stocks and hence the evolution of future output levels via the aggregate supply equation. At each date there is only one level of investment which clears the goods market and if we sketched in the rest of the model the real interest rate would have to adjust to ensure that this was indeed the planned investment level. Nor is there anything restrictive about the log-linear specification. Begg (1980) argues that the same result is found in any model in which goods market clearing takes the form

$$Y(K_t) = C[Y(K_t)] + (K_{t+1} - K_t) + \phi K_t$$

where Y and K denote the absolute levels of real output and capital.

Let us now examine the effects of systematic monetary policy. If we augment the IS equation (6.1.9) by specifying an LM equation such as (3.2.7) and a money supply rule, we can solve the model under Perfect Foresight. This solution will determine a path for the endogenous variables, prices and capital, from which other variables may be inferred. Since the path of capital is entirely determined by equation (6.1.9), the Strong Neutrality Theory is confirmed. The adoption of a particular systematic monetary policy can have no effect on the path of real capital or real output. Although it has implications for prices, expected inflation, and nominal interest rates, these do not feed through into the goods market, for we have seen that the real interest rate must always accommodate the level of planned investment required to clear the goods market at the temporarily fixed stock of real capital.

Now consider fiscal policy. Assume that real government spending on goods and services at time t is g_t. Again g_t is measured in logarithms. The IS equation is amended to

$$\alpha_0 + \alpha_2 k_t = c(\alpha_0 + \alpha_2 k_t) + (k_{t+1} - k_t) + \phi k_t + g_t \quad (6.1.10)$$

In addition, we require a fiscal policy rule which explains the path of g_t. This amended model can be solved under Perfect Foresight. The solution has two properties. First, at time t the level of output is predetermined, because supply depends on the inherited capital stock. Suppose the economy had been following a particular Perfect Foresight path, but at the end of time $t - 1$ there was an unanticipated change in the fiscal rule. Individuals immediately recompute the Perfect Foresight solution and thereafter the economy evolves along this new path. However, at time t the capital stock has not yet had time to adjust. Because of the one period gestation in investment, the capital stock at time t is still based on investment plans are made under the old policy rule. Thus a change in fiscal policy has no immediate effect on real output. Notice the importance of the assumption that the policy change was unanticipated: had the change been foreseen, the level of investment would have been different even before the policy change was actually put into operation. Provided the fiscal shift is unanticipated, short-run output is predetermined and the consequence of, say, a higher level of government expenditure under the new policy is to crowd out investment by raising interest rates. Thus at period t, the composition of aggregate demand is affected by the policy shift, even though aggregate supply is predetermined. By affecting the level of investment at period t, the shift in fiscal policy will affect future capital stocks and, in general, future values of all real variables. Unlike monetary policy, fiscal policy is impotent only in the short run, a result noted by Sargent and Wallace (1975), Shiller (1978) and many other authors.

It is time to summarise the analysis of this section. Systematic policy, whether monetary of fiscal, cannot manipulate $(p_t -_{t-1} p_t^e)$ under Rational Expectations and hence cannot cause systematic deviations of output and employment from their Natural Rates. Implicit in this view is the belief that changes in systematic components of policies will be detected by the private sector sufficiently quickly that transitional periods may be ignored. Previously unanticipated changes in fiscal policy will not immediately affect the Natural Rate of Output, but in the longer run may affect full employment capacity by affecting current investment. However, this is likely to be a slow process, since investment levels are small relative to the existing capital stock. In the model of this section, monetary policy cannot affect output even in the long run. The economy can be completely dichotomised into a real sector and a nominal sector, such that the real sector evolves in a way which is independent of monetary variables, whose only role is to determine the price level and its rate of change.

This analysis explains the Monetarist pessimism about demand management or fine tuning. Active intervention is likely to lead to large changes in the price level with little consequence for output or employment. To the extent policies are unpredictable, they may increase the uncertainty in the economy and lead to larger fluctuations around the Natural Rates. Thus, it is inferred, policies should be predictable and, if any weight is attached to the desirability of a low and stable inflation rate, should be directed primarily towards this end.

The analysis of this section thus substantiates the claim at the beginning of this book that, in Rational Expectations, Monetarists have found an assumption which allows their intuitive beliefs to be elegantly set out and formally derived. The remainder of this chapter examines whether we should be convinced by the arguments presented above. One might wish to argue that the Rational Expectations hypothesis is not appealing, in which case monetary and fiscal policies remain powerful because it is possible systematically to fool the private sector. I have already indicated why I find this position unattractive.

I shall continue to assume that expectations are Rational, but emphasise the need to distinguish the expectations assumption from the assumptions about the structure of the model in which that assumption is embedded. In Section 6.2 I argue that the model of Section 6.1 is a special case and that in more general specifications, monetary policy can affect future Natural Rates of Output by affecting current investment. The symmetry between monetary and fiscal policy is then restored. In Section 6.3 I allow the government to manipulate the forecasting error under Rational Expectations by assuming that the government has an informational advantage over the private sector. Nevertheless, these models are still within the Monetarist tradition of full market clearing. In Section 6.4 I consider a more fundamental departure which recognises that the labour market may not clear. It is still possible to derive a Rational Expectations path along which individuals' expectations are not knowably incorrect. Since this model admits the possibility of involuntary unemployment and spare capacity, it is Keynesian in spirit and generates Keynesian policy prescriptions.

6.2 A Long-Run Role for Monetary Policy

The Strong Neutrality Theorem asserts that systematic monetary policy cannot affect real variables such as capital, output and employment, even in the long run. To illustrate how this argument may break down, it is sufficient to consider a steady state: if monetary policy can alter the real steady state it will generally have real effects. As in the previous section, it is convenient to work with the assumption of Perfect Foresight.

I continue to assume that equation (6.1.8) describes aggregate goods market clearing. However, when the capital stock is at its steady state level k^*, net investment must be zero to maintain this level of capital. In the steady state, equation (6.1.8) becomes

$$\alpha_0 + \alpha_2 k^* = c(\alpha_0 + \alpha_2 k^*) + \phi k^* \qquad (6.2.1)$$

Following the discussion of Section 3.2, I now add a simple log-linear LM equation

$$m_t - p_t = \delta_1 y_t - \delta_2(\alpha_2 + \pi_t) \quad \delta_1 > 0 \quad \delta_2 > 0$$

in which the demand for real money balances depends positively on output and negatively on nominal interest rates, the latter being decomposed into perfectly foreseen inflation π and the real interest rate which again I take to be the marginal product of capital in the output equation. Assume a constant rate of money growth θ. If real money balances are to be constant in the steady state, the steady state inflation rate must also be θ. The LM equation may then be rewritten as

$$(m - p)^* = \delta_1(\alpha_0 + \alpha_2 k^*) - \delta_2(\alpha_2 + \theta) \qquad (6.2.2)$$

where $(m - p)^*$ denotes the steady state level of real money balances. In this simple framework θ describes the systematic monetary policy. As we discovered in the previous section, changing θ has no effects on capital or output, since it does not enter equation (6.2.1) which solves uniquely for k^*. A policy of perpetually faster monetary expansion increases the steady state inflation rate and nominal interest rates, leading to a lower steady state demand for real money balances, but this has no effect on goods market equilibrium.

However, as I have argued, the above model is rather special. Before the discovery of Rational Expectations, the most important mechanism for Monetarist dynamics of the price level was the *Real Balance Effect* which is analysed at great length in Patinkin (1956). This literature assumes that consumption expenditure is not a simple function of real income, but also depends on real money balances:

$$C_t = c_1 y_t + c_2(m_t - p_t) \quad c_1 > 0 \quad c_2 > 0$$

where C_t is the logarithm of consumption expenditure. For a given real income, higher real money balances induce higher real consumption. Amending the IS equation to recognise the

Real Balance Effect, equation (6.2.1) becomes

$$\alpha_0 + \alpha_2 k^* = c_1 (\alpha_0 + \alpha_2 k^*) + c_2 (m - p)^* + \phi k^* \qquad (6.2.3)$$

Let us re-examine the consequences of an increase in the steady state rate of money growth θ. Suppose first that k^* was unaffected as in the previous case. Tracing through the argument, we find that higher inflation and nominal interest rates reduce $(m - p)^*$, the steady state level of real money balances. However, in the amended model this feeds back into the goods market condition (6.2.3): consumption is reduced and k^* must change if the goods market is to clear in the new steady state. The dichotomy between real and monetary sectors is broken. In this model monetary policy can be used to affect the steady state level of all real variables, in particular the level of output, employment and the real rate of interest. The invariance of Natural Rates of these variables disappears.

Begg (1980) extends this analysis to economies which are not in the steady state. Provided there remains a real balance effect on consumption, systematic monetary policy will feed through into the goods market, thereby affecting the level of investment required for market clearing. Like fiscal policy, monetary policy can crowd out investment, gradually affecting the path of future capital stocks and the Natural Rate of Output.

Nor will Irving Fisher's proposition that the real rate of interest is constant be upheld in more general models. Once non-linear models are adopted, anything which changes the level of the capital stock will alter the marginal product of capital. If this bears any relation to the real rate of interest, the latter will surely be affected by changes in fiscal or monetary policy. Alternatively, since cash pays a zero nominal rate of interest, any policies which alter the expected inflation rate must alter the real rate of return on money. Simple considerations of portfolio or asset equilibrium then suggest that real rates of return on substitutes such as real capital will also have to change.

Archibald and Lipsey (1958) argue that the Real Balance Effect is a disequilibrium phenomenon which vanishes in the steady state. In their model the dichotomy between real and monetary sectors eventually re-emerges. However, this is not sufficient to re-establish the Strong Neutrality Theorem: since the Real Balance Effect continues to operate when the economy is not in the steady state, Fischer (1979b) has shown that systematic monetary policy will still affect the path along which the economy converges to the steady state under Perfect Foresight or Rational Expectations. I conclude that the Strong Neutrality Theorem holds only in the very special model in which the Real Balance Effect is completely ignored.

6.3 Multiperiod Wage Contracts

Having argued that systematic, and therefore anticipatable, monetary and fiscal policies can crowd out investment, thereby affecting future levels of the Natural Rate of Output, I now wish to re-examine the Weak Neutrality Theorem that the government cannot generate systematic deviations from the current levels of the Natural Rate under Rational Expectations, i.e. the government can influence the *composition* of current output but not its overall level. McCallum (1980b) terms this the impossibility of pure stabilisation policy. In the stochastic model considered in Section 6.1 in which output supply deviates from its Natural Rate only because of errors in forecasting the price level, this result follows immediately from the assumption of Rational Expectations.

Thus far I have assumed that all individuals have access to the same information. I now assume that the government has an *Informational Advantage* over the private sector. A simple example will clarify this idea. Consider again equation (6.1.1) describing aggregate goods supply

$$y_t = y_n + \alpha_1 (p_t - {}_{t-1}p_t^e) + \epsilon_{1t} \quad \alpha_1 > 0 \quad \epsilon_{1t}: \text{mean zero and}$$
$$\text{serially uncorrelated}$$

Since in this section I wish to examine only the role of forecasting errors, I revert to the simpler assumption that y_n is constant. Suppose, as before, that individual wage bargainers must form expectations about the price level conditional on information available at $t - 1$, but now suppose that the government does not have to make a policy decision about the level of current policy variables until after the beginning of period t, by which time values of the current disturbance terms in the model can be observed. To be specific, I assume the simple monetary policy

$$m_t = \bar{m} + \epsilon_{3t} \qquad (6.3.1)$$

where $\bar{m}$ is a constant and, conditional on information at $t-1$, ϵ_{3t} has mean zero and no serial correlation. Individuals solve the Rational Expectations problem in the usual way and their expectations still have the property that

$$p_t = {}_{t-1}p_t^e + \eta_t$$

such that, conditional on information available at time $t-1$, η_t has mean zero and no serial correlation. The government now has an informational advantage over the private sector. At the beginning of time t, the government observes the structural disturbances, such as ϵ_{1t} in the goods supply equation, and can therefore calculate the Rational Expectations forecasting error. Of course, η_t depends partly on ϵ_{3t}, the extent to which individuals fail to forecast government monetary policy. However, the government knows its own policy. Thus the government can choose ϵ_{3t}, and hence η_t, such that from equation (6.1.1)

$$\alpha_1 \eta_t + \epsilon_{1t} = 0 \qquad (6.3.2)$$

The government is able to stabilise output at the Natural Rate. This policy is feasible here because ϵ_{3t} can be chosen after the private sector has had to form expectations ${}_{t-1}p_t^e$ and after the government receives the additional information about the values of current disturbances such as ϵ_{1t}. Even though the private sector understands the nature of the policy in operation, there is no way this knowledge can be used at time $t-1$ to improve forecasts. The actual government intervention ϵ_{3t} at time t depends only on the *ex post* deviations of other random disturbances at time t from their zero means. Since at $t-1$ the best guess about the values of these other disturbances is that they will attain their mean values, individuals can do no better than assume that ${}_{t-1}\epsilon_{3t}^e = 0$. They know that intervention will take place, but they have no basis for predicting its direction.

Notice what the government can achieve and what it

cannot. The above argument suggests that the government can use its informational advantage over the private sector to reduce the fluctuations of output around its Natural Rate. One might call this very fine tuning. The success of such a policy depends crucially on the ability to make quick and accurate inferences about the precise nature of current shocks. Friedman's caveat that such a policy may be counter-productive if inferences are incorrect remains relevant. Any economist who has studied the extent to which economic data series are revised over time by central statistical departments might wonder whether such an informational lead is really an advantage. Notice too that the above argument does not imply that the government can hold output at a level other than the Natural Rate for any length of time. If the government sets ϵ_{3t} systematically above zero in an attempt to generate a sequence of positive private sector forecasting errors, individuals will quickly recognise the basis of the policy and incorporate this information in $_{t-1}p_t^e$. Putting this argument in a different form, individuals quickly learn that the average level of m_t is higher than they were previously expecting and reassess their view of $\bar{m}$ in equation (6.3.1), such that the unforecastable component ϵ_{3t} once more has conditional expectation zero at $t-1$ when expectations are formed.

While this simple example is useful as an expositional device for illustrating how stabilisation may be conducted when the government has an informational advantage, it is not a very plausible example: even the most sophisticated government economists are unlikely to have a significant time advantage in their access to information. A more plausible model is developed by Fischer (1977). Imagine there are two groups of workers and firms such that the first group nego-tiates nominal wage settlements in September, the second group in March. A period lasts six months. A nominal wage contract for either group is in force for two periods, though it may specify a different nominal wage in each of the two six month periods over which the contract lasts. Thus there are overlapping two period nominal wage contracts. It is still assumed that the aim in settling a nominal wage contract is to clear the labour market in the sense defined earlier.

Under Rational Expectations, a group settling at the end

of time $t - 1$ forms its best guesses about p_t and p_{t+1} in order to fix, at time $t - 1$, the wages w_t and w_{t+1} for that group of workers. The other group settles a period later, having formed expectations $_tp^e_{t+1}$ and $_tp^e_{t+2}$. Unlike the above example, it is not assumed that the government can set its policy for time t after observing the current values of the random disturbances; rather, the informational advantage accrues because it is assumed that the government can change its policy before the start of each period, whereas part of the private sector is allowed to make use of new information only every second period. When a group of workers and firms set a contract at the end of time $t - 1$ they will be locked into this contract for two periods. The government can react one period later to partly offset disturbances which have occurred since the contract was set. As in the previous example, any systematic attempt to hold output at a level other than the Natural Rate will quickly be discovered and is usable information when the two period contracts are set. Such attempts by the government will fail. However, by reacting to shocks which occur after the contract for some group of workers is set, the government can reduce the fluctuations of output around the Natural Rate. Such interventions do not affect expectations formation, because *ex ante* the best guess about the shocks, and hence about the intervention, is that they will attain their zero means.

If multiperiod wage contracts extend over few periods of short duration, the quality of the recent information over which the government has an informational advantage is unlikely to justify an active stabilisation policy. The longer is the duration of wage contracts, the more plausible it is that active policy might reduce the fluctuations around the Natural Rate. For example, in economies such as the UK in which wage agreements are negotiated annually, the scope for intervention is likely to be less than in economies such as the USA in which many wage contracts extend over three years.

6.4 Demand Management in Disequilibrium Models

The models of Sections 6.1–6.3 are distinctly Monetarist in spirit: even in the absence of active government intervention, output and employment deviate only temporarily from their Natural Rates. Since the impact of an unforeseen shock lasts only as long as the longest outstanding contract, the economy is buffeted by an unending succession of unforeseeable shocks, but exhibits no tendency in either direction to persistent deviations from the Natural Rate. I now wish to depart from the framework of stochastic market clearing.

To illustrate how Rational Expectations may be applied within a disequilibrium framework, I examine the model set out in Begg (1982) which formalises the analysis of Keynes (1936) in Chapter 19 of the General Theory. This argument assumes neither complete wage rigidity nor money illusion. Rather, Keynes asserts:

> 'There may exist no expedient by which labour as a whole can reduce its *real* wage to a given figure by making revised money bargains with entrepreneurs. We shall endeavour to show that primarily it is certain other forces which determine the level of real wages.'[1]

The central assumption is that while money wages are flexible, goods prices are more flexible; thus, the real wage is determined by firms not workers. For any level of money wages, firms choose prices and real wages to clear the goods market, as is recognised in Solow and Stiglitz (1968). Keynes regarded it as self-evident that the transactions costs of negotiating wage changes outweigh the transactions costs of changing prices. It is this asymmetry in real transactions costs which generates asymmetric wage and price behaviour.

To formalise this idea, I assume that there are two period overlapping contracts for nominal wages with the additional constraint, not imposed in the model of Fischer (1977), that a contract must specify the *same* nominal wage in both subperiods of the contract. Similar ideas may be found in the work of Taylor (1979b)(1980a).

Details of the model are given in Begg (1982). The typical firm has a production function $Y = (1/a)L^a$, where the parameter a lies between zero and unity. Whatever the level of nominal wages, competitive firms then equate the real wage to the marginal product of labour. There are two cohorts of

---

1. Keynes (1936), Chapter 2, part II.

firms and workers, cohort A settling two period wage contracts at times $t-1, t+1, t+3 \ldots$ and cohort B at times $t, t+2, t+4 \ldots$ Aggregate demand is given by

$$Y_t = cY_t + b(M_t/P_t) + Z_t \quad 0 < c < 1 \quad b > 0 \quad (6.4.1)$$

where Y, M, P and Z denote respectively real output, nominal money, the price level and exogenous components of aggregate demand. The two cohorts produce the same good whose price P_t clears the goods market at time t. Labour demand and output supply equations for each cohort are derived from competitive profit maximisation.

Suppose the economy begins in a steady state at full employment. Both cohorts have the same nominal wage. We now imagine that there is a downward shock to real aggregate demand which disturbs the steady state. For convenience, we measure variables in deviations from their original steady state levels. Suppose cohort B settles at date t when the shock first occurs, cohort A being locked into the previous nominal wage for one more period. Begg (1982) shows that goods market clearing at time t implies

$$\left(\frac{1}{a-1}\right)(w_t^B - p_t + w_{t-1}^A - p_t) =$$
$$\left(\frac{c}{a-1}\right)(w_t^B - p_t + w_{t-1}^A - p_t) + d_t - ep_t \quad e > 0 \quad (6.4.2)$$

where w_t, p_t and d_t now denote the deviations of nominal wages, prices, and $(Z_t + b(M_t/P^*))$ from their steady state values, P^* being the original steady state price level. Superscripts A and B refer to cohorts and e is a positive constant. The left hand side represents output supply by firms in the two cohorts and is straightforwardly neoclassical: higher real wages in either cohort reduce desired output supply. Recall that the parameter a is less than unity. The first term on the right hand side captures consumption, depending on output. d_t is the exogenous downward shock to real aggregate demand and is negative. The final term captures the idea that lower prices will increase aggregate demand by increasing real money balances.

Conventional neoclassical microeconomics also suggests that labour demands for the two cohorts will be given by

$$L_t^A = -\left(\frac{1}{1-a}\right)(w_{t-1}^A - p_t)$$

$$L_t^B = -\left(\frac{1}{1-a}\right)(w_t^B - p_t)$$

(6.4.3)

where L_t^A and L_t^B are measured in deviations from the steady state levels. Suppose this economy begins in the steady state. Thus, in deviations, $w^A = w^B = p = L^A = L^B = 0$. At time $t = 1$, there is an unanticipated, but immediately recognised, permanent negative shock d to aggregate demand. In the model of equations (6.4.1) and (6.4.2), it does not matter whether this shock is exogenous or is the result of a contractionary monetary or fiscal policy. Assume cohort B is the settling cohort at time $t = 1$ when shock occurs; cohort A is locked into its previous wage contract for another period. How the economy evolves depends on the intertemporal preferences of wage bargainers. The simplest assumption is that the settling cohort B chooses nominal wage w_1^B to ensure its immediate full employment at $t = 1$. Since cohort A is still at its old steady state nominal wage, $w_1^A = 0$ (all variables are measured in deviations from the original steady state). Equation (6.4.3) implies that cohort B will achieve full employment at $t = 1$ by solving the model under Perfect Foresight and choosing $w_1^B = p_1$. At any date at which cohort B settles for a wage ensuring its own full employment, equations (6.4.3) and (6.4.2) imply

$$w_t^B = \left(\frac{1-c}{D}\right)w_{t-1}^A + \left(\frac{1-a}{D}\right)d \quad D \equiv e(1-a) + (1-c) > 0$$

(6.4.4)

Hence at $t = 1$, given $w_1^A = 0$, cohort B settles for

$$w_1^B = \left(\frac{1-a}{D}\right)d < 0$$

(6.4.5)

which is negative given that d, the shock to aggregate demand, is negative. If at time $t = 2$, cohort A then settles for w_2^A to ensure its own full employment, wages are determined by equation (6.4.4) with the cohort superscripts reversed. In fact, ignoring the superscripts, equation (6.4.4) determines the evolution of the wage of the settling cohort thereafter.

It is easily checked that the settlement wage of equation (6.4.4) eventually converges to

$$w^{A**} = w^{B**} = d/e < 0 \qquad (6.4.6)$$

From equation (6.4.2), if p^{**} also equals d/e, then the goods market clears and $(w^{**} - p^{**})$ equals zero: the model eventually converges to the full employment steady state where, from equation (6.4.3), $L^{A**} = L^{B**} = 0$. Employment of both cohorts has reverted to its original steady state. All deviations are eventually eliminated.

Consider what this implies for the path of employment. It is simple algebra to confirm that w_1^B in equation (6.4.4) is less negative than the new steady state level w^{**} given in equation (6.4.6). Faced with the initial downward shock to aggregate demand, cohort B does cut its nominal wages, but it does not have to cut them all the way to the new steady state level d/e. Since cohort A is temporarily locked into a nominal wage which is 'too high', cohort B can secure a higher market share for its output and employment while cutting wages only a little. Since full employment of cohort B at time 1 implies $p_1 = w_1^B$, prices do not fall all the way to their new steady state level d/e. Nevertheless, prices do fall. The real wage of cohort A at time 1 is increased and it suffers unemployment. At time 2, cohort B is locked into the wage w_1^B which it settled for a period earlier; cohort A achieves its own full employment without cutting its wage all the way to the new steady state level d/e. Cohort B then faces unemployment, since p_2 equals w_2^A which is more negative than w_1^B. The economy claws its way slowly back to full employment with each cohort facing unemployment every second period.

This model exhibits involuntary unemployment. There is no policy of wage setting which will allow both cohorts to maintain full employment. Of more importance, the effects of the shock, although correctly perceived from time $t = 1$ onwards, persist long after each cohort has had the opportunity to renegotiate. Only asymptotically is full employment of both cohorts restored, with the relative wages of the cohorts equalised once more. In the new steady state, nominal wages and prices have fallen just sufficiently to raise the value of real money balances to offset the initial downward shock to aggregate demand.

In assuming that cohorts set wages to ensure their short-run full employment, I have selected a particularly simple assumption. What would actually happen depends on the intertemporal preferences of cohorts. For example, if cohort B were to proceed directly to the new steady state wage d/e at time $t = 1$, the steady state wage would be attained one period later when cohort A also settles for wage d/e. However, such a policy by cohort B at $t = 1$ involves short-run sacrifice by that cohort: it can be shown that this implies a large fall in their real wage at this date relative to the real wage in equation (6.4.5), which is sufficient to guarantee the full employment of cohort B. Thus cohort B has the choice of trading-off lower real wages in the short run to avoid un-employment in the future. More complicated preferences may be allowed. The general principle remains that whatever the current wage settlement, it will affect the wage inherited by the economy in the following period. Under Rational Expectations, cohorts can solve this intertemporal problem and decide which path to follow once their preferences have been specified. Except in the extreme case in which settling cohorts proceed immediately to the new steady state wage, the effect of a shock will persist after all cohorts have had the opportunity to renegotiate. Given the structure of transactions costs in this economy, persistent involuntary unemployment may arise even under Rational Expectations.

From the date the shock is first perceived, individuals do not make systematic forecasting errors. They understand that this model admits involuntary unemployment and they use the knowledge of equations (6.4.2) and (6.4.3) in forming expectations. Rather, the problem is that once a shock leads cohorts' relative wages to get out of line, the constraint of having to settle a single wage for two periods prevents the correct relative wages being quickly re-established, unless one or other cohort incurs very large short-term sacrifices.

I now consider the role of demand management in this model. I suppose this takes the form of fiscal policy, though the above specification would allow an identical role for monetary policy. In equation (6.4.2) I now decompose d_t

into two components $d**$ and g_t. The former is the exogenous downward shock to aggregate demand which occurs unexpectedly at $t = 1$, is immediately recognised, and remains constant thereafter; the latter measures deviations of real government spending from its original steady state level. Thus, if $g**$ is the level of real government spending to which fiscal policy eventually converges, the new steady state price level is $(d** + g**)/e$. With w^{A**} and w^{B**} also at this level, the goods market clears at full employment. I assume that the government and the private sector have access to the same information. Since at $t = 1$ cohort B recognises the shock $d**$ has occurred, I assume that the government also uses this information in setting fiscal policy g_1 at this date. By setting $g_1 = -d**$, the shock may be immediately neutralised, leaving the economy at full employment at the original nominal wages and prices. Even if the government faces a decision lag, the problem is complicated only a little. If the government takes one period to react to new information, g_1 will equal zero, since fiscal policy will not yet have deviated from its former steady state level. From equation (6.4.5), cohort B settles for

$$w_1^B = \left(\frac{1-a}{D}\right)d** > 0 \quad D \equiv e(1-a) + (1-c) > 0$$

if it wishes to ensure its own immediate full employment. At $t = 2$, the government is now able to react. By setting

$$g_2 = -d** + e(1-a)d**/D$$

it ensures that w_1^B is the new steady state nominal wage. Hence cohort A can settle for the same nominal wage w_2^A and convergence to the new steady state is achieved in period 2. The economy remains in this steady state, provided government spending is maintained at this level and no new shocks occur.

I have studied this model at some length to establish two propositions. Rational Expectations can be applied in models which do not impose continuous market clearing and conventional stabilisation policy will then have conventional Keynesian effects, even though the policy is understood and incorporated into the process of expectations formation. In such models the notion of a Natural Rate of Output or Employment is somewhat ambiguous, for it could be defined in one of two ways: we might mean the level of output or employment which occurs if expectations formed in the previous period are indeed fulfilled, or the level of output or employment which corresponds to Walrasian market clearing in all markets. Only in the market clearing world in which Friedman coined the term do the two definitions reduce to the same thing.

The possibility of effective stabilisation policy thus rests not on the nature of expectations formation, though the assumption of Rational Expectations precludes policies which rely on systematically fooling the private sector, but rather on the question of whether or not markets clear continuously. Proponents of market clearing argue that theoretical disequilibrium models require the assumption of institutional arrangements such as long-term contracts, whose existence is incompatible with serious microeconomic analysis: if it is only the presence of such institutions which generates undesirable consequences such as involuntary unemployment, surely there exist incentives to alter these institutions? Moreover, even where such institutions appear to exist, the use of price discounts and overtime wage payments in practice may give sufficient effective flexibility to validate the market clearing assumption.

If this argument seems appealing, the reader should consult Hahn (1971)(1980) who is a vigorous advocate of the view that the presence of transactions costs and informational uncertainty removes the presumption that disequilibrium models cannot be given legitimate microeconomic foundations. The model above, which I attributed to Keynes, argued that transactions costs of changing wages outweigh the transactions costs of changing prices; firms cannot forever be arguing with workers about what the wage should now be. Other microeconomic foundations are possible and I mention just two.

The first derives from the seminal paper by Akerlof (1970) on the market for 'lemons' which he originally applied to the used car market, but may equally be applied to the market for labour. The presumption that excess supply will lead to a speedy fall in the wage rests on the belief that unemployed workers will offer to undercut employed workers, bidding down the wage. However, workers are not of uniform skill and less productive workers tend to work for lower wages. A skilled, unemployed worker may be deterred from submitting a low wage offer because the firm, lacking any other means of cheaply establishing the worker's characteristics, may infer that the worker must be unskilled to be prepared to work for such a wage. When the relevant information is expensive to collect, the smooth working of the market cannot be taken for granted.

A second class of microfoundations for temporary wage stickiness emphasises the long-run nature of implicit contracts between firms and workers and is usefully surveyed in Hall (1980a). Training on the job confers important firm-specific human capital to workers, forcing both parties to the wage bargain to take a longer-run view: human investment is as irreversible as investment in plant. If firms are to retain skilled workers in whom they have invested, and if workers are to be prepared to undertake a period of skill acquisition, a credible if only implicit schedule of long-run wage payments must be established and this may preclude short-run variation of wages to reflect the temporary state of the labour market. When firms are able to borrow more easily than households, it may be mutually advantageous for firms to act as financial intermediaries, reinforcing the incentive to adopt cyclical wage smoothing.

The relevance of the market clearing assumption remains a contentious issue. Until this debate is resolved it will not be possible to reach a definitive conclusion on whether conventional stabilisation policy or demand management is possible. In this context, the empirical research on stabilisation policy under Rational Expectations is of particular interest and it is to that evidence that I now turn.

6.5 Empirical Research on Stabilisation Policy Under Rational Expectations

We have seen that observable equations require the specification of joint hypotheses about the process of expectations formation and the structure of the underlying economic model. Since it is the latter on which I wish to focus, the empirical studies which I discuss follow the previous sections in assuming the validity of the Rational Expectations hypothesis. I begin by examining the large body of literature whch takes the market clearing assumption as its point of departure, relying either on the aggregate supply equation (6.1.1) or its companion equation for unemployment (6.1.2). I begin with the latter.

Variations in actual unemployment U_t are to be explained by variations in the Natural Rate of Unemployment U_{nt} and by variations induced by errors in forecasting the current price level. The first step is to determine the empirical magnitudes of these two components. Since we know that the real economy is fairly sluggish, a simple hypothesis is that the current value of the unobservable Natural Rate may be forecast by extrapolating past values of actual unemployment.[2] Suppose that this relation takes the form

$$U_{nt} = \beta_1 U_{t-1} + \beta_2 U_{t-2} + v_t' \tag{6.5.1}$$

where v_t' is a random disturbance with mean zero and no serial correlation. Substitution into equation (6.1.2) yields

$$U_t = \beta_1 U_{t-1} + \beta_2 U_{t-2} + v_t$$
$$v_t = \epsilon_{2t} + v_t' - \beta[p_t - (_{t-1}p_t^e)] \tag{6.5.2}$$

Since each component of v_t has mean zero and is serially uncorrelated, v_t must have similar properties. By confronting unemployment data with equation (6.5.2) we may estimate the coefficients $\hat{\beta}_1$ and $\hat{\beta}_2$ which best fit the data and let $(\hat{\beta}_1 U_{t-1} + \hat{\beta}_2 U_{t-2})$ be our estimate of $\hat{U}_{nt}$. Since U_{t-1} and U_{t-2} are known at the date individuals must form expectations $_{t-1}p_t^e$, individuals forming Rational Expectations at time $t - 1$ could certainly have undertaken this calculation.

---

2. Possible explanations of the dependence of U_t on its lagged values are studied in Lucas (1975) who emphasises the effect of previous investment on the current capital stock and in Blinder and Fischer (1978) who emphasise a similar mechanism operating through inventory accumulation.

Using quarterly data for the USA from 1954 to 1974, Hall (1975) found that this estimate $\hat{U}_{nt}$ explained 93% of the actual variation in unemployment U_t. Thus, at most, 7% of variation in unemployment is explained by variation in v_t. Since the Rational Expectations forecasting error $(p_t - {}_{t-1}p_t^e)$ is only one component of v_t, Hall concluded that if equation (6.1.2) is to be an adequate model of unemployment variation, the source of this variation must be sought not in the failure to forecast the price level but in changes in the Natural Rate itself.

Proponents of almost continuous market clearing must therefore explain large changes in the Natural Rate of Unemployment without resort to disequilibrium phenomena such as deficient aggregate demand. Among the phenomena which might be examined are changes in microeconomic incentives to work, such as marginal income tax rates or the value of social security payments, social and demographic changes such as increased female participation in the labour force or the post war 'baby boom', the cumulative effect of previous levels of investment on the current capital stock, and the possibility that when real wages are thought to be temporarily low, workers take a voluntary holiday as the current price of leisure falls. Such empirical explanations have been attempted and have sometimes been suggestive — for example, Hall (1980c) found a surprisingly large propensity to substitute between current and future leisure which might go some way towards explaining the rise in the Natural Rate within this framework.

Although such evidence bears indirectly on the issues in which we are interested, I must confine my discussion to evidence which directly relates to the possibility of stabilisation policy under Rational Expectations. Sargent (1976a) postulated an augmented version of equation (6.5.2)

$$U_t = \sum_{i=1}^{4} \beta_i U_{t-i} + \sum_{i=1}^{k} \Gamma_i Z_{t-i} + v_t \tag{6.5.3}$$

allowing four lagged values of unemployment and up to k lagged values of other variables Z_t which include policy variables, such as real government spending and the nominal money supply, and variables such as wages and prices which all theories accept can be systematically manipulated by government policy. If stabilisation policy is completely ineffective, all the coefficients Γ_i ought to be zero. Unemployment then follows a trend which may be extrapolated from its own past values, but which cannot be affected by stabilisation policy. Notice that unanticipated policy surprises may still affect current unemployment through the random term v_t, whose definition in equation (6.5.2) makes clear its dependence on the current forecasting error $(p_t - {}_{t-1}p_t^e)$ in equation (6.1.2).

Using quarterly US data to fit equation (6.5.3), Sargent concluded that past levels of real government spending and past prices had no effect on current unemployment, but that past levels of money supply and past wages did have a significant effect.[3]

However, it has since been realised that equations such as (6.5.3) can never discriminate between the competing hypotheses. Even if the data confirm that past values of the Z_t variables do affect current unemployment, the equation does not distinguish between anticipated and unanticipated components of these Z_t variables. For simplicity, assume that the only Z_t variable is M_{t-1}, the nominal money stock in the previous period. As a matter of definition, we can decompose M_{t-1} into two parts

$$M_{t-1} \equiv {}_{t-2}M_{t-1}^e + (M_{t-1} - {}_{t-2}M_{t-1}^e)$$

We wish to consider the hypothesis that systematic government policy (here represented by the anticipatable component ${}_{t-2}M_{t-1}^e$) has no effect on current unemployment. Since both Monetarists and Keynesians accept that the unanticipated component of policy should have real effects, M_{t-1} should affect unemployment if only because it includes this unanticipated component. Non-zero estimates of the coefficient on M_{t-1} convey no information about the effects of the anticipated component ${}_{t-2}M_{t-1}^e$.

We have now reached the following position. Proponents

---

3. For an extension of this approach, see Cuddington (1980).

of the view that only unanticipated policy matters assert that the current level of unemployment may be adequately explained by the equation

$$U_t = \sum_{i=1}^{4} \beta_i U_{t-i} + \sum_{i=1}^{k} \Gamma_i (Z_{t-i} - {}_{t-i-1}Z_{t-i}^e) + v_t \quad (6.5.4)$$

in which only current and past surprises cause unemployment to deviate from its exogenous trend path which may be extrapolated from previous values of U_t. Current surprises enter directly through v_t and past surprises may have lingering effects because of the dynamic structure of the economy, as for example when a previous surprise contemporaneously alters investment and hence the current capital stock. If equation (6.5.4) is correct, systematic stabilisation policy is powerless, because it is anticipated under Rational Expectations. Whether or not equation (6.5.5) is correct can only be empirically tested if empirical studies distinguish anticipated and unanticipated components of government policy and cannot be determined from equations such as (6.5.3) which confuse the two components. This argument was first set out in Sargent (1976a).

In a series of papers, Barro (1977a)(1978) and Barro and Rush (1980) have attempted to meet this challenge by distinguishing between anticipated and unanticipated components of monetary policy. Let DM_t denote $(m_t - m_{t-1})$, where m_t is the logarithm of the nominal money stock at time t. The first step is to discover a useable equation for predicting money supply growth. After much trial and error using annual US data, Barro and Rush (1980) conclude that for the period 1941–77 a satisfactory empirical specification is

$$DM_t = \gamma_0 + \gamma_1 DM_{t-1} + \gamma_2 DM_{t-2} + \gamma_3 G_t +$$
$$\gamma_4 \log\left(\frac{U_{t-1}}{1 - U_{t-1}}\right) + \epsilon_t \quad (6.5.5)$$

where ϵ_t is a random disturbance with mean zero and no serial correlation, U_{t-1} denotes measured unemployment at time $t - 1$, and G_t denotes the deviation of government spending from its trend level, capturing the idea that unusually large budget deficits, as in the Korean War, lead to unusual monetary expansion. It is assumed that individuals understand this implicit money supply rule and use it to form Rational Expectations of the future money supply growth, forming $_{t-1}DM_t^e$ by setting $_{t-1}\epsilon_t^e$ equal to zero. Notice that the contemporaneous variable G_t is not strictly known at time $t-1$ when expectations are formed, so the interpretation of equation (6.5.5) as the Rational Expectations forecasting rule is questionable. Barro (1977a) defends its inclusion on the grounds that aberrant wartime expenditure is quickly understood, perceived and forecast. Detailed criticisms of equation (6.5.5) may be found in the Appendix to Chapter 2 in Fischer (1980a).

By choosing coefficients $\hat{\gamma}$ to best fit the data, Barro and Rush form the estimate

$$_{t-1}DM_t^e = \widehat{DM}_t = \hat{\gamma}_0 + \hat{\gamma}_1 DM_{t-1} + \hat{\gamma}_2 DM_{t-2} +$$

$$\hat{\gamma}_3 G_t + \hat{\gamma}_4 \log\left(\frac{U_{t-1}}{1 - U_{t-1}}\right)$$

and hence estimate the forecasting errors $(DM_t - _{t-1}DM_t^e)$ by $(DM_t - \widehat{DM}_t)$, and I denote the residuals DMR_t. Having an operational estimate of the forecasting errors, it is now possible to estimate a model in which current employment depends on current and lagged forecasting errors as equation (6.5.4) suggests. Barro and Rush report the estimates for 1949–77

$$\log\left(\frac{U_t}{1 - U_t}\right) = -2.7 - 4.6DMR_t - 10.9DMR_{t-1}$$

$$- 5.5DMR_{t-2} - 5.3MIL_t \qquad (6.5.6)$$

where *MIL* is a variable capturing the labour market implications of conscription and other military employment. All the coefficients are significantly different from zero according to standard statistical criteria and the equation explains 87% of the variation in the left hand side variable.

Barro (1977a) then adds two lagged values $\widehat{DM}_{t-1}$ and $\widehat{DM}_{t-2}$ capturing the past *systematic and anticipatable* components of money supply growth and re-estimates equation

(6.5.6), concluding that the estimated coefficients on these additional variables are not significantly different from zero. Barro and Rush (1980) adopt a slightly different approach, but again conclude that the data are consistent with the view that only unanticipated money growth affects unemployment. Similar results are presented for an output equation based on equation (6.1.1) rather than (6.1.2). Barro's approach has also been adopted by other authors. Attfield, Demery and Duck (1982a & b) have examined data from the UK, confirming the usefulness of unanticipated money growth in explaining output changes and the insignificant additional contribution of past values of $\widehat{DM}_t$ derived from a money supply rule which is broadly similar to equation (6.5.5). Canadian evidence has been studied by Wogin (1980).

At first sight this evidence looks impressive, but it does not avoid the pitfall noted by Sargent (1976b), whose central point may be made within a highly simplified model comprising two equations

$$U_t = \beta' DM_{t-1} + v_t \tag{6.5.7}$$

$$DM_t = \gamma_1 DM_{t-1} + \epsilon_t \tag{6.5.8}$$

in which the random variables v_t and ϵ_t have mean zero and no serial correlation. Equation (6.5.8) describes a simple money supply rule. Equation (6.5.7) describes a model in which, by hypothesis, past money supply growth affects current unemployment, whether or not that money growth is unanticipated. Thus the model is constructed to allow an effect for systematic monetary policy.

From equation (6.5.8)

$$\begin{aligned}
DM_{t-1} &= \gamma_1 DM_{t-2} + \epsilon_{t-1} \\
&= \epsilon_{t-1} + \gamma_1 (\epsilon_{t-2} + \gamma_1 DM_{t-3}) \\
&= \epsilon_{t-1} + \gamma_1 \epsilon_{t-2} + \gamma_1^2 (\epsilon_{t-3} + \gamma_1 DM_{t-4}) \\
&= \epsilon_{t-1} + \gamma_1 \epsilon_{t-2} + \gamma_1^2 \epsilon_{t-3} + \gamma_1^3 \epsilon_{t-4} + \ldots
\end{aligned}$$

Hence the model given by equations (6.5.7) and (6.5.8), constructed to allow a role for anticipatable stabilisation policy, can *always* be expressed in the form

$$U_t = \beta' \epsilon_{t-1} + \beta' \gamma_1 \epsilon_{t-2} + \beta' \gamma_1^2 \epsilon_{t-3} + \ldots + v_t \tag{6.5.9}$$

in which it appears that only past *unanticipated* money growth matters.[4] Thus the Barro procedure will never shed light on the efficacy of stabilisation policy, for it is always possible to interpret equations such as (6.5.6) as versions of equation (6.5.9) derived from a model in which policy is effective. Adding additional variables DM_{t-i} then merely duplicates the information already available and should not be expected to contribute any additional explanatory power.

A more promising approach is that suggested by Sargent (1976a). Consider again equation (6.5.9) derived from equation (6.5.8). Systematic and therefore anticipatable monetary policy is reflected in the parameter γ_1 which determines the Rational Expectation $_{t-1}DM_t^e$ given information on DM_{t-1}. Equation (6.5.9) differs from the Natural Rate specification (6.5.4) in asserting that the *coefficients* on monetary surprises ϵ_{t-i} depend systematically on the stabilisation policy in force. If equation (6.5.9) really does describe the world in which we live, if offers an example of the Lucas Problem discussed in Section 4.4, since a change in the nature of the systematic policy rule will alter the coefficients on past monetary surprises in equation (6.5.9). In contrast, the Natural Rate specification (6.5.4) predicts that coefficients will be invariant with respect to policy changes, since coefficients describe only the inevitable structural lags in a dynamic economy. If we can find a data sample in which different subperiods have clearly distinct policy rules, we may be able to test whether the coefficients depend on policy or not.

6.6 Conclusion

In this chapter I have examined the proposition that stabilisation policy will be ineffective because its effect is completely

4. Readers with some knowledge of econometric theory may suspect that the Keynesian assumption that stabilisation policy works implies the existence of testable coefficient restrictions in the unemployment equation. For example, in equation (6.5.9) successive coefficients on lagged ϵ_t are γ_1 times the previous value. Sargent (1976b, 1976c) points out that it is always possible to conceive of a sufficiently general money supply rule that no testable restrictions are implied in the observable equation. A similar pessimistic conclusion is reached in Buiter (1980b).

discounted under Rational Expectations. Market clearing models will be characterised by a Natural Rate of Output or Unemployment from which actual levels of these variables deviate chiefly because of errors in forecasting the price level in a world in which many settlements are in nominal rather than real terms.

Unless the government has some kind of informational advantage over the private sector, it will not be possible systematically to manipulate these forecasting errors if expectations are Rational. Nevertheless, under quite weak assumptions, both monetary and fiscal policy may be used to affect the present composition of output and hence future levels of these Natural Rates. Explicit microeconomic considerations such as the incentive effects of marginal tax rates or social security payments will of course also bear on the Natural Rates, but these are not conventionally deemed part of macroeconomic stabilisation policy.

Once the assumption of market clearing is relaxed, stabilisation policy may have standard Keynesian effects, even if expectations are Rational. Such models must offer a convincing account of the failure of market clearing. Recent work on differential transactions costs, informational or signalling confusion, and the longer-term incentives which arise through training on the job or other mobility costs, suggest that it may be possible to elaborate the reasons for market failure and involuntary unemployment. Whether such effects are important in practice is therefore an empirical question.

Even if the market clearing framework is accepted, current forecasting errors at best explain only a small part of the variation in output or employment. However, in a dynamic and somewhat sluggish economy characterised for example by gestation lags for investment, past forecasting errors might cumulatively be of sufficient magnitude to explain movements in the current Natural Rate, especially when these are superimposed on a worsening trend whose explanation is to be sought not in macroeconomic but in microeconomic developments. Empirical studies suggest that such a thesis is consistent with the data.

However, as we have seen, the Natural Rate assumption

can be theoretically challenged: at least in the short run, there remains the possibility of involuntary unemployment which would allow a role for macroeconomic stabilisation. Within the framework typically adopted in the empirical literature, the two models are observationally equivalent, so that the results cited above are also compatible with a Keynesian interpretation. Although more sophisticated tests can be devised, they are not trivial to conduct, requiring for example the ability to partition a sample period into subperiods in which distinct systematic policies were pursued. As yet, it is impossible to reach an unambiguous conclusion and the reader, like other economists, must continue to be guided by *a priori* beliefs. The difficulties which I have tried to convey should not be judged a weakness of the Rational Expectations approach, for it is pointless to gloss over genuine difficulties which arise in economic research. It is only by encouraging a rigorous statement of the competing positions that we can consider how to design empirical research which is truly informative.

Notes on the Literature

The Natural Rate hypothesis is set out in Friedman (1968) and elaborated in Phelps (1970) and Friedman (1977). Minford and Peel (1981) classify the various supply equations used to capture the Natural Rate hypothesis.

The neutrality of stabilisation policy in general, and monetary policy in particular, is a theme developed at length in Lucas (1972b, 1975), Sargent (1973), Sargent and Wallace (1975) and Barro (1976). Papers which dispute the neutrality result without rejecting the basic assumption of market clearing include Fischer (1977, 1979a & b), Phelps and Taylor (1977), McCallum (1977), Shiller (1978), Begg (1980) and Buiter (1980a). Many of these issues are surveyed in McCallum (1980) and Fischer (1980b). The efficacy of stabilisation policy in disequilibrium models has been argued by Taylor (1979b, 1980a), Begg (1982) and Neary and Stiglitz (1982). Such models are also discussed in Buiter (1980a).

In addition to the empirical work cited in Section 6.5, direct tests of the disequilibrium hypothesis by Rosen and Quandt (1978) and Fair (1979c) are relevant. Taylor (1980a) argues that a version of the overlapping contracts model of Section 6.4 is consistent with unemployment data for the USA. The papers by McCallum (1979c), Sargent (1979c) and Buiter (1980b) extend the original work by Sargent (1976b) on observational equivalence.

7
Rational Expectations and Aggregate Demand

In the previous chapter I examined the proposition that aggregate supply might be tied to a Natural Rate sufficiently closely that attempts to manipulate some components of aggregate demand would necessarily be offset or crowded out in order to preserve goods market clearing at the predetermined Natural Rate. Since I wished to analyse the behaviour of aggregate supply, it was convenient to adopt a simple specification of aggregate demand in order to complete the model. The purpose of this chapter is to consider whether the traditional treatment of aggregate demand itself must be amended when it is recognised that individuals have Rational Expectations.

In Section 7.1 I discuss the application of Rational Expectations to the well established Permanent Income—Lifecycle model of aggregate consumption in which current household expenditure is assumed to be related to expected future incomes. Section 7.2 surveys empirical research on this new approach to aggregate consumption expenditure. In Section 7.3 I develop a theoretical model of aggregate investment under Rational Expectations, emphasising the role of anticipated capital gains on the price of new machines as a mechanism for slowing the response of investment to changes in the level of the capital stock which firms desire. Empirical evidence is presented in Section 7.4.

7.1 The Random Walk Model of Aggregate Consumption

The modern theory of aggregate consumption recognises that households make intertemporal decisions which need not be severely constrained by current income, since any discrepancy between flow income and flow expenditure can be offset by lending or borrowing, or by augmenting or depleting whatever stocks of marketable assets these households possess. Rather, a more appropriate view of the budget constraint may be the condition that the Present Discounted Value (PDV) of planned expenditure should equal the PDV of expected income plus the initial wealth on which households can draw.

The Permanent Income Hypothesis (PIH) developed by Friedman (1957) argues that diminishing marginal utility of consumption creates an incentive to even out planned consumption across future periods, since the marginal utility of extra consumption in years of high consumption would not compensate for the marginal disutility of less consumption in years of low consumption. Precisely how much it is optimal to smooth consumption in the face of anticipated variation in income depends on the costs and benefits of borrowing or lending, the relation between the rate of time preference at which future utility is discounted and the real rate of interest at which households borrow and lend. When the real rate of interest exceeds the rate of time preference, it will generally be optimal, in the sense of maximising the PDV of expected future utility, to plan a rising consumption stream over time since the return on saving now for future consumption exceeds the cost. Nevertheless, if the difference between the rate of time preference and the real rate of interest is small, it may be a reasonable simplification to suppose that households plan a constant level of consumption. Permanent Income is that constant annual stream whose PDV just equals initial wealth plus the PDV of expected future incomes. The simplest version of the PIH asserts that current consumption should be proportional to, and very nearly equal to, the current evaluation of Permanent Income.

The Lifecycle Hypothesis (LCH) of Ando and Modigliani (1963) differs from the PIH only in allowing households a wider menu of lifetime choices. Households may anticipate changes in their preferences and plan accordingly, as for example when they anticipate a temporary period of higher consumption expenditure while their children are being privately educated. Individual households make the lifetime consumption plan which best fulfils their anticipated preferences, subject only to the constraint of lifetime budget balance taking account of lending and borrowing. If the tastes and age structure of the population remain roughly constant over time, the aggregate consumption function derived from such individual behaviour will closely resemble that implied by the PIH.

Since the PIH—LCH model places great importance on the current expectations of future incomes, the process of expectations formation plays a central role in this analysis of consumption behaviour. Originally, this model was cast within the framework of Adaptive Expectations, but recently several authors have examined the consequences of replacing this assumption by the hypothesis of Rational Expectations. As Hall (1978) first discovered, a striking result is then obtained.

I simplify by assuming that households can lend and borrow at a real interest rate δ which is constant over time. Let Y_t^p be the assessment of Permanent Income at time t, given real wealth W_t, current real income Y_t and Rational Expectations of future incomes $_tY_{t+i}^e$ conditional on current information. By the definition of Permanent Income

$$
W_t + Y_t + \sum_{i=1}^{\infty} \frac{_tY_{t+i}^e}{(1+\delta)^i}
$$

$$
= Y_t^p \left[1 + \left(\frac{1}{1+\delta}\right) + \left(\frac{1}{1+\delta}\right)^2 + \left(\frac{1}{1+\delta}\right)^3 + \ldots \right]
$$

$$(7.1.1)$$

For simplicity I assume an infinite planning horizon, though the analysis may be extended to the case in which lives are finite. The left hand side of equation (7.1.1) is the expectation at time t of the PDV of potential spending power over the planning horizon. Since the definition of Permanent Income is the constant annual income which equates in PDV to the expected spending power over the planning horizon, the right hand side is simply the PDV of Y_t^p over the infinite future. Although at time t the above equation implies a particular constant stream Y_t^p over the infinite future, it is essential to include the time subscript: as new information becomes available at time $t + 1$ individuals will reassess their potential spending power and form a new evaluation of the constant stream Y_{t+1}^p which equates to the PDV of this spending power.

The series of terms inside the brackets on the right hand side form a geometric series which converges to $(1 + \delta)/\delta$. The equation may therefore be rearranged to yield an explicit expression for Permanent Income

$$Y_t^p = (\frac{\delta}{1+\delta}) \ [W_t + Y_t + \sum_{i=1}^{\infty} \frac{{}_t Y_{t+i}^e}{(1+\delta)^i}] \qquad (7.1.2)$$

Now consider households at time $t-1$ forming expectations conditional on information available at this date. From equation (7.1.1)

$$_{t-1}(Y_t^p)^e = (\frac{\delta}{1+\delta}) \ [_{t-1}W_t^e + {}_{t-1}Y_t^e + \sum_{i=1}^{\infty} \frac{{}_{t-1}Y_{t+i}^e}{(1+\delta)^i}]$$

By the definition of Permanent Income, individuals at time $t-1$ do not expect their Permanent Income to change, for it is the *constant* stream which they envisage over the planning horizon. Hence, whether or not expectations are Rational and purely from the definition of Permanent Income, it must be true that $_{t-1}(Y_t^p)^e = Y_{t-1}^p$. Making this substitution into the above equation, and subtracting from equation (7.1.2), we obtain

$$Y_t^p - Y_{t-1}^p = (\frac{\delta}{1+\delta}) \ [(W_t - {}_{t-1}W_t^e) + (Y_t - {}_{t-1}Y_t^e)$$

$$+ \sum_{i=1}^{\infty} \frac{({}_t Y_{t+i}^e - {}_{t-1}Y_{t+i}^e)}{(1+\delta)^i}] \equiv u_t \qquad (7.1.3)$$

Now let us assume the hypothesis of Rational Expectations. Each and every term on the right hand side is then a pure Rational Expectations forecasting error, the first two terms being the difference between actual variables at time t and their Rational Expectations one period earlier, the terms in the summation being the revisions of expectations of future variables in response to new and previously unanticipated information first available at time t. Let us collectively denote the right hand side forecasting errors by the random variable u_t. By the properties of Rational Expectations discussed in Section 4.1, u_t must be serially uncorrelated and have mean zero conditional on information available at time $t-1$. Any other properties would imply that expectations at time $t-1$ were systematically and knowably mistaken.

We may thus write

$$Y_t^p = Y_{t-1}^p + u_t \qquad _{t-1}u_t^e = 0 \qquad (7.1.4)$$

Summarising the above argument, the definition of Permanent Income implies that individuals ought not to expect their Permanent Incomes to change, for if they did, this knowledge should already have been used to reassess Permanent Income. When expectations are Rational, individuals will discover *ex post* that revisions in Permanent Income could not indeed have been predicted one period earlier.

Suppose we adopt the simple PIH model of consumption

$$C_t = k Y_t^p$$

where C_t is aggregate consumption at time t and k is a positive fraction close to unity. Equation (7.1.4) implies

$$C_t = C_{t-1} + ku_t \qquad _{t-1}(ku_t)^e = 0 \qquad (7.1.5)$$

Consumption follows a Random Walk: the best guess about next period's consumption is this period's consumption, because it is based on the latest assessment of Permanent Income which embodies all knowable information at the current date. Equation (7.1.5) has the testable implication that adding lagged values of income, unemployment, or any of the other variables conventionally believed to affect consumption, should not improve our ability to predict consumption at t given variables known at $t-1$. This is the striking result which Hall (1978) first discovered.[1]

In practice, we may wish to modify the above analysis a little. Consider first the implication of the fact that households

---

1. Rather than merely asserting the proportional dependence of consumption on Permanent Income, Hall derives the Random Walk model within a framework of explicit intertemporal utility maximisation.

have finite lives. If households really did live forever, all future growth in real income should already be discounted in the current assessment of Permanent Income. However, Ando and Modigliani (1963) stress that aggregate Permanent Income will tend to increase over time because of population growth and growth in real income. As yet unborn households are not represented in the aggregate Permanent Income calculation; in a growing economy, new households can look forward to higher lifetime incomes than the old households they replace.

Thus Permanent Income in the aggregate tends to trend upwards over time and Hall's result should be interpreted to mean that the best guess about next period's consumption is that it will attain this period's level adjusted for the trend rate of growth. Other consequences of the LCH model may modify the result still further. Households may plan seasonal variations in consumption such as Christmas spending sprees. Bilson (1980) emphasises two departures from the simple assumption that consumption is proportional to Permanent Income. First, since households can substitute between leisure and consumption by varying the hours they work, fluctuations in real wages may induce a more complicated dependence of consumption on Permanent Income. Secondly, changes in household wealth induced for example by changes in the stock market may alter planned bequests and hence the relation between consumption and Permanent Income.

One final point deserves some attention. It has been assumed that households may lend and borrow as much as they choose at the prevailing real interest rate. Capital markets are perfectly competitive. If the actual incomes of the young, or the temporarily unemployed, are expected to be significantly higher in the future than in the present, the implication of the PIH–LCH model may be that such households should currently consume more than their current income. In practice, capital markets tend to be highly imperfect so that it is difficult to borrow against future expected labour incomes unless some liquid assets can currently be offered as collateral. This phenomenon is stressed by Flemming (1973). Under these circumstances, there may be an asymmetry between the effective real interest rate for lending and borrowing and the latter rate may be extremely high for some households. Future

incomes will then have a very low weight in the PDV calculation and actual consumption will be severely constrained by
current income and liquid assets. Moreover, it may then be
optimal for households to undertake emergency saving to
replenish the real value of their precautionary stock of liquid
assets when these are reduced, a phenomenon emphasised by
Davidson *et al.* (1978).

As in other areas, it is necessary to distinguish the Rational
Expectations assumption from the assumed structure of the
model in which that assumption is embedded. The Random
Walk model of aggregate consumption depends on the
proposition that desired consumption is proportional to
Permanent Income as well as the assumption of Rational
Expectations and may be falsified by the data if any of the
complications cited above obtain, even if expectations are
Rational. On the other hand, it is such a strikingly sharp
assertion and so much at variance with previous models of
consumption that even broad conformity with the data would
justify an extension of the approach to attempt to model
these complicating factors.

Before turning to that empirical evidence, I wish to consider
the ways in which traditional macroeconomic analysis would
have to be amended if the Random Walk model of consumption is broadly correct. In the simple Keynesian model with
a stable marginal propensity to consume out of current
income, autonomous changes in aggregate demand have large
multiplier effects, whereas the PIH–LCH model has been
used to argue that the multiplier should be very small since
the marginal propensity to consume out of *current* income is
correspondingly reduced. Bilson (1980) emphasises that this
latter argument is much more easily sustained if expectations
are Adaptive than if expectations are Rational. We have seen
in Chapter 3 that a discrete piece of new information may
require the complete re-evaluation of the convergent Rational
Expectations path. Quite frequently, unanticipated changes
in current income will be associated with a complete reassessment of Permanent Income, provided only that the unanticipated development is expected to persist. Short-run multipliers
may then be quite large, restoring the Keynesian instability
from which the PIH–LCH models had seemed to free the

economy. Such effects are likely to be more important if two conditions are met. First, effective real interest rates must be low so that reassessments of expected future incomes make a considerable difference to the evaluation of Permanent Income in the PDV calculation. Secondly, aggregate supply must be reasonably elastic so that households do not expect changes in aggregate demand to be choked off by supply constraints: the more valid is the Natural Rate hypothesis studied in the previous chapter, the less is the scope for households to alter assessments of future income levels.

7.2 Empirical Evidence on the Random Walk Model of Aggregate Consumption

Empirical studies of this model typically confine their attention to the consumption of non-durable goods for which the proportional dependence of consumption on Permanent Income is a strong but admissible simplification. The explanation of expenditure on durable consumer goods is necessarily more complicated, since a consumption plan must consider not only whether and what quantity of a durable to purchase, but also at what date the purchase should be made. Temporary discounts, taxes, or anticipated changes in prices or real interest rates may affect the timing decision and suggest that these factors may be too important to ignore. Indeed, household investment decisions about consumer durables are analytically much closer to the investment decisions of firms considered in the next section in which anticipated changes in the price of the asset play a key role in the timing decision.

Hall (1978) examined detrended and seasonally adjusted quarterly USA data on non-durable consumer goods for the period 1948–77. The simple prediction of equation (7.1.5) is that current consumption on non-durables C_t should depend on C_{t-1} with a coefficient close to unity, but should not depend on any other information known before the start of time t. Hall began by examining previous consumption data and reported the estimates

$$C_t = 8.2 + 1.13\, C_{t-1} - 0.04\, C_{t-2} \\ + 0.03\, C_{t-3} - 0.01\, C_{t-4}$$

Only the coefficient on C_{t-1} was statistically significant. To assess whether information from previous levels of real income helps explain current consumption, the equation was then augmented to include such variables:

$$C_t = b_0 + b \ C_{t-1} + \sum_{i=1}^{12} b_i Y_{t-i} + u_t$$

where u_t is a random disturbance with mean zero and no serial correlation, and Y_t denotes real disposable income at time t. Hall reported the estimates

$$b_0 = -25 \quad b = 1.11 \quad \sum_{i=1}^{12} b_i = 0.08$$

Since previous values of disposable income are known at time $t-1$, any information which they contain about future income levels should already have been incorporated in the assessment of Permanent Income on which C_{t-1} is based. The Random Walk model thus predicts that each of the b_i coefficients should be zero. Taken together, Hall's estimates of the b_i coefficients are close to the level at which standard statistical tests reject the hypothesis that these parameters are all zero. On the other hand, their effect both singly and jointly is very small and does not bear out the approach usually taken in textbooks and by macroeconomic model builders. Nor are Hall's results much comfort for those who believe in Adaptive Expectations, which suggests that extrapolation of past incomes should be a useful guide to future income levels. Hall therefore concluded that the evidence was compatible with the spirit of his analysis. The Random Walk model of consumption is a surprisingly good approximation.

Hall discovered only one other variable which was known at time $t-1$, but did contribute to the explanation of current consumption of non-durables — an index of the real value of the stock market adjusted for inflation. Denoting this index S_t, Hall reported the estimates

$$C_t = -22 + 1.01 \ C_{t-1} + 0.22S_{t-1} - 0.26S_{t-2}$$
$$+ 0.17S_{t-3} - 0.12S_{t-4}$$

where all coefficients were statistically different from zero. Allowing for the units in which the stock market index is measured, its additional contribution to the explanation of current consumption is quite small and the Random Walk model remains a reasonable simplification. Two explanations for Hall's empirical result seem possible. Both hinge on the fact that the largest part of the additional predictive power essentially derives from a term $(S_{t-1} - S_{t-2})$ with a coefficient of around 0.25. The first interpretation is that participants in the stock market have access to better information, or are faster at processing existing information, so that a previously unanticipated piece of optimistic news about future output and profits leads to an upward revaluation of stock prices one quarter before households make a corresponding revaluation of their Permanent Incomes. The weight of evidence suggesting that participants in the stock market have Rational Expectations and adjust quickly to new information is presented more fully in Section 8.1. The second explanation for Hall's findings is that households immediately adjust their evaluation of their Permanent Incomes, but cannot translate this immediately into consumption expenditure, either because commitments have already been undertaken, or because habits, the need to search for the goods now desired, and other departures from the more naive textbook description of consumer behaviour, impose a short lag on actual spending decisions. In any case, Hall found that the usefulness of the stock market index in supplementing the basic Random Walk model was confined to the recent observations whose coefficients are cited above. Values of the index more than three-quarters prior to C_{t-1} contributed no additional power to explain movements in C_t.

Bilson (1980) examined quarterly data from 1963 I to 1978 IV for the USA, UK and West Germany. For each country, he estimated the optimal extrapolative predictor of changes in per capita real disposable income over the sample period. Having found a convenient summary measure of the way disposable income actually changed over the period, his idea was to test whether the assessments of Permanent Income implicitly revealed in consumption decisions squared with the actual path of disposable income. The fitted extrapolative equations were quite complicated — technically known as 10th order moving averages — but the basic approach may be illustrated using a simplified model. Let D_t be the growth of real per capita disposable income between times $t-1$ and t. Consider the simple equation

$$D_t = \gamma_0 + \gamma_1 D_{t-1} + v_t \qquad (7.2.1)$$

where v_t is a random disturbance with mean zero and no serial correlation. Choose the coefficient estimates $\hat{\gamma}_0$ and $\hat{\gamma}_1$ which best fit the data and let the unobservable Rational Expectation $_{t-1}D_t^e$ be estimated by

$$_{t-1}D_t^e = \hat{\gamma}_0 + \hat{\gamma}_1 D_{t-1} = \hat{D}_t$$

which uses only information available at time $t-1$ as equation (7.2.1) suggests. Using the Chain Rule of Forecasting we can build up estimates of expectations at time $t-1$ of values of D_t further into the future. For example,

$$_{t-1}D_{t+1}^e = {}_{t-1}(\gamma_0 + \gamma_1 D_t + v_{t+1})^e = \gamma_0 + \gamma_1 ({}_{t-1}D_t^e)$$
$$= \gamma_0(1 + \gamma_1) + \gamma_1^2 D_{t-1}$$

which we may estimate using the estimates $\hat{\gamma}_0$ and $\hat{\gamma}_1$. Other terms may be built up in a similar manner.

Once the real interest rate has been specified, these estimates can be used to estimate the revision in Permanent Income which should theoretically have occurred at time t under Rational Expectations, given the new information $(D_t - {}_{t-1}D_t^e)$ which can be used to update expectations of future incomes. For each country, Bilson then estimated the equation

$$C_t - C_{t-1} = c_0 + c_1(D_t - {}_{t-1}D_t^e) + c_2 Z_t + c_3 Z_{t-1} + u_t \qquad (7.2.2)$$

where Z_t and Z_{t-1} include data on real wages and the real value of the stock market index, whose significance in explaining deviations from the proportional dependence of consumption on Permanent Income I discussed in the previous section. Again, $\hat{D}_t$ is used to estimate $_{t-1}D_t^e$. The test of the Rational Expectations PIH–LCH model rests on comparison of the estimated value $\hat{c}_1$ obtained by fitting equation (7.2.2) directly to the data and the theoretical correlation between $(D_t - \hat{D}_t)$ and revisions in Permanent Income derived from the optimal predictor of changes in per capita real disposable income. Bilson concluded that the two estimates agreed closely, provided the relevant real interest rate was less than two per cent per quarter. Commenting on this result, Hall (1980b) argues that such a low real interest rate cannot be compatible with the view that households face serious capital market constraints of the kind discussed in Flemming (1973).

In a second battery of tests, Bilson augments equation (7.2.2) by adding to the right hand side an estimate $\hat{D}_t$ obtained from a prior regression on a more complicated specification of equation (7.2.1). This estimate is the optimal predictor of D_t, given information available at time $t-1$. If C_{t-1} already embodies this information, the coefficient on $\hat{D}_t$ in the augmented regression should be zero. Bilson found that this hypothesis was confirmed for the UK and West Germany, but rejected for the USA. A possible reason for the discrepancy between the conclusions of Hall and Bilson is that the latter uses consumption data which include expenditure on durables. Since households may anticipate changes in the real price of durables over time, speculation on the price of household investment goods may destroy the proportional dependence of consumption on Permanent Income which forms the cornerstone of the Random Walk model.

These findings have been further disputed by Davidson and Hendry (1981). Using UK data, they show that a more sophisticated specification discovers yet more variables which are known at time $t-1$, but which empirically contribute to the explanation of C_t even when C_{t-1} is included in the equation. Their second point is perhaps even more significant, since it concerns the methodology of the empirical test procedures commonly employed. The Rational Expectations– Permanent Income model provides one explanation for the data approximately following a random walk. Even if empirical econometricians agreed that this property was confirmed by the data, it does not confirm the Rational Expectations – Permanent Income model, for there may be other theories which lead to the same empirical prediction. This methodological point is not new, but it should be stressed since it is easily forgotten. Similar remarks are relevant to the interpretation of empirical evidence in the next chapter. Drawing on their earlier work presented in Davidson *et al.* (1978),

Davidson and Hendry (1981) argue that a different model of consumption behaviour may lead approximately to the Random Walk property. In their analysis, households plan a constant relation between consumption and income in the long run, but not necessarily in the short run. As new information becomes available, households recognise that their behaviour in the previous period was inappropriate and undertake what these authors call 'error correction' to amend their plans. Although very similar to the expectations revision in the Rational Expectations–Permanent Income model, the error correction mechanism stresses reaction to past information, rather than to current information about future variables. Since these authors do not elaborate the exact role of information or expectations, it may be possible to recast their analysis so that it reduces to something akin to the Permanent Income model. In any case, it is desirable that the relation between the two models should be clarified, since the model of Davidson *et al.* has proved to explain UK consumption data very well. The case for the Permanent Income–Rational Expectations model should therefore be given the verdict commonly employed in law courts in Scotland: not proven.

This should be interpreted merely as a call for further research. Critics of the model have doubtless been surprised that the data conforms as closely as it does to the simple Random Walk proposition. Proponents of Rational Expectations might reasonably argue that the elaboration of a more sophisticated theory of intertemporal household choice, embracing varying discount rates, market imperfections especially for borrowing, and explicit consideration of the timing of expenditure on durables and semi-durables, might yield a model which fits the data even more closely.

It should not be inferred from this that Random Walk models, or their generalisations, are adequate descriptions of aggregate consumption, even though they may be useful in making clear the implications of Rational Expectations.[2] Even if the Random Walk model was exactly correct, it

2. The comment by Davidson and Hendry notwithstanding, it remains expositionally convenient to abbreviate the 'Rational Expectations– Permanent Income model' to the Random Walk model.

would still be open to the Lucas Problem. A hypothetical policy change, being unanticipated and not reflected in previous consumption, would alter individuals' expectations of future incomes and hence their consumption. It requires a full structural model to estimate what the evaluation of Permanent Income would be once the policy change was recognised and to estimate how consumption would respond to this revision in Permanent Income. Such models can and should be constructed along the lines Bilson suggested. Given a past data sample, we can estimate the optimal extrapolative predictor of future income levels and hence estimate the left hand side of equation (7.1.1) under the assumption of Rational Expectations, thereby inferring estimates of Permanent Income period by period over that sample period. This allows the direct estimation of the consumption response to Permanent Income and allows us to solve the Lucas Problem by recomputing the future path of actual incomes, and hence modelling the revision of Permanent Income, when a new policy is adopted.

It may be helpful to relate the discussion of this section to the more traditional approach to modelling consumption, in which a key variable is current income. It is convenient to restate equation (7.1.3) which describes the revision of Permanent Income between times $t-1$ and t

$$Y^p_t - Y^p_{t-1} = (\frac{\delta}{1+\delta}) [(W_t - {}_{t-1}W^e_t) + (Y_t - {}_{t-1}Y^e_t)$$

$$+ \sum_{i=1}^{\infty} \frac{{}_t Y^e_{t+i} - {}_{t-1} Y^e_{t+i}}{(1+\delta)^i}]$$

Permanent Income is revised because individuals receive new information about wealth, income and future incomes. Although it is possible to decompose new information into the above components, in practice it is likely that the different components will be highly correlated. An unanticipated increase in current income is likely to be positively correlated with increased optimism about future incomes. Since actual income may be decomposed as

$$Y_t = {}_{t-1} Y^e_t + (Y_t - {}_{t-1} Y^e_t)$$

inclusion of current income in a consumption equation ought to yield a non-zero coefficient, because the unanticipated component of income reflects new information on which the revision of Permanent Income will be based. In the framework of this section, current income is an imperfect but effective proxy for the random disturbances which are not directly observable. There is nothing in this argument which denies that the inclusion of current and lagged incomes will yield an equation which fits any particular data sample reasonably well.

Whilst current and lagged incomes may be used as the basis for an extrapolation to capture future incomes and hence Permanent Income, the Random Walk model asserts that if lagged consumption is additionally included, lagged incomes will now become insignificant, since lagged consumption reflects Permanent Income at time $t-1$ more accurately than an extrapolation of past income levels; and it is only the unanticipated component of current income which contains any additional information.

7.3 Rational Expectations and the Dynamics of Aggregate Investment

Modern theories of aggregate Investment recognise that the flow demand for new capital goods must be derived from an analysis of changes in the capital stock which firms wish to hold. This analysis may be viewed in two stages. First, we require a model determining K_t^*, the capital stock which firms currently believe they wish to hold in the long run. This will have the property that q^*, the marginal cost of purchasing an additional unit of capital in the steady state, just equals the Present Discounted Value (PDV) of Operating Profits (OP) on this marginal unit over its lifetime of T periods. Thus competitive profit maximisation implies

$$q^* = \sum_{i=1}^{T} \frac{OP_i^*}{(1 + \delta)^i} \qquad (7.3.1)$$

where δ is the relevant discount rate. Given diminishing marginal productivity of capital, it is assumed that a higher value of K^* will bid down the stream of returns OP on the marginal unit of capital. Secondly, we require an adjustment rule or function

$$I_t = f(K^*_t - K_{t-1})\qquad(7.3.2)$$

which determines the rate at which I_t, investment at time t, eliminates the discrepancy between K_{t-1}, the capital stock carried over from the end of the previous period, and K^*_t, the capital stock to which firms currently wish to converge. Without some kind of sluggish adjustment, firms would continuously hold their desired long-run capital stocks and it would be hard to explain a continuous flow of investment without supposing perpetually changing views about the steady state itself.

Within this framework, the standard models of investment behaviour may be reviewed briefly. In Chapter 2, I argued that Keynes (1936) assumed that current expectations of the values of economic variables in the future were given exogenously. In equation (7.2.1) the current expectations of q^*, and of long-run demand and cost conditions in the industry on which the stream of operating profits depend, are exogenously given in the short run. For this given state of expectations, a lower discount rate δ increases the value of capital at the margin and implies a higher choice K^*_t thus bidding down the expected PDV of operating profits, restoring the equality (7.3.1). This relation is Keynes' Marginal Efficiency of Capital. Notice that it is not an implication of this model that actual investment depends chiefly on the interest rate, for Keynes emphasises that shifts in the Marginal Efficiency due to exogenous shifts in opinion about future profitability, especially future demand conditions, will be large; rather, within the framework of exogenous expectations, the only remaining endogenous relation of any significance is the discounting relation between K^*_t and δ.

Consider an economy which begins in the steady state in which capital is at the desired level and net investment is zero. The only investment which occurs is replacement investment to offset depreciation of the capital stock. Let there be an exogenous increase in optimism about future profits: the Marginal Efficiency of Capital shifts upwards.

Keynes supposes that there is a separate industry manufacturing new capital goods and that the supply of these is less than perfectly elastic in the short run. If all firms immediately make effective their wish for a higher capital stock, the short-run price q_t of new capital goods will rise sharply. Those firms with lucrative short-run opportunities to use a higher capital stock will be prepared to pay a high price for the new capital, but other firms will find it more profitable to hold off for a time: as the demand for additional capital is gradually met, the pressure on the capital goods industries will fall and q_t will fall back towards its original level. Thus, in Keynes' model, the mechanism (7.3.2) by which changes in desired steady state capital stocks are spread over many periods relies on short-term speculation on the price of new capital goods.

Whereas Keynes simplifies equation (7.3.1) by assuming exogenous the expected future market conditions which determine the numerator of the PDV calculation, Accelerator models of investment simplify by treating the denominator as exogenous while emphasising endogenous changes in the numerator. Suppose that the discount rate, relative factor prices and output prices all remain constant and that the production function exhibits constant returns to scale. The desired capital output ratio will then be constant. Thus the steady state capital stock K^* may be written as λY^*, where Y^* is the steady state output level and λ is a constant. Suppose expectations are extrapolative, using past values of Y to predict future values of Y. In the simplest case of static expectations, which assumes that future values of Y are simply given by current output Y_t, $Y_t^* = Y_t$. Hence we derive the simple Accelerator model in which firms instantaneously adjust capital stocks to their desired levels

$$I_t = K_t^* - K_{t-1}^* = \lambda(Y_t - Y_{t-1})$$

More generally, invoking a linear version of equation (7.3.2) in which some fraction θ of the gap $(K_t^* - K_{t-1})$ is eliminated at time t

$$I_t = \theta(K_t^* - K_{t-1}) = \theta\lambda Y_t - \theta K_{t-1} \qquad 0 < \theta < 1$$

which is known as the Flexible Accelerator. More general formulations of this expression may include further lagged values of Y_t which may be given one of two interpretations: either further lags of Y_t are required to obtain a more sophisticated extrapolative forecast of future output levels from past output levels, or the adjustment rule has a more complicated dynamic specification than the simple formulation (7.3.2). These models share the idea that extrapolation of past output levels, or rates of change, sheds light on expected future output and hence expected future profits. The motivation for sluggish adjustment of actual capital to the desired capital stock no longer rests on speculation on capital goods prices. The literature emphasises delivery lags and the increasing marginal cost of changing quickly, for example because a scarce supply of management resources finds it increasingly difficult to co-ordinate the firm's activities.

Jorgenson (1963)(1971)(1972) models changes both in the numerator and the denominator of equation (7.3.1). By assuming a particular production function he derives the desired capital output ratio as a function of relative goods prices and factor costs when firms maximise the PDV of expected future profits in competitive markets. Since this calculation is intertemporal, it involves the specification of a future path for the capital stock and requires firms to form expectations about future variables. Nevertheless, the dynamic equation which Jorgenson derives is less rich in structure than one might have supposed for two reasons. First, by assuming that all investment decisions are completely reversible he ensures that the maximisation of long-run profits is simply maximisation of profits period by period, so that many future variables drop out of the current calculation. Secondly, the one remaining intertemporal feature, the timing decision about whether to purchase equipment now or next period, a calculation which depends on the expected change in the price of new machines in the short run, is played down by adopting convenient but *ad hoc* assumptions about firms' expectations. Moreover, the analysis is open to a more fundamental objection. Smooth investment streams are derived by invoking adjustment costs to impose *ex post* the gradual adjustment of actual capital to the level which the analysis predicts firms will desire. If such costs are real, they ought to be an explicit part of the intertemporal calculation.

Tobin (1961)(1969) argues that the stock market valuation of firms may be used to infer the current evaluation of the PDV of future profits. When this exceeds the short-run supply price of new capital goods, there will be an incentive to invest. Again, the existence of adjustment costs is taken to explain temporary deviations between the desired capital stock and the actual capital stock, or equivalently between the stock market valuation of capital and its current supply price.

Having reviewed existing theories of investment, I now examine the consequences of recognising the Rational Expectations hypothesis. Equation (7.3.1) may be amended in a relatively simple manner, but equation (7.3.2) requires more discussion. If sluggish adjustment is assumed to depend on the existence of delivery lags, surely we must distinguish between anticipated and unanticipated changes in the desired capital stock? Indeed, if all increases in desired capital were anticipated, delivery lags should be irrelevant, since the equipment could have been ordered in advance. If adjustment costs depend on the scarce supply of managers to organise the changes, cannot firms hire additional managers in advance of anticipated investment? Because of the ambiguities which surround such treatments of equation (7.3.2), the insights allowed by the Rational Expectations approach are seen most clearly if one adopts an interpretation of adjustment costs which is readily amenable to standard economic analysis: speculation by firms on short-run changes in the price of new capital goods, the mechanism emphasised by Keynes (1936). The application of Rational Expectations is then straight-forward. Firms expect the market for new capital goods to clear and use this information to form expectations about the sequence of equilibrium prices for new capital goods. For expositional convenience, I shall discuss a model in which firms behave as if they had Perfect Foresight but are occasionally subject to unanticipated shocks.

I shall follow the treatment of Precious (1979) which draws directly on Keynes' model of the *General Theory*. The treatment by Abel (1979) is essentially similar, but follows Tobin more closely. I imagine that there are two competitive industries producing consumer goods and capital goods whose equilibrium prices are p_t and q_t respectively. For simplicity I suppose that all new capital goods are purchased by the consumer goods industry, though the analysis may be extended to more complicated cases. Following Jorgenson I also assume that capital labour ratios may be altered even after equipment has been installed, so that the intertemporal profit maximisation calculation is conveniently simplified. I assume a constant real discount rate δ and a constant proportional depreciation rate ϕ.

A competitive firm in the consumer goods industry compares the marginal benefits and costs of an additional unit of new capital and need only consider directly the single period planning horizon because of the assumption that decisions are reversible in subsequent periods. In the literature this assumption of *ex post* as well as *ex ante* flexibility is known as *Putty-Putty* technology whereas the assumption that capital labour requirements are irreversible once equipment has been installed is known as *Putty-Clay* technology. In the Putty-Putty case, investment will proceed to the point at which

$$\dot{q}_t + p_t f_{kt} = (\delta + \phi)q_t \qquad (7.3.3)$$

The one period benefit of a marginal unit of investment is shown on the left hand side and has two components: the capital gain $\dot{q}_t$ in the price of new machines, reflecting the extent to which the firm makes a return by purchasing new capital now when it is cheap, rather than next period when it is more expensive; and the value of operating profits which the higher capital stock allows in the current period. Operating profits are given by f_{kt}, the marginal product of capital K_t at time t assumed to be a diminishing function of the level of the capital stock K_t, multiplied by p_t, the price for which the firm sells its output. The right hand side denotes the opportunity cost of spending q_t on an additional unit of new capital at time t, the interest foregone plus the depreciation which occurs during the period. To be specific, I assume that the diminishing marginal product relation takes the form

$$f_{kt} = c - eK_t \qquad c > 0 \qquad e > 0$$

although a more general formulation would be easily incorporated. I assume that the parameter c is sufficiently large that the marginal product f_{kt} remains positive for all relevant values of K_t. Rearranging equation (7.3.3) we obtain the first equation from which the phase diagram may be constructed

$$\dot{q}_t = (\delta + \phi)q_t - p_t(c-eK_t) \qquad (7.3.4)$$

The supply of new capital goods is assumed to be an increasing function of (q_t/p_t) and provides capital goods for net investment and replacement investment. Thus

$$\dot{K}_t + \phi K_t = I_t = a(q_t/p_t) \qquad a > 0 \qquad (7.3.5)$$

where I_t denotes gross investment and it is assumed that the market for new machines clears.

Following the discussion of Section 3.2, I construct the phase diagram for q_t and K_t. Since I wish to emphasise the role of anticipated capital gains $\dot{q}_t$, I make the simplifying assumption that p_t is constant over time at the level p. From equation (7.3.5), the locus along which $\dot{K}$ is zero is given by

$$q = \frac{p\phi}{a} K \qquad (7.3.6)$$

Along this locus, a higher price q which increases the supply of new capital goods must be matched by a higher capital stock to ensure that replacement investment takes up this additional supply while maintaining net investment at the zero level. Thus the locus $\dot{K} = 0$ slopes up in Figure 7.3.1. Consider any point on this locus and imagine increasing q while holding K fixed. Replacement investment is unaffected so the additional supply response to a higher value of q must be taken up by positive net investment, increasing the capital stock. Thus, above the locus $\dot{K} = 0$, arrows point horizontally to the right in the K direction. Below the locus, arrows point horizontally to the left.

From equation (7.3.4), the locus $\dot{q} = 0$ is given by

$$q = \frac{p(c-eK)}{\delta + \phi} \qquad (7.3.7)$$

which slopes downwards in Figure 7.3.1 overleaf. A higher capital stock leads to a lower marginal product of capital,

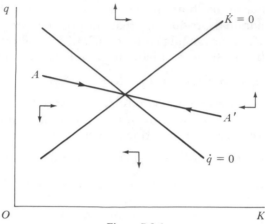

Figure 7.3.1

reducing operating profits and requiring a lower purchase price for new machines if the investment is to yield the going rate of return $(\delta + \phi)$. Beginning from a point on this locus and increasing q while maintaining K, a positive capital gain $\dot{q}$ must now be anticipated if the required return is to be earned. Hence arrows point vertically upwards in the q direction above the locus $\dot{q} = 0$ and point vertically downwards below this locus.

The intersection of the two loci depicts the steady state. From the analysis of Section 3.2 this steady state is a Saddle-point: one set of arrows (in the K direction) points towards the relevant locus $(\dot{K} = 0)$, while the other set of arrows (in the q direction) points away from the relevant locus $(\dot{q} = 0)$. There is thus a unique convergent path AA' and this must have a negative slope if it is to obey the arrows of motion in Figure 7.3.1. The phase diagram may now be used to analyse the investment response to previously unanticipated shocks.

Consider first a fall in the discount rate which was previously unanticipated, but is immediately recognised and is expected to persist. The steady state capital stock is given by the solution of equations (7.3.6) and (7.3.7)

$$K^* = \frac{ac}{ae + \phi(\delta + \phi)} \qquad (7.3.8)$$

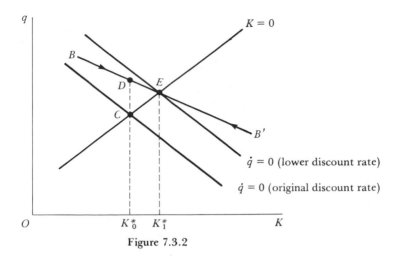

Figure 7.3.2

and is increased by a fall in δ. Since equation (7.3.6) is un-affected, the adjustment takes the form of an upward shift in the $\dot{q} = 0$ locus given by equation (7.3.7).

Relative to the new loci the arrows of motion remain as before and the new convergent locus is given by BB' in Figure 7.3.2. If the economy began at the steady state C with capital stock K_0^*, and if it is assumed that prices q adjust fractionally more quickly than the output of investment goods, the unanticipated fall in the discount rate occurs when the capital stock is instantaneously predetermined at the level K_0^*. The impact effect is therefore a vertical jump from C to the point D to place the economy on the unique Perfect Foresight path BB' vertically above K_0^*. Thereafter, the economy converges along this path to the point E.

The implications for aggregate investment may now be analysed. In the original steady state the capital stock is constant and all investment is replacement investment at the rate ϕK_0^*. When the interest rate unexpectedly falls there is an immediate jump in q after which the price of new machines gradually falls back to its new steady state level, where net investment ceases and replacement investment occurs at the rate ϕK_1^*. Since the supply of investment goods is an increasing function of q this analysis allows us to derive the time path

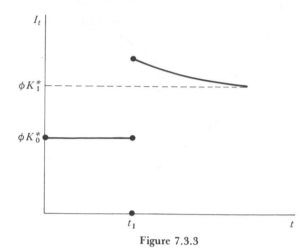

Figure 7.3.3

of investment shown in Figure 7.3.3, in which t_1 is the date at which the unanticipated fall in the discount rate occurs.

This analysis illustrates the mechanism by which anticipations of future changes in the price of new capital goods induce firms to spread investment plans over several periods. Net investment begins when the interest rate is altered but dies out only gradually although replacement investment is permanently higher. The initial desire for new investment bids up the supply price of new machines. While some investment opportunities can be profitably exploited even when machines are expensive to purchase, other investment becomes profitable only when the price of new machines gradually falls as the demand for net investment falls off and supply bottlenecks ease. Notice the precise manner in which expectations enter the analysis. Even though the intertemporal investment decision has been simplified by assuming a Putty-Putty technology in which firms need only assess the short-run returns, the Perfect Foresight solution to determine q and $\dot{q}$ requires the evaluation of the whole future course of investment decisions period by period.

It is important to stress that the investment response first occurs when new information becomes available. In the above example, new information and the change in the interest rate

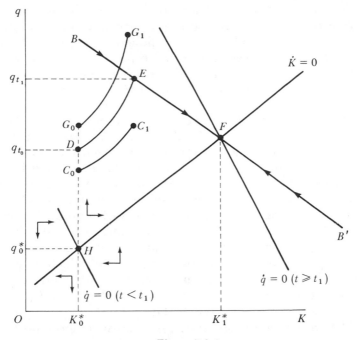

Figure 7.3.4.

were assumed to coincide, but this is not necessary: it is possible that at some date t_0 individuals first appreciate that there will be a permanent fall in the interest rate at some future date t_1. Under Rational Expectations, individuals respond to this news at t_0, rather than waiting until t_1 when the anticipated fall in interest rates takes effect. This general property of Rational Expectations models may be analysed in the present context using Figure 7.3.4.

Assume that the economy begins in the original steady state at the point H at time t_0. The discount rate is δ and the arrows of motion are as drawn in Figure 7.3.1. At t_0 individuals first realise that a lower discount rate δ_1 will become relevant at the future date t_1. From the analysis based on Figure 7.3.2, the new steady state will be at the point F with capital stock K_1^*. Since the arrows of motion depend on equations (7.3.4) and (7.3.5), the new arrows of motion take effect only when the discount rate has actually changed. From time t_1 onwards, these new arrows will be as drawn in Figure 7.3.2 and imply that a unique convergent path BB' is then relevant. However, between times t_0 and t_1 the original arrows of motion, drawn in Figure 7.3.4, must be obeyed.

If individuals remain at the point H until time t_1, a vertical jump will then be required to place the economy on the new convergent path BB'. However, this discrete jump in q, the price of new machines, is anticipatable from t_0 onwards and it must be profitable to purchase new machines before the price shoots up at time t_1. This speculative demand for new machines must bid up q before time t_1. Suppose individuals react immediately to the new information at time t_0 by bidding the price to the point C_0. The arrows of motion then imply that the economy will move to the north east, reaching the point C_1 at time t_1. A discrete jump is still required at time t_1 to place the economy on the path BB' which is relevant from this date onwards. Similarly, if the economy reacts to new information at t_0 by jumping to the point G_0, it will have reached the point G_1 at date t_1 and a discrete fall in q will then be required at time t_1. It must be more profitable to postpone investment until this fall has occurred, so this path is not sensible either. The unique Perfect Foresight path requires a jump to the point D at time t_0. Following the original arrows of motion during the period between t_0 and t_1, the economy exactly reaches the path BB' at time t_1. The complete path is therefore DEF. The Perfect Foresight path is necessarily continuous to rule out speculative opportunities for supernormal profits. Jumps occur only as new information is immediately reflected in asset market prices, a theme elaborated in the following chapter. Other examples of this general proposition may be found in Blanchard (1981) and Wilson (1979). The latter also gives a clear mathematical analysis of the solution procedure displayed diagramatically in Figure 7.3.4.

The precise magnitude of the initial jump in capital goods prices will depend on the structural parameters of the model. The price q_{t_0} corresponding to the point D may lie above or below the new steady state price q_1^* corresponding to the point F. Wherever the precise location of the point D on the line vertically above H, Figure 7.3.4 guarantees that q rises steadily between times t_0 and t_1. At t_1 the price q reaches its maximum, after which it falls back along BB' until the new steady state price q_1^* is reached. Equation (7.3.5) promises us that the rate of gross investment is an increasing function of the price q and allows us to infer the path of investment from the above analysis of the time path of q. If, as in Figure 7.3.4, the initial jump to D leaves q_{t_0} below q_1^*, the corresponding time path for gross investment will be as depicted in Figure 7.3.5.

The economy begins in the steady state in which all investment is replacement investment at the rate ϕK_0^*. When information about the impending fall in interest rates first becomes available there is an immediate increase in investment and further increases in investment steadily accrue between t_0 and t_1, after which net investment gradually dies off. Eventually there is only replacement investment at the rate ϕK_1^* corresponding to the new higher steady state capital stock in Figure 7.3.4.

This analysis implies that it will be totally inappropriate to attempt to model dynamic investment responses by any mechanistic rules of the form (7.3.2). Such rules assume that the pattern of adjustment always takes the same form. Not

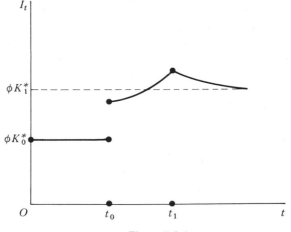

Figure 7.3.5

only will such rules fail to capture the jumps implicit in Figures 7.3.3 and 7.3.5, they cannot be compatible with the very different shapes which these figures imply. The Lucas problem is acute and must again be solved by recalculating the Perfect Foresight path by the method discussed in this section. It will be essential to distinguish between anticipated and unanticipated changes. These remarks apply not only when investment dynamics depend on speculative behaviour, but also when Rational Expectations analysis is applied in models which rely on other adjustment assumptions. The model developed by Abel (1979) is one such example.

I now consider the consequences of a change in expectations about future profits. In the model given by equations (7.3.3) and (7.3.5) we might expect an increase in expected future profits, captured by an increase in the output price p of the industries demanding new capital goods as production inputs, to have expansionary effects similar to those derived from a fall in the rate at which these profits are discounted. Yet this does not occur. The expression for the steady state capital stock given in equation (7.3.8) is independent of the output price p. It is important to understand why this occurs. The supply of new investment goods is assumed to depend on (q/p), the relative price of investment goods to consumer goods. A possible interpretation is that the real value of nominal wages paid in the investment goods industry depends on the general price level for consumer goods. In a highly aggregated macroeconomic model, an increase in p matched by an increase in q leaves all real variables unaltered and hence has no effect on the steady state capital stock. Conversely, if we try to model a rise in expected profits in the consumer goods industry by an exogenous rise in p, an equivalent jump in q will immediately negate the real consequences of this assumption.

If we wish to capture the idea that anticipated profitability rises, we shall have to allow relative output prices to change. A simple device which has this consequence is to imagine that p now refers to the output price of a single industry which is small relative to the production of consumer goods as a whole. It is then plausible that nominal wages in the investment goods industry will be unaffected and we may capture this idea by replacing the investment supply equation (7.3.5) by the equation

$$I_t = \dot{K}_t + \phi K_t = a \, q_t \qquad (7.3.9)$$

so that output price rises in the industry demanding investment goods have no effect on the supply curve for investment goods.

It is now straightforward to analyse the consequences of a rise in p which was previously unanticipated but is expected to persist. The locus $\dot{K} = 0$ is given not by equation (7.3.6) but by the equation $q = (\phi/a)K$, which still slopes upwards and is now independent of the output price p. The locus $\dot{q} = 0$ is still given by equation (7.3.7) and will be shifted upwards by a rise in p, since this increases the value of q corresponding to any particular capital stock K. The response to a previously unanticipated increase in p is therefore qualitatively similar to the fall in the discount rate depicted in Figures 7.3.2 and 7.3.3. When anticipated future profits are unexpectedly revised upwards before demand conditions actually improve, a phase diagram qualitatively similar to Figure 7.3.4 will describe the behaviour of the output and price of investment goods and the time path of investment will correspond to Figure 7.2.5.

This simple model allows an illustration of the type of analysis which is possible when the hypothesis of Rational Expectations is applied to the study of investment behaviour. The standard features of Rational Expectations analysis are present. New information induces a jump in the most flexible variables, here the price of new capital goods, in order to place the model on the new convergent path. This jump causes q to overshoot its new long-run equilibrium level. Once the new information is available no further jumps are planned, though the subsequent continuous evolution of the economy may involve quite elaborate dynamic behaviour as in Figure 7.3.4. One would not expect previous approaches to economic modelling to offer convincing accounts of such dynamic behaviour, nor to suggest equations which easily tracked actual data if individuals do indeed form Rational Expectations.

The approach can be extended to more complicated models such as the Putty-Clay model mentioned earlier. A start to this problem is made in Abel (1979). Since many economists believe that the Putty-Clay assumption is considerably more plausible than the assumption of Putty-Putty, I would expect this to prove a fruitful area for further research.

7.4 Empirical Evidence on the Rational Expectations Approach to Investment

In the previous section I adopted the framework which most conveniently simplified the exposition of the Rational Expectations approach to investment behaviour; in particular, I analysed a model in which time was continuous and firms had Perfect Foresight. Since economic data are collected only at intervals and since uncertainty is an important feature of the real world, the first task is to derive an observable equation specified in discrete time under the weaker assumption of Rational Expectations.

Equation (7.3.3) is easily amended to yield

$$(_t q_{t+1}^e - q_t) + p_t f_{kt} = (\delta + \phi)q_t \tag{7.4.1}$$

As in Section 4.1, the *ex post* value q_{t+1} will differ from its Rational Expectation one period earlier only by a forecasting error η_{t+1}, which is serially uncorrelated and has conditional expectation zero, given information available at time t when the Rational Expectation $_t q_{t+1}^e$ is formed. Thus

$$q_{t+1} = {}_t q_{t+1}^e + \eta_{t+1} \tag{7.4.2}$$

where η_{t+1} reflects new information available at $t + 1$. Combining these equations

$$q_{t+1} = (1 + \delta + \phi)q_t - p_t f_{kt} + \eta_{t+1} \tag{7.4.3}$$

I assume that the supply of investment goods is given by

$$I_t = a_0 + a_1 q_t + \epsilon_t \qquad a_1 > 0 \tag{7.4.4}$$

where ϵ_t is a random disturbance with mean zero and no serial correlation. As in equation (7.3.9), it is assumed that a higher value of q_t elicits a larger output from the suppliers of investment goods. From equations (7.4.3) and (7.4.4)

$$I_t = a_0(1-\gamma) + \gamma I_{t+1} + a_1 \gamma p_t f_{kt} - a_1 \gamma \eta_{t+1}$$
$$+ \epsilon_t - \gamma \epsilon_{t+1} \tag{7.4.5}$$
$$\gamma \equiv \frac{1}{1 + \delta + \phi}$$

This equation has two parts: the first three terms in observable variables from whose coefficients the parameters a_0, a_1, and γ may be disentangled; and the last three terms which are random.[3] While this equation may be estimated from the relevant economic data, as yet I am unable to report the results of any empirical work.

Abel (1979) does present empirical results for a model of investment whose structure, while differing in some points of detail from the model discussed above, is essentially the same. In particular, the application of Rational Expectations in Abel's model generates phase diagrams which are qualitatively similar to those presented in Section 7.3 and implies an empirical relation which has the same basic form as equation (7.4.5) which owes its simplicity to the definition of η_{t+1}, the revision in expectations between time t and time $t + 1$, as a serially uncorrelated random variable with mean zero reflecting new information at time $t + 1$.

Before reporting Abel's empirical results it is useful to consider the differences between his model and the model of Section 7.3. Following the approach of Tobin, he treats q not as the purchase price of investment goods, but as the ratio between the PDV of the net benefits of a marginal unit of new capital to its purchase price. Some unspecified adjustment costs are therefore required to explain why the value of q may deviate from unity in the short run. Firms are then assumed to evaluate q by forming Rational Expectations about future profits and hence the net benefit of acquiring

---

3. The econometric estimation of this equation is complicated by the correlation between the right hand side variables and the compound disturbance term, particularly the correlation between η_{t+1} and I_{t+1}. General econometric issues and the appropriate instrumental variable estimation techniques are discussed in Abel (1979).

new capital goods. As I have pointed out, the implications of the two models are very similar in theory and make even less difference to empirical work based on equations such as (7.4.5) from which q has been substituted out.

Other differences are relatively minor. Whereas I associate the direct benefit of new capital with higher output, reflected in the term f_{kt} denoting the marginal product of capital, Abel assumes that firms seek to minimise the cost of producing a given output so that the direct benefit is measured by the labour saving which the additional capital allows. In either case, the assumption of a particular production function such as Cobb—Douglas allows the direct benefit to be estimated from observable variables such as output and the capital stock. Abel is also careful to include the effects of investment tax incentives such as depreciation allowance, an extension which could easily be admitted within the framework generating equation (7.4.5). Finally, instead of using I_t and I_{t+1} in equation (7.4.5), Abel uses values at t and $t + 1$ of the logarithm of (I/K), the ratio of gross investment to the capital stock. This difference comes merely from a different assumption about the precise functional form of equation (7.4.4).

I turn now to the empirical results which he reports. His amended version of equation (7.4.5) appears to fit the data reasonably well and satisfies obvious cross checks. For example, when the estimation is most sophisticated, his quarterly data for the USA from 1948 I to 1976 IV imply a value of γ of 0.907 which seems plausible for quarterly data. From the estimated value of the crucial parameter a_1, Abel calculates the implied elasticity of I/K with respect to his q variable and concludes that this elasticity is just over 0.5.

In the theory of investment the variable q, however defined, performs a role analogous to that which Permanent Income performs in the theory of consumption. It is the consequence of undertaking a PDV calculation, in the one case to determine net benefits of investment, in the other to determine the lifetime spending power available to a household. The application of Rational Expectations allows us to develop dynamic theories of consumption and investment which are greatly simplified by the property that future revisions in expectations reflect only new information and may be modelled by random variables with mean zero and no serial correlation. The parallel extends further. Just as the Random Walk consumption model is subject to the Lucas Problem, so is the model of investment based on the variable q: a previously unanticipated change in policy will alter the PDV calculation on which q depends, leading to jumps in q as in Section 7.3. If one wishes to undertake policy evaluation, one must alter the initial level of Permanent Income in the consumption function and the initial level of investment in equations such as (7.4.5). Just as Bilson (1980) attempted to model directly the path of future disposable income from which households calculate Permanent Income, Abel attempts to model the path of future net profits or cost savings which a marginal unit of investment allows in order to provide an independent check that his valuation ratio q is close to its hypothetical long-run value of unity. Using *a priori* guesses about the discount rate δ and the depreciation rate ϕ, he estimates that q varies between 1.27 and 2.17 over his sample period, an average value he concludes is too high. Using the estimate of γ obtained from the data and reported above would reduce the value of q a little, but not sufficiently to leave its average value close to unity.

In my judgment, this work is an important beginning to the task of elaborating a theory of investment under Rational Expectations. The reader will appreciate that much remains to be done. Abel (1979) has also made a start on the question of applying Rational Expectations in a Putty-Clay model of technology in which capital labour decisions on installed plant are subsequently irreversible. Abel (1980) presents a useful summary of his recent work on investment equations.

7.5 Conclusion

In this chapter, I have analysed the application of the Rational Expectations hypothesis to the principal private sector components of aggregate demand in a closed economy, consumption and investment. In each case, individuals are assumed to make intertemporal decisions in which expectations play a central role. Because expectations revision is easily characterised under Rational Expectations, it is possible to develop simple dynamic relations describing consumption and investment which draw heavily on the stochastic properties of Rational Expectations models. In the absence of new surprises, the implied paths for consumption and investment are very different from those predicted by conventional analyses, yet the initial empirical work on these new models is quite encouraging. Although less publicised than the famous stabilisation debate discussed in the previous chapter, these applications of the Rational Expectations hypothesis may have consequences for positive economics which are just as important.

Notes on the Literature

The Random Walk model of consumption and its extensions are studied by Hall (1978), Sargent (1978a), Flavin (1978) and Bilson (1980). Although writing before the introduction of Rational Expectations, Friedman (1957) seems in places to anticipate subsequent developments. The empirical specification currently used by the UK Treasury is based on Davidson *et al.* (1978) and relies heavily on their 'error correction mechanism'. The relation of this mechanism to the revisions of Rational Expectations as new information becomes available may be of interest to some readers; see Davidson and Hendry (1981).

Chapters 11 and 12 of Keynes (1936) form the basis of many macroeconomic models of investment. The stock market approach to q set out in Tobin (1961) (1969) and Brainard and Tobin (1968) is extended in Abel (1979) (1980). The discussion of Section 7.3.3 follows Precious (1979). Sargent (1980) has also written on this subject, emphasising the irreversibility of investment decisions. Blinder and Fischer (1978) extend Rational Expectations analysis to the determination of inventories. Blanchard (1981) combines the analysis of consumption and investment to recast IS/LM analysis within the framework studied in this chapter. Blanchard (1980) summarises his empirical investigation of this approach.

8
Rational Expectations and Efficient Asset Markets

In this chapter I consider the application of Rational Expectations to the analysis of highly organised financial markets. Since asset trading is almost continuous and transactions costs are small, these markets most closely resemble the textbook paradigm of the continuously clearing market in which prices immediately respond to any imbalance between demand and supply.

In Section 8.1 I introduce the notion of an Efficient Market in which asset prices fully reflect available information. I then develop a theoretical model of the Stock Exchange and examine the empirical evidence. The data is consistent with the hypothesis that individuals do not make knowable forecasting errors. In Sections 2 and 3 the model is extended to the market for government bonds and forward cover in the foreign exchange market. Again, there is considerable empirical support for the hypothesis of Rational Expectations. Section 4 discusses the determination of floating exchange rates. Recent theoretical analysis plays down the role of floating exchange rates as a mechanism of adjustment for eliminating imbalances in the net flow of traded goods and services, emphasising instead the role as a mechanism of adjustment for eliminating imbalances in the net demand for stocks of international assets. The implications under Rational Expectations are analysed. These implications are testable and cmpirical evidence is surveyed in Section 8.5.

8.1 The Theory of Efficient Markets and its Application to the Stock Exchange

An asset market is said to be *Efficient* if asset prices fully reflect available information, thus eliminating knowable opportunities for supernormal profit. Since assets are durable and may be purchased in one period for resale in a subsequent period, the rate of return comprises not merely a dividend or interest payment but also a capital gain or loss over the holding period. Asset markets are speculative in the technical sense that expectations of future asset prices affect current supply and demand and hence the current asset price. The hypothesis of *Efficient Markets* therefore has two components: the hypothesis that expectations are Rational so that individuals avoid knowable forecasting errors given current information and the hypothesis that any discrepancy between the expected rates of return of different assets is quickly arbitraged to eliminate expected supernormal profit. As Grossman and Stiglitz (1976) (1980) emphasise, it is the possibility of obtaining supernormal profits in the course of arbitraging which provides the incentive to collect and process new information: we cannot mean that market prices literally reflect all information at every instant. Given data collected at discrete intervals, the Efficient Markets hypothesis assumes that the process of arbitrage has already occurred within the period. We may then analyse the implication of available information being fully reflected in the price data we collect, without modelling the process of arbitrage itself.

Although the Efficient Markets model is an interesting application of Rational Expectations, the two literatures are partly distinct. Although the Rational Expectations hypothesis was first stated formally by Muth (1961), it was only adopted widely in macroeconomics after the pathbreaking papers by Lucas (1972b) (1973), Sargent (1973) and Sargent and Wallace (1973a)(1973b)(1975). In contrast, empirical tests of something akin to the Efficient Markets hypothesis have been undertaken ever since Bachelier (1900), although the model was not formally stated until Samuelson (1965) and Mandelbrot (1966). These led to a profusion of papers on Efficient Markets surveyed by Fama (1970). Thus for some years in the late 1960s and early 1970s, macroeconomists were irrational in modelling expectations, failing to take account of all available information on how this task might be approached.

I now wish to apply the Efficient Markets hypothesis to the analysis of the Stock Exchange in which securities of quoted companies are continuously traded. I assume that the market clears continuously and that the equilibrium price p_t of a security depends on the security's expected return which has two components: dividend payments during the period and capital gain or loss between this period and next period. It is convenient to suppose that any dividends are ploughed back to purchase yet more of the security and that p_{t+1} denotes the value at time $t + 1$ of the original security augmented by any accruals due to ploughback. I define the expected one period return $_t\delta^e_{t+1}$ by

$$_t p^e_{t+1} = (1 + {}_t\delta^e_{t+1})p_t \tag{8.1.1}$$

I assume that the subjective expectations $_t p^e_{t+1}$ and $_t\delta^e_{t+1}$ satisfy Rational Expectations given information at time t.

To complete the model we require a theory of the equilibrium expected rate of return for each asset. This question is the focus of modern portfolio theory based on Markowitz (1959), which assumes that the desirability of different assets cannot be described solely in terms of their expected return. Risk averse individuals care also about the *ex post* variability or risk of their portfolios. By analysing the principles of optimal portfolio diversification, this theory derives the relation between the equilibrium expected rates of return on different assets and their contribution to the overall variability of portfolio returns. If these 'hedging' properties remain constant over time, a simple model of the expected return on a particular asset is that it should remain constant over time. Let δ be the constant value of the expected rate of return. Since actual stock prices p_{t+1} differ from their Rational Expectations $_t p^e_{t+1}$ only by a forecasting error η_{t+1}, which is serially uncorrelated with mean zero, the evolution of stock prices is given by

$$p_{t+1} = {}_t p^e_{t+1} + \eta_{t+1} = (1 + \delta)p_t + \eta_{t+1} \tag{8.1.2}$$

If δ is close to zero, as will be the case when studying daily or even weekly data, equation (8.1.2) is a Random Walk whose structure is similar to the consumption model studied in Section 7.1. The model asserts that the best guess about next period's price is the current price. If markets are Efficient, any information suggesting a high future price should immediately drive up the current price to eliminate supernormal rates of return which are knowable at the current date. All available information is already in the price of such assets.

Letting δ_t be the *ex post* return, equation (8.1.2) implies

$$\delta_t = \frac{p_{t+1} - p_t}{p_t} = \delta + (1/p_t)(\eta_{t+1}) = \delta + \xi_{t+1} \qquad (8.1.3)$$

where ξ_{t+1} is also serially uncorrelated with mean zero. Hence *ex post* returns deviate only randomly from their expected return, which is assumed to remain constant.

I turn now to empirical tests of the *Efficiency of the Stock Exchange*, beginning with work which is directly based on the Random Walk model. If individuals expect the current rate of return to remain constant and if individuals have Rational Expectations, there should not exist any trading rule which utilises previous data to make supernormal profits. Fama (1970) surveys a large empirical literature which overwhelmingly concludes that data on past returns and past asset prices cannot be used to predict changes in actual asset returns. No trading rule would beat the simple policy of buying a security and holding it in perpetuity. In particular, this evidence suggests that extrapolative rules such as the Chartist analysis favoured by many Stock Market analysts cannot be used to suggest when to switch between securities.

While this evidence is consistent with Rational Expectations, it does not provide a very powerful test of the hypothesis, for there are many other sources of available information besides data on past prices and past rates of return. One example is when companies split their shares by offering additional shares to existing shareholders. If this involves merely a renumbering of the shares outstanding, the only consequence should be a corresponding reduction in the price of each share to reflect the diluted entitlement of each share to the aggregate dividend. However, Fama notes that in 940 share splits on the New

York Stock Exchange between 1927 and 1959, more than two-thirds were quickly followed by an announcement that the aggregate dividend had been increased. Thus an Efficient Market should recognise that the announcement of a forth-coming share split signals a good chance of a dividend increase and this information should be reflected in share prices from the moment the market gets wind of the forthcoming share split. Using the more complex formula for the equilibrium expected rate of return implied by portfolio theoretic analysis, and using the data on share splits cited above, Fama, Fisher, Jensen and Roll (1969) examined deviations of share prices from their normal levels in the months before and after the share split. They conclude that share prices *do* show unusual growth *before* the share split occurs, but *after* the announce-ment of the forthcoming split; moreover, by the date the split occurs, all the relevant information has been included in the price. Similar studies of other announcements effects are discussed in Fama. They too find in favour of Rational Expectations.

In Section 6.3 I introduced in a different context the idea that some individuals might have an informational advantage. This idea may be applied in asset markets. Presumably port-folio advisers are employed by investors because they are thought to have an informational advantage which, even under Rational Expectations, enables them to make systematic profits: they are the faceless individuals who first change the price to reflect the new information when it becomes available, and in the process of bidding the price up by their purchases or forcing it down by their sales they make profits relative to the rest of the market. Fama (1970) concludes that no empirical studies support the view that Mutual Fund managers are better at acquiring or processing new information; they do no better than the average. One group who could system-atically outperform the market are specialist brokers who make the market. Neiderhoffer and Osborne (1966) find that information on as yet unexecuted orders to buy and sell could be used to turn a small profit systematically. The fact that such 'insider information' represents one of the examples in which a profitable trading rule exists is quite compatible with the theory of Rational Expectations and suggests that current research on models with differential access to information may bear fruit in many areas.

In this section, I have introduced the notion of Efficient Markets and considered the application of this version of the Rational Expectations hypothesis to the analysis of the Stock Exchange. This topic is not addressed in all macroeconomics courses, but macroeconomists cannot neglect this branch of Portfolio Theory which has pioneered many of the tests of Rational Expectations subsequently adopted elsewhere. Moreover, whilst largely microeconomic in nature, this analysis allows a reasonably robust test of the Rational Expectations hypothesis. As we have seen, the empirical evidence provides surprisingly uniform support for the hypothesis.

8.2 The Market for Government Bonds and the Term Structure of Interest Rates

In this section, I discuss the market for government bonds. A bond is described by its redemption date and its coupon yield. A 1995 bond with a 10% coupon will be repurchased by the government in 1995 at the 'par' value of £100 and from the first date of issue until 1995 will pay £10 fixed interest per annum. The current price at which the bond is traded between individuals during its lifetime is simply the present discounted value of the stream of £10 per annum over the remaining life or term to maturity of the bond, plus the present discounted value of the final capital repayment. An N period bond is a bond with N periods remaining until it matures. Let R_t^N be the average discount rate which the market applies to an N period bond at time t. If the coupon rate is c, the price of the bond at time t is

$$p_t^N = \sum_{i=1}^{N} \frac{c}{(1 + R_t^N)^i} + \frac{100}{(1 + R_t^N)^N} \qquad (8.2.1)$$

(The superscript N denotes the term to maturity. It does not mean that p_t and R_t are raised to the power N.)

If an investor purchases the bond for p_t^N at time t and holds it to maturity, there is perfect certainty at the purchase date about the nominal yield, since c, p_t^N and the par value are all known; the bond yields an annual rate of return of R_t^N for N years. The date at which the bond was first issued is not relevant. Bonds issued at different dates, but with the same coupon and the same term outstanding at t, will have the same price p_t^N and the same redemption yield R_t^N. Assuming that market equilibrium depends on expected returns, the yield on all N period bonds must be the same, even if they have different coupons; equation (8.2.1) tells us how their current prices must differ to ensure that this is the case. Low coupon bonds will have a lower price, since the present value of the stream of interest payments is less. Interpreting this result a little differently, if low coupon bonds have low current prices, this has two effects: first it raises the fixed coupon interest as a fraction of the purchase price; secondly, since all N period bonds mature at the same date for the same par value, the lower initial price of the low coupon bond allows a larger capital gain over the term to maturity. Together, these effects enable the low coupon bond to offer prospective buyers the same redemption yield R_t^N as higher coupon N period bonds.

A casual glance at the financial pages of a newspaper will reveal that this story is not quite correct: low coupon bonds typically have lower redemption yields than higher coupon bonds of the same maturity. Because the lower coupon bonds take a larger share of their total return in the form of capital gains, and because capital gains are less heavily taxed than dividends and interest, equalisation of after tax rates of return implies that the gross redemption yield on low coupon bonds must be lower. While differential taxation has important implications for bond yields, its effects may be minimised by comparing bonds with approximately equal coupon rates. Henceforth, I abstract from the problem of taxation and consider only gross yields.

At any date, the bond market includes a spectrum of outstanding bonds of differing maturities, from the short end at which bonds are about to be redeemed, to the long end where perpetuities are never redeemed, being commitments merely to pay the coupon interest rate forever. By the *Term Structure of interest rates* at time t we mean the relation between the yields R_t^N for different terms to maturity N. The

Term Structure provides the essential link between the short interest rates on which monetary policy impinges directly and the long interest rates which affect corporate investment decisions. I wish to develop a model of the Term Structure and examine the implications of Rational Expectations for this analysis.

Consider first a world with complete certainty and perfect foresight. An investor compares the rates of return on two investment strategies, the first to buy an N period bond and hold it to maturity, the second to buy a one period Treasury Bill, reinvest the proceeds (principal plus interest) in a Treasury Bill the following period, and keep rolling over Treasury Bills for N periods. A Treasury Bill is a pure discount bond with no coupon which is issued below par at the beginning of the period and redeemed at par at the end of the period. The percentage capital gain on the purchase price is called the interest rate on Treasury Bills. Let r_t be the Treasury Bill rate at time t. For each £1 invested, the first strategy yields a terminal wealth after N periods of $(1 + R_t^N)^N$, while the second yields $(1 + r_t)(1 + r_{t+1}) \ldots (1 + r_{t+N-1})$. Thus, under perfect foresight, market equilibrium implies

$$(1 + R_t^N)^N = (1 + r_t)(1 + r_{t+1}) \ldots (1 + r_{t+N-1})$$
$$(8.2.2)$$

Many authors use the approximation

$$R_t^N = (1/N)(r_t + r_{t+1} + \ldots + r_{t+N-1}) \tag{8.2.3}$$

which may be derived from equation (8.2.2) in the following way. Taking logarithms of both sides

$$N \log(1 + R_t^N) = \log(1 + r_t) + \log(1 + r_{t+1}) + \ldots$$
$$+ \log(1 + r_{t+N-1})$$

When x is small, $\log(1 + x)$ is close to x itself. Measuring all interest rates as decimals, and using this approximation, equation (8.2.3) follows from equation (8.2.2).

Thus, long interest rates are simply averages of future rates over the term to maturity. For any given path of future short rates, equation (8.2.3) allows us to read off the different redemption yields R_t^N for bonds at t with different terms N to maturity. If short rates remain constant over the indefinite future, all longer bond rates R_t^N will be equal to the current short rate r_t. If short rates rise steadily in the future, long bond rates will lie above the current short rate, whilst falling future short rates imply that current long rates lie below the current short rate. Drawing a graph of current redemption yields for bonds of different maturity, we may depict this Term Structure of interest rates as a *Yield Curve*. Figure 8.2.1 depicts the shape of the yield curve at t when future short rates are rising, so that R_t^N increases steadily with N.

I now relax the assumption of perfect certainty and assume that individuals at t form Rational Expectations of future short rates in order to determine the equilibrium set of long rates R_t^N. At the time expectations must be formed, individuals know r_t, the current short rate, and R_t^N, the redemption yield, if they buy a long bond and hold to maturity. Thus I amend equation (8.2.3) to

$$R_t^N = (1/N)(r_t + {}_t r_{t+1}^e + \ldots + {}_t r_{t+N-1}^e)$$

There remains one final complication. In Section 8.1, I argued that risk averse investors would assess not merely by the expected return, but also by the risk of *ex post* deviations of the return from its expected level. This suggests we amend the above equation to

$$R_t^N = (1/N)(r_t + {}_t r_{t+1}^e + \ldots + {}_t r_{t+N-1}^e) + k_t^N \quad (8.2.4)$$

where k_t^N denotes the 'risk premium' on an N period bond at

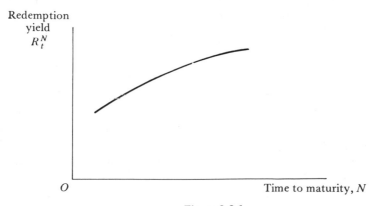

Figure 8.2.1

time t. The literature on the Term Structure distinguishes three possible assumptions about this risk premium. The *Pure Expectations Hypothesis* advanced by Meiselman (1962) asserts that risk aversion is not an important phenomenon, so that risk premia may be ignored; thus k_t^N equals zero. The *Preferred Habitat Hypothesis* advanced by Modigliani and Sutch (1966)(1967) takes an agnostic view of the risk premia. Bonds of different maturities will be attractive or unattractive depending on the other commitments of participants in the bond market; the only requirement that should be imposed is that bonds which mature at dates close together should be reasonably close substitutes and have similar risk premia. The *Liquidity Preference Hypothesis* associated with Keynes (1936), and Hicks (1939) suggests that the risk premium on long bonds should typically increase as the term to maturity increases. I have some sympathy with this third position.

Recall from Chapter 6 the assertion of Irving Fisher that increases in expected inflation are typically fully reflected in short interest rates. There I argued that this hypothesis was unlikely to be exactly fulfilled. Nevertheless, there is impressive evidence that short-term interest rates do broadly keep up with short-term inflationary expectations; see Fama (1975). Let us recognise that investors without money illusion care chiefly about the expected real rate of return: from any given nominal interest rate they subtract their inflation expectation over the same period. Consider the two strategies whose comparison yielded equation (8.2.3). The policy of rolling over short Treasury Bills for N periods now becomes relatively safe in real terms. As of time t, individuals with Rational Expectations cannot predict how inflation and short interest rates at time $t + k$ will deviate from their current best guesses. Nevertheless, they may have some confidence that when time $t + k$ arrives, short-term interest rates will basically reflect the relatively accurate assessment at the beginning of $t + k$ of the inflation rate during that period. In contrast, the policy of buying an N period bond at t and holding to maturity N periods later, while guaranteeing with certainty the nominal redemption yield R'^N_t, implies that all deviations of *ex post* inflation over the period from the Rational Expectation at t are reflected in the real redemption yield. In a world of uncertain inflation, the riskiest policy is to commit oneself to a long nominal contract and this risk increases the longer the commitment. In my judgment, this argument increases the likelihood that risk premia k_t^N will be an increasing function of the term to maturity.

Having developed a model of the Term Structure of interest rates I turn now to empirical evidence designed to shed light on this approach and to test the assumption of Rational Expectations within this model. I begin with the work of Modigliani and Shiller (1973). I simplify their model to clarify the arguments they use. For example, they use a more sophisticated approximation than equation (8.2.3), but the details need not concern us here. Suppose we imagine a fully specified macroeconomic model which can be solved under Rational Expectations once the policy rules are specified. Suppose the policy rules are fairly simple so that it turns out the Rational Expectations solution implies

$$i_t = a_1 i_{t-1} + a_2 i_{t-2} + v_{i,t} \qquad {}_t v_{i,t}^e = 0 \qquad (8.2.5)$$

$$\pi_t = b_1 \pi_{t-1} + b_2 \pi_{t-2} + v_{\pi,t} \qquad {}_t v_{\pi,t}^e = 0 \qquad (8.2.6)$$

π_t is the inflation rate at time t and i_t is the *ex post* real interest rate $(r_t - \pi_t)$. Even though r_t may be observed at the beginning of period t, individuals are not yet certain of π_t and hence do not yet know how i_t will deviate from its Rational Expectation. As of time t, individuals use the *Chain Rule of Forecasting* to form guesses about future values of i_t and π_t conditional on information at t. For example

$$_t i_t^e = a_1 i_{t-1} + a_2 i_{t-2}$$

This estimate may now be used to form $_t i_{t+1}^e$ using equation (8.2.5)

$$i_{t+1} = a_1 i_t + a_2 i_{t-1} + v_{i,t+1}$$

$$_t i_{t+1}^e = a_1 (_t i_t^e) + a_2 i_{t-1} = a_1 (a_1 i_{t-1} + a_2 i_{t-2}) + a_2 i_{t-1}$$

$$= (a_1^2 + a_2) i_{t-1} + a_1 a_2 i_{t-2}$$

In turn this estimate may be used to forecast $_t i_{t+2}^e$ and hence $_t i_{t+3}^e$ and so on. Each Rational Expectation $_t i_{t+k}^e$ can thus be expressed as a weighted sum of i_{t-1} and i_{t-2}, the relevant information available at t; only the weights change as we change k. Rational Expectations for future inflation rates π_{t+k} may be built up in similar fashion and depend only on π_{t-1} and π_{t-2}. Since $_t r^e_{t+k} = {}_t i^e_{t+k} + {}_t \pi^e_{t+k}$, it follows that $_t r^e_{t+k}$ depends only on $(i_{t-1}, i_{t-2}, \pi_{t-1}, \pi_{t-2})$. Moreover, since $i_{t-1} = r_{t-1} - \pi_{t-1}$ and $i_{t-2} = r_{t-2} - \pi_{t-2}$, we can also express $_t r^e_{t+k}$ in the form

$$_t r^e_{t+k} = c_1 r_{t-1} + c_2 r_{t-2} + c_3 \pi_{t-1} + c_4 \pi_{t-2} \qquad (8.2.7)$$

However, in equation (8.2.4), R^N_t is basically an average of expected future short rates $_t r^e_{t+k}$. Since each of these can be expressed using equation (8.2.7), their average may be written as a weighted average of $(r_{t-1}, r_{t-2}, \pi_{t-1}$ and $\pi_{t-2})$. Hence Modigliani and Shiller rewrite equation (8.2.4)

$$R^N_t = d_1 r_{t-1} + d_2 r_{t-2} + d_3 \pi_{t-1} + d_4 \pi_{t-2} + k^N_t + u_t$$

$$_{t-1} u^e_t = 0 \qquad (8.2.8)$$

where u_t is a purely random term whose Rational Expectation is zero. By using a measure of the recent volatility of short interest rates to proxy k^N_t, Modigliani and Shiller estimate the coefficients of this Term Structure equation from data on short and long interest rates and on inflation. They use quarterly USA data from 1955 to 1971.

Before discussing their results, two remarks are in order. First, the only way in which this simplified exposition differs from their actual model is that they allow a larger number of lagged terms in equations (8.2.5)–(8.2.6) since, under policies typically followed, the Rational Expectations solution of the full macroeconomic model will not be as simple as in the equations cited. This does not change the method of the analysis; it only complicates the demonstration of how the Chain Rule of Forecasting may be used to express Rational Expectations as weighted averages of relevant past rates of inflation or interest. Secondly, since equations (8.2.5) and (8.2.6) are imagined to be the Rational Expectations equilibrium solution under a particular set of policy rules, the coefficients in these equations will change, and hence the coefficients in equation (8.2.8) will change, if a different policy rule is adopted. Modigliani and Shiller use this to justify terminating their sample data in 1971, when government intervention to control prices in the USA would have altered equation (8.2.5) immediately. While the Modigliani and Shiller study may be a valid application of Rational Expectations, the earlier work of Modigliani and Sutch, who derive an equation such as (8.2.8) from the hypothesis of Adaptive Expectations and use the estimated results for policy simulations, falls into the trap pointed out by Lucas (1976) and discussed in Section 4.4.

Modigliani and Shiller estimate equation (8.2.8) and find it explains long yields extremely well. Estimates of the relevant parameters differ from zero by amounts which are statistically significant according to conventional criteria. The inclusion of lagged inflation terms in equation (8.2.8) contributes significantly to the explanatory power and justifies the view in equations (8.2.5) and (8.2.6) that decomposing nominal interest rates into real rates and inflation rates and modelling these separately offers a better description than modelling the combined variable r_t. The evidence for the variable risk premium is also significant.

Having estimated the model, Modigliani and Shiller test whether Expectations are Rational. While the coefficients d_i in equation (8.2.8) are justified by applying Rational Expectations to equations (8.2.5) and (8.2.6) through the Chain Rule of Forecasting, the computer chooses estimates of d_i merely to fit best the data by equation (8.2.8). If expectations are Rational, these coefficients should be precisely the coefficients implied by equations (8.2.4) and the Chain Rule of Forecasting. Hence Modigliani and Shiller adopt a procedure which is equivalent to the direct estimation of the parameters of equations (8.2.5)(8.2.6), using $(r_t - \pi_t)$ to measure i_t, the mathematical solution of the Chain Rule of Forecasting equations, and hence the construction of the implied estimates of d_i. They conclude that these artificially constructed estimates are very similar to the estimates obtained by fitting equation (8.2.8) directly to the data. This evidence provides further support for the contention that Expectations are Rational.

Whereas Modigliani and Shiller work within the tradition of empirical macroeconomics in which part of the economic structure is estimated and tested, Mishkin (1978a) (1980) has examined the more direct Efficient Markets approach discussed in section 8.1. The evidence of Modigliani and Shiller notwithstanding, suppose that short-run changes in the risk premia k_t^N are not important determinants of changes in long bond rates. Equation (8.2.4) may then be written

$$R_t^N = (1/N)\,(r_t + {}_t r_{t+1}^e + \ldots + {}_t r_{t+N-1}^e) + k^N$$

where the risk premium k^N depends on the term to maturity, but does not change over time. Thus, one period earlier,

$$R_{t-1}^N = (1/N)\,(r_{t-1} + {}_{t-1} r_t^e + {}_{t-1} r_{t+1}^e + \ldots$$
$$+ {}_{t-1} r_{t+N-2}^e) + k^N$$

By subtraction

$$R_t^N - R_{t-1}^N =$$
$$(1/N)\,[(r_t - {}_{t-1} r_t^e) + ({}_t r_{t+1}^e - {}_{t-1} r_{t+1}^e) + \ldots + ({}_t r_{t+N-2}^e - {}_{t-1} r_{t+N-2}^e)]$$
$$+ (1/N)\,({}_t r_{t+N-1}^e - r_{t-1}) \tag{8.2.9}$$

By Property I of Section 4.1, the Rational Expectation at $t-1$ of the Rational Expectation ${}_t r_{t+k}^e$ at t is simply ${}_{t-1} r_{t+k}^e$ the best guess at $t-1$ of r_{t+k}. Expectations of r_{t+k} are revised between $t-1$ and t only because of new information at t which cannot be anticipated at $t-1$. Thus at $t-1$ the Rational Expectation of all the terms in the first large bracket on the right hand side of equation (8.2.9) is zero. Consider the second bracket on the right hand side of this equation. If the bond is a perpetuity, N is infinite and this term will be zero unless $({}_t r_{t+N-1}^e - r_{t-1})$ is also infinite. Provided the model converges to a steady state as the Saddlepoint property of Section 3.2 requires, ${}_t r_{t+N-1}^e$ must be expected to converge to this steady state value and must be finite. Hence for perpetuities this second term is zero. For bonds with a finite but lengthy term to maturity, N will be sufficiently large that this term is still negligible. Hence, given only the assumption that risk premia are roughly constant over time, equation (8.2.9) implies

$$R_t^N - R_{t-1}^N = \eta_t \qquad {}_{t-1}\eta_t^e = 0 \qquad\qquad (8.2.10)$$

Again we derive the Random Walk model.[1] No information available at time $t - 1$ should allow us to predict systematically changes in the N-period interest rate R_{t-1}^N.

This may seem a bit confusing: we have just examined the Modigliani–Shiller model which explains R_t^N extremely well. However, the two results square perfectly. As in the Stock Exchange, the implication of Efficient Markets theory is that all systematic information available at $t - 1$, such as the Modigliani–Shiller equation, is used to determine R_{t-1}^N. The entire content of economic theory is already in the bond price or bond yield. Failure to incorporate fully this information immediately would leave unexploited profit opportunities which the theory of Efficient Markets asserts will not occur. Once available information has been optimally used, economic theory cannot contribute to predicting changes in R_t^N over time. Such changes will occur in an Efficient Market only when new and previously unanticipatable information becomes available, at which instant the relevant economic theory may be used to assess how the price and yield of a bond must change to reflect fully this new information. Once these have been quickly revised, further changes once more become unpredictable.

Many studies claim to have found evidence in support of equation (8.2.10). Prell (1973) found that professional forecasters' guesses about changes in long bond rates were less accurate than the Random Walk hypothesis that the best guess about all future N period bond rates is the current N period bond rate. Other studies finding in favour of the hypothesis include Bierwag and Grove (1971), Laffer and Zecher (1975), Sargent (1976a)(1979b) and Pesando (1978). This seems a formidable list.

---

1. Clearly, the Random Walk model of stock market prices may also be derived by this elegant route. We need only recognise that the market price of a stock is the discounted present value of expected future dividends, and that revisions in expected dividends cannot be forecast under Rational Expectations.

Recently, Shiller (1979) has cast doubt on these findings. His arguments are threefold. First, a few empirical studies have questioned the conformity of bond market data with the Rational Expectations/Efficient Markets hypothesis. Secondly, he argues that, since the Term Structure equation is a weighted average of expected future short rates, R_t^N ought to change only very slowly, whereas long bond rates in the USA and the UK are quite volatile in the short run. To demonstrate this, he uses *ex post* data on short interest rates to construct

$$R_t^N = (1/N)\,(r_t + r_{t+1} + \ldots + r_{t+N-1})$$

which changes only very slowly over time. Since Rational Expectations are supposed to be best guesses at t of these future short rates, this term ought not to contribute much to variations in measured R_t^N. Thirdly, Shiller provides direct evidence that the Random Walk hypothesis is incorrect. He argues that previous investigators have not discovered the variables which do systematically explain changes in R_t^N. Their evidence, while necessary for the validity of Rational Expectations, is not sufficient. Shiller presents estimates for the USA and the UK using quarterly data for 1966—77 and 1956—77 respectively. The coefficient estimates are given in Table 8.2.1 below. R denotes the long bond rate and r the short-term rate on Bills.

Table 8.2.1

USA	$R_t - R_{t-1}$	$= 0.211 - 0.125$	$(R_{t-1} - r_{t-1})$
UK	$R_t - R_{t-1}$	$= 0.164 - 0.120$	$(R_{t-1} - r_{t-1})$

All coefficients are statistically significant. Since the information on the right hand side of these equations is available at $t - 1$, individuals with Rational Expectations should be able to utilise this to predict changes in long bond rates. Shiller concludes that the empirical evidence is not favourable to the Rational Expectations/Efficient Market model of the Term Structure which has been developed in this chapter. Other empirical work reported in Shiller (1979) suggests it is likely to be the presence of R_{t-1} on the right hand side of the equations of Table 8.2.1 which largely explains the effect of $(R_{t-1} - r_{t-1})$ on changes in the long bond rate.

There can be no dispute that this evidence calls into question the Random Walk model (8.2.10). Whether it casts serious doubt on the Rational Expectations model of the Term Structure is another matter. Recall that the Random Walk model follows only if the risk premium k^N_t is assumed constant over time. Shiller assumes this even though his previous work with Modigliani established a variable risk premium. This raises the possibility that the terms in Table 8.2.1 are really modelling the change in the risk premium $(k^N_t - k^N_{t-1})$. If so, Shiller's results would be quite compatible with the Rational Expectations Term Structure equation (8.2.4); only the Random Walk simplification of this theory would be rejected.

Let us study this possibility more closely. The positive constants in Table 8.2.1 might be interpreted to mean that risk premia were increasing over the period. If an important source of risk in the real return on long bonds is the error in forecasting inflation, this requires only that inflation uncertainty increased over the period, which I find quite plausible. The second term in Table 8.2.1 shows that when long rates are high relative to short rates at time $t - 1$, long rates typically fall between $t - 1$ and t. Suppose we model the risk premium by a constant plus a random variable with mean zero describing temporary deviations from the normal risk premium. A large positive deviation at $t - 1$ implies that R_{t-1} is abnormally high: on average R_t will be lower than R_{t-1}. Thus the second terms in Shiller's equations may be given the interpretation of temporary panics about inflation uncertainty.

A more systematic interpretation is also possible. The expectations part of the Term Structure equation (8.2.4) implies that R_{t-1} will most exceed r_{t-1} when short-term interest rates, and by implication short-term inflation rates, are expected to rise sharply. Shiller's results may therefore be interpreted to mean that risk premia and inflation uncertainty are greatest when inflation is accelerating sharply. The view that Shiller's results suggest the importance of the risk premium, confirming his earlier work with Modigliani, is thus easy to maintain. The reader must choose between this interpretation and the view that Shiller's evidence casts doubt on the assumption of Rational Expectations.

To sum up, the proposition that bond market participants have Rational Expectations has been extensively tested, with many authors claiming empirical support for this proposition. As usual, we observe only data generated jointly by the expectations formation process and the model in which that process is embedded. Until the portfolio-theoretic model of risk premia is more fully incorporated into bond market studies, the evidence in favour of Rational Expectations cannot be regarded as conclusive. Nevertheless, I would guess that the early proponents of Rational Expectations would happily have settled for the bond market evidence which has subsequently been accumulated.

8.3 The Forward Market for Foreign Exchange

Since much of the ensuing analysis deals with percentage changes in the exchange rate, it is convenient to work with a log-linear model. Let s_t be defined as the logarithm of the current or spot exchange rate at time t, measuring the exchange rate as the number of units of domestic currency which exchange for one unit of foreign currency. The exchange rate is the domestic price of foreign currency. Although this definition is the natural one for an economist, and is widely adopted in the literature, it is at variance with much popular usage which takes the exchange rate to refer to the number of units of foreign currency which exchange for a unit of the domestic currency. Thus a *rise* in s_t, by making foreign currency more expensive, implies a *depreciation* in the foreign value of the domestic currency, and in common parlance is a devaluation.

I assume that individuals at time $t-1$ use the relevant model of exchange rate determination to form Rational Expectations $_{t-1}s_t^e$ of the exchange rate s_t (in logarithms). By the usual property of Rational Expectations

$$s_t = {}_{t-1}s_t^e + \eta_t \qquad {}_{t-1}\eta_t = 0 \qquad (8.3.1)$$

where again I use η to denote the Rational Expectations forecasting error.

In addition to the spot market for foreign exchange, suppose that there exists a forward market for foreign exchange in which at time $t - 1$ individuals can trade foreign currency to be exchanged at time t, but at a rate agreed at time $t - 1$. Let f_{t-1} be the logarithm of this one period forward exchange rate set at time $t - 1$ for exchange at time t. Given perfect certainty and perfect foresight, intertemporal arbitrage would then ensure $f_{t-1} = s_t$. Notice that no interest rate or discounting need be considered, since forward market transactors do not have to put up the money in advance. Now let us recognise that the world is risky and weaken the assumption of Perfect Foresight to that of Rational Expectations. The above reasoning then suggests the model

$$f_{t-1} = {}_{t-1}s_t^e + v_{t-1}' \qquad (8.3.2)$$

where v_{t-1}' is the risk premium at time $t - 1$. If all individuals were risk neutral, evaluating assets in terms of expected return alone, v_{t-1}' would be identically zero and the model then asserts that forward exchange rates are precisely the current Rational Expectation of future spot rates.

As in the previous section, we may wish to develop a more general model which recognises risk aversion and the possible existence of risk premia. Equation (8.3.2) is compatible with this more general assumption. The forward market allows international traders with unavoidable future foreign exchange commitments to hedge the exchange rate risk by making advance contracts at exchange rates of which they can currently be sure. The risk premium is thus the expected profit margin of a dealer providing forward cover now with foreign exchange which will actually be acquired in the following period at the then prevailing spot exchange rate. If, for example, there are roughly equal numbers of British and American firms seeking forward cover at time $t - 1$ for the Sterling/Dollar rate at time t, forward dealers will be able to balance their books so that the residual risk in their portfolios will be zero. The expected profit margin should then reflect only the transactions costs of organising the forward market. Even if books are sometimes unbalanced, so that dealers have to take what is called an open position, the risk premium v'_t may still be close to zero if dealers are reasonably risk neutral.

Since I do not wish to prejudge the issue, I shall assume that v'_{t-1} may be modelled by

$$v'_{t-1} = a + v_{t-1} \qquad (8.3.3)$$

where the parameter a denotes the mean value of the risk premium, which I take to be positive, but possibly quite close to zero, and v_{t-1} is a serially uncorrelated random variable with mean zero reflecting transient deviations of the risk premium from its mean value. Equations $(8.3.1)$–$(8.3.3)$ imply

$$s_t = -a + f_{t-1} + (\eta_t - v_{t-1}) \qquad (8.3.4)$$

As viewed from time $t-1$, the future spot rate s_t deviates systematically from the forward rate f_{t-1} because of the average or normal risk premium a and deviates randomly because of forecasting errors η_t and random fluctuations v_{t-1} in the risk premium.

The testable implication of the Rational Expectations Efficient Markets model is that changes in the forward rate reflect all systematic knowable information at $t-1$ about the likely value of the future spot rate s_t. By confronting the data with the general specification

$$s_t = b_0 + b_1 f_{t-1} + u_t$$

where u_t is a random disturbance term, the coefficients b_0 and b_1 may be estimated. The model predicts that b_0 should be negative, since it is the negative of the average risk premium. Of more importance, the coefficient b_1 should be unity, since the model assumes that all information about s_t is incorporated in the forward rate at time $t-1$. Readers familiar with econometric theory will recognise that equation $(8.3.2)$ implies that f_{t-1} is stochastically correlated with v_{t-1}, so that estimation of the coefficients by the method of Ordinary Least Squares is not appropriate; however, consistent estimates may be obtained by the method of instrumental variables. Frenkel (1980c) presents estimates for the Dollar/Sterling, Dollar/French Franc, and Dollar/Deutsche Mark rates for

Table 8.3.1

	b_0	b_1
Dollar/Pound	0.030	0.961
Dollar/Franc	−0.236	0.844
Dollar/Deutsche Mark	−0.021	0.973

monthly data for June 1973–July 1979. The coefficient estimates are given in Table 8.3.1.

None of the estimates of b_1 differ from unity by a statistically significant amount. The only estimate of b_0 which differs significantly from zero is the estimate in the Dollar/Franc equation, and this variable has the expected sign if a small risk premium exists on average. This rather weak test of the Efficient Markets hypothesis is consistent with the theory. A more powerful test involves adding extra variables, such as f_{t-2}, to the right hand side of the equation and re-estimating the coefficients. If the Efficient Markets model is valid, the coefficient on b_1 should still be unity and the coefficients on additional variables should be zero: the forward rate at $t-1$ should embody all the relevant information for the systematic prediction of s_t. Frenkel's experiments confirm this result for the first and third equations. When f_{t-2} is added to the second equation, its own coefficient is insignificantly different from zero, but the coefficient b_1 is reduced to 0.706 which does differ significantly from unity. For this equation, the joint hypotheses that expectations are Rational and that these expectations are immediately reflected in the forward rate are statistically rejected. Moreover, the caveat of Shiller (1979) discussed in the previous section still remains relevant: merely because existing experiments fail to discover additional variables which help predict s_t does not mean that other experiments might not discover such variables.

Many other studies have conducted experiments similar to those of Frenkel and are cited in the Notes on the Literature at the end of the chapter. Many conclude that the Efficient Markets model passes the tests which they devise, some find that the full implications of the model are not quite satisfied, but few conclude that the model is seriously at odds with the data.

8.4 The Determination of Floating Exchange Rates

Efficient forward markets are compatible with any process of exchange rate determination, since Efficiency requires only that true process be understood, used as a basis for expectations formation, and quickly incorporated into the equilibrium forward rate. I now take up the more important question of how flexible spot rates themselves are determined.

Consider first the view that exchange rates adjust to equilibrate the net flows of goods and services on the current account of the balance of payments. The hypothesis which has been studied most extensively is *Purchasing Power Parity,* or the *Law of One Price.* To the extent that we can ignore transport and other transactions costs, international arbitrage in goods should ensure that the price of a traded good is the same in all countries. If a particular country has a general inflation which leaves all its prices higher than elsewhere, a depreciation of its exchange rate will restore the world price of its traded commodities, preserving real competitiveness. This view is most easy to maintain if one believes generally in flexible goods prices and market clearing. In the absence of money illusion, economies may then conveniently be characterised by Natural Rates of real variables such as output and employment and it is straightforward to add the Natural Real Exchange Rate, or constant level of international competitiveness, to this list. The nominal or measured exchange rate is merely another flexible endogenous variable which must adjust to maintain the economy in real equilibrium. The implication of this model is that systematically higher inflation than the rest of the world will be accompanied by steady depreciation of the foreign value of the domestic currency. If, as in the hyperinflation model, one believes that nominal changes are sufficiently large relative to real changes that the latter can be ignored, differential inflation becomes the sole determinant of changes in nominal exchange rates, maintaining real competitiveness at the level required to balance the current account of the balance of payments. This simple prediction is the consequence of the strong assumption of Purchasing Power Parity (PPP).

Letting s_t be the logarithm of the spot exchange rate

measured not as the foreign price of domestic currency but rather as the domestic price of foreign currency, pure PPP thus implies

$$s_t = p_t - p_t^* \tag{8.4.1}$$

where p_t denotes the logarithm of the domestic price level and p_t^* the logarithm of the foreign price level. A slightly weaker version of PPP would not insist that traded goods prices were literally equalised throughout the world, but would still require differential inflation to be offset by changes in nominal exchange rates, a hypothesis which may be written as

$$s_t = \alpha + p_t - p_t^* \tag{8.4.2}$$

where the constant α denotes the logarithm of the equilibrium real exchange rate $(s - p + p^*)$.

Since domestic and foreign price levels are themselves endogenous variables, a model of price determination is still required to complete the theory of exchange rate determination. Given the assumptions already implicit in the analysis, it seems quite natural to add a simple log linear LM equation

$$m_t = p_t + \gamma_1 y_t - \gamma_2 r_t \tag{8.4.3}$$

where m_t and y_t are the logarithms of the domestic money stock and real output and r_t is the domestic nominal interest rate. A similar equation describing the rest of the world then allows $(p_t - p_t^*)$ to be inferred from $(m_t - m_t^*)$, $(y_t - y_t^*)$ and $(r_t - r_t^*)$, the starred superscripts again denoting variables in the rest of the world. A yet more complete macroeconomic model would allow an explanation for the current levels of interest rates and output. The use of LM equations, essentially money demand equations, to augment the PPP hypothesis as a theory of exchange rate determination has become known as the *Monetary Approach to exchange rate determination*, though Buiter and Miller (1981) more accurately label this model as *Current Account Monetarism* to emphasise the contrast with the models I shall shortly describe.

If this model represented the last word on the theory of floating exchange rates, it would allow a role for Rational Expectations only indirectly as part of the general equilibrium solution for interest rates and the current price level in the manner discussed in Chapters 3 and 6. However, many economists now reject this model of exchange rate determination for two distinct reasons. First, the empirical evidence cited in the following section is rather discouraging, not only to the model of Current Account Monetarism, but also to more direct test of PPP. Secondly, economists thinking about exchange rate determination have become increasingly convinced that short-term movements are to be sought not in changes in the current account, but in the capital account of the balance of payments.

In the Bretton Woods system of fixed exchange rates set up after World War II, private sector capital account transactions between countries were often discouraged by various forms of exchange control. Although direct foreign investment by companies and foreign aid transactions by governments were important components of the capital account, short-term money movements were less important. The growth of multinational corporations with international portfolios of assets increased the importance of speculative transactions, but the quantitative significance of such transactions altered dramatically in the 1970s when the accumulated surplus funds of OPEC countries began to be invested in international asset markets, a process accentuated by the parallel elimination of exchange controls in a world no longer committed to defending fixed exchange rates.

Thus, instead of simplifying by focusing on the current account alone, economists began to develop simple models of exchange rate determination which adopted the opposite simplification, that the short-run behaviour of the exchange rate might be captured by considering only the capital account. On this view, exchange rates adjust to leave international investors indifferent as to where they hold their funds. Given the volume of international investment funds outstanding, a disequilibrium exchange rate would induce an immediate and vast flow of funds on the capital account which would swamp short-term current account flows and it is to prevent such vast capital flows that the exchange rate continuously adjusts. This analysis focuses on asset stocks rather than goods flows and by treating foreign exchange as a financial asset allows a direct role for Rational Expectations, just as in earlier sections of this chapter.

Before analysing the market for foreign exchange, it is important to dispel a popular misunderstanding. Consider any asset market which is Efficient, the asset price reflecting all information currently available. Suppose a new piece of information becomes available to all traders at the same instant. As we have seen, the asset price will instantaneously jump to its new 'correct' price, but no trading will occur: everyone with the new information agrees that the new price is correct. Trading in asset markets occurs only when traders disagree about the correct price, either because they have access to different information, or because they process the same information differently. Thus the assumption that it is primarily capital account forces which determine the exchange rate cannot be empirically tested by comparison of the magnitudes or elasticities of capital account movements and current account movements. Rather, it is the threat of large capital flows in response to new information which leads to a change in the exchange rate without the flow necessarily taking place. Moreover, in the absence of intervention by central banks, by definition the current and capital accounts must sum to zero, since the floating exchange rate clears the market for foreign exchange. Thus the observation that capital account flows are not in practice enormous does not of itself constitute evidence against the asset market models of exchange rate determination.

As in previous sections, I begin by making a strong assumption which greatly simplifies the structure of the model, allowing us to explore the insights which Rational Expectations analysis provides. In the current context, the strong assumption is that of perfect capital mobility between countries. This has two aspects, first that transactions costs and exchange controls are negligible and secondly that international assets such as bonds are perfect substitutes. Given this assumption, exchange rates must adjust to equate the rate of return on different international assets. In Sections 8.2 and 8.3 I argued that different financial assets were unlikely to be perfect substitutes and drew on modern portfolio theory to explain the existence of risk premia reflecting the degree to which expected rates of return might differ between assets. Later in this section I shall re-introduce this assumption and show how it restores a role for the current account in determining short-term movements in exchange rates. Initially however it will be simpler to consider the stronger assumption of perfect international capital mobility.

Let d_t denote $(r_t - r_t^*)$, the differential between domestic and foreign nominal interest rates on the assets in which international wealth holders are assumed to invest. If the assets are perfect substitutes, asset market equilibrium at time $t-1$ requires that the expected rate of return on the two assets be equalised

$$_{t-1}s_t^e - s_{t-1} = d_{t-1} \qquad (8.4.4)$$

The expected rate of return has two components, the interest payment which I assume to be known at time $t-1$ and the expected capital gain or loss in holding the currency during the period. Equation (8.4.4) points out that the expected capital gain must offset the known interest differential. For example, if the foreign country pays zero interest, a domestic investor buying foreign currency at the start of the period and converting back at the end of the period will finish with a quantity of domestic currency high enough to match the alternative strategy of holding domestic interest bearing bonds, provided the domestic currency depreciates sufficiently over the period. Since this depreciation implies a rise in s_t, the domestic price of foreign exchange, that is precisely what equation (8.4.4) asserts as an *ex ante* equilibrium condition.

Again using η_t to denote the Rational Expectations forecasting error, the observable spot exchange rate therefore obeys

$$s_t = _{t-1}s_t^e + \eta_t = s_{t-1} + d_{t-1} + \eta_t \qquad _{t-1}\eta_t^e = 0 \ (8.4.5)$$

which has the testable implication that no information at time $t-1$ should help explain s_t, provided s_{t-1} and d_{t-1} are included on the right hand side. Moreover, these last two variables should have unit coefficients.

The idea that higher nominal interest rates are associated with a depreciating currency seems contrary to much of the conventional wisdom in which rises in interest rates are held to lead to appreciation of the foreign value of the domestic currency. Dornbusch (1978) argues that these two views may be reconciled as follows. Consider individuals at time $t-1$ contemplating a two period decision. The expected capital gain over two periods must just offset the interest differential over the same time:

$$_{t-1}s^e_{t+1} - s_{t-1} = {}_{t-1}d^e_t + d_{t-1} \qquad (8.4.6)$$

which recognises that individuals at time $t-1$ are not yet certain about interest rates prevailing at time t. From equation (8.4.4)

$$_ts^e_{t+1} - s_t = d_t$$

Subtracting this equation from equation (8.4.6)

$$s_t = s_{t-1} + d_{t-1} - (d_t - {}_{t-1}d^e_t) + ({}_ts^e_{t+1} - {}_{t-1}s^e_{t+1}) \qquad (8.4.7)$$

Thus we have decomposed the forecasting error η_t in equation (8.4.5) into two components — failure at $t-1$ to forecast the interest rate differential at t and failure to foresee at $t-1$ how expectations about s_{t+1} would be revised at t. Under Rational Expectations, each of these components has mean zero; if in fact no new information becomes available, these two terms will attain their zero mean and the actual capital gain will indeed have exactly offset the interest differential.

Of more importance, equation (8.4.7) implies that an *unanticipated* increase in the differential d_t will reduce s_t and lead to an *appreciation* of the foreign value of the domestic currency relative to the movement anticipated at $t-1$. In contrast, known high differentials d_{t-1} are expected to and on average do lead to a *depreciation* of the currency. As usual, the distinction between anticipated and unanticipated is crucial. Anticipated high interest rates are already in the price and it is only a high exchange rate s_{t-1} which acts to stem the potential inflow of funds by inducing an anticipated capital loss; unanticipated rises in interest rates make the currency unexpectedly attractive and require an additional rise in its foreign value.

This analysis is instructive but incomplete, since it explains neither how individuals form expectations of future interest rates nor how the initial level of the exchange rate is determined. We require a complete macroeconomic model and the following discussion is based on Dornbusch (1976a) whose work has subsequently been extended by many authors. Again, I assume continuous time and Perfect Foresight to simplify as much as possible.

Since I wish to emphasise the international aspects of the model I assume that domestic aggregate demand for goods obeys

$$y^d_t = h(s_t - p_t + p^*_t) \qquad h > 0$$

where y^d is the logarithm of real aggregate demand and $(s_t - p_t + p^*_t)$ the relevant measure of real competitiveness. Imagine that consumption, depending on current output, has already been substituted out of this equation as in the traditional IS equation and that investment is exogenously constant. An increase in real competitiveness $(s_t - p_t + p^*_t)$ increases export volume and reduces imports leading to a net increase in aggregate demand. Suppose aggregate goods supply is fixed at the level y. Let θ be the constant rate of domestic money growth and the long-run domestic inflation rate. I assume that goods prices adjust according to

$$\dot{p}_t = \phi \left[h(s_t - p_t + p^*_t) - y \right] + \theta \qquad \phi > 0 \quad (8.4.8)$$

When aggregate goods demand equals the fixed supply y, inflation is at the rate θ. Excess goods demand causes goods prices to rise faster than the rate of money growth, thereby reducing real competitiveness and acting as a mechanism of adjustment in the domestic goods market. If the parameter ϕ is small, price adjustment is sluggish and goods market disequilibrium persists for some time. Higher values of ϕ imply faster clearing of the goods market and in the limit as ϕ tends to infinity, market clearing may be instantaneous. Although I treat ϕ as a constant, by imagining different values for that parameter we may capture the complete spectrum from extreme Monetarist to extreme Keynesian. In the exposition I shall assume that ϕ is finite so that the goods market does not necessarily clear.

To complete the model, I assume the continuous time Perfect Foresight version of the perfect substitutes assumption (8.4.4)

$$\dot{s}_t = r_t - r_t^* \tag{8.4.9}$$

and the money demand equation (8.4.3). Provided the domestic country is small relative to the rest of the world, it will be reasonable to assume that foreign variables are exogenous to the analysis. I assume that foreign output is constantly at the level y^*, that foreign prices and nominal money grow at the constant rate θ^* and that foreign interest rates are constant at the level r^*.

From Section 3.2, the Perfect Foresight solution path is constructed in two stages. First we derive the steady state, then we derive the unique convergent path to this Saddlepoint. Since I use the superscript $*$ to denote the rest of the world, I denote the steady state by suppressing the time subscript t. When the domestic economy is in the steady state real money balances are constant, whence as usual $\dot{p} = \theta$. Since the goods market clears in the steady state, equation (8.4.8) implies

$$s - p + p^* = y/h \tag{8.4.10}$$

is the steady state level of real competitiveness. Precisely because this is constant, the nominal exchange rate s must then be changing continuously to offset differential international inflation

$$\dot{s} = \theta - \theta^* \tag{8.4.11}$$

Since equation (8.4.9) holds at all dates, it must be true in the steady state that

$$r - r^* = \theta - \theta^* \tag{8.4.12}$$

Thus, in the steady state this model exhibits both PPP — equation (8.4.11) — and the Irving Fisher property that higher inflation is completely reflected in higher nominal interest rates though, as we shall shortly discover, neither property holds in the short run. Finally, from equation (8.4.3) the steady state level of domestic real money balances is given by

$$m - p = \gamma_1 y - \gamma_2 (\theta - \theta^* + r^*) \tag{8.4.13}$$

I now construct the phase diagram relating real money balances $(m_t - p_t)$ to real competitiveness $(s_t - p_t + p_t^*)$. Since real money balances are constant only when $\dot{p}_t$ equals θ, the rate of money growth, equation (8.4.8) implies that the locus along which real money balances are constant is given by the equation for goods market clearing

$$s_t - p_t + p_t^* = y/h \tag{8.4.14}$$

depicted in Figure 8.4.1 as a horizontal line through the steady state level of real competitiveness y/h. If the level of real competitiveness exceeds this value, excess goods demand bids up prices and reduces real money balances. Hence, above the locus $\dot{m}_t - \dot{p}_t = 0$ the arrows of motion point horizontally to the left, below the locus they point to the right.

Now construct the locus along which real competitiveness is unchanging. Equation (8.4.8) describes the behaviour of $\dot{p}_t$ and equation (8.4.9) the behaviour of $\dot{s}_t$. Recalling that $\dot{p}_t^*$ is assumed to equal θ^*, we may write the locus along which real competitiveness is constant as

$$0 = \dot{s}_t - \dot{p}_t + \dot{p}_t^*$$
$$= (r_t - r^*) - \{\phi[h(s_t - p_t + p_t^*) - y] + \theta\} + (\theta^*)$$

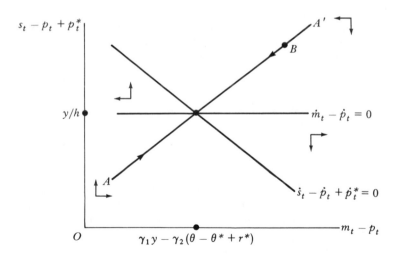

Figure 8.4.1

Eliminating r_t using the money demand equation (8.4.3)

$$0 = [(1/\gamma_2)(p_t - m_t + \gamma_1 y) - r^*]$$
$$- \{\phi [h(s_t - p_t + p_t^*) - y] + \theta\} + (\theta^*)$$

and rearranging

$$\phi h \gamma_2 (s_t - p_t + p_t^*) = [\gamma_1 y - \gamma_2 (\theta - \theta^* + r^*)]$$
$$+ \gamma_2 \phi y - (m_t - p_t) \qquad (8.4.15)$$

Notice that the first term is just the steady state level of real money balances given in equation (8.4.13). Hence along the locus $\dot{s}_t - \dot{p}_t + \dot{p}_t^* = 0$, a higher level of real balances $(m_t - p_t)$ is associated with a lower level of real competitiveness $(s_t - p_t + p_t^*)$ as in Figure 8.4.1. Higher real balances require a lower nominal interest rate r_t, which reduces the capital gain $\dot{s}_t$ which clears the asset market in equation (8.4.9). To maintain real competitiveness there must be a corresponding reduction in $\dot{p}_t$ which can be achieved only by the excess goods supply which a lower level of real competitiveness generates.

For a given level of $(m_t - p_t)$ nominal interest rates must be constant, whence a higher level of real competitiveness increases $\dot{p}_t$ without any corresponding change in $\dot{s}_t$. Above the locus $\dot{s}_t - \dot{p}_t + \dot{p}_t^* = 0$, real competitiveness must be falling (downward vertical arrows) and below the locus it must be rising. From the analysis of Section 3.2 the steady state is therefore a Saddlepoint and there is a unique convergent locus AA' which must have a positive slope if the arrows of motion in Figure 8.4.1 are to be obeyed.

If ϕ is infinite goods market clearing is instantaneous, the economy is always in the steady state, and the convergent path is simply irrelevant. Whereas goods market data on variables such as GNP are available only at discrete intervals so that it *might* be possible to live with the assumption that one should model the behaviour of such data by imposing market clearing, what is distinctive about asset markets is that they are known to trade continuously and data is quickly available. We can read today how yesterday's interest rates and exchange rates changed. Empirical work on asset markets might be conducted using daily, weekly, or even monthly data. Within the spirit of this analysis, it may be reasonable to highlight the special nature of asset markets by imagining a period sufficiently short in length that asset markets clear within the period, but goods markets do not. Thus I assume a finite value of ϕ which recognises that goods market clearing may not be instantaneous within the period length we have in mind. In the analysis of short-run exchange rate determination, the convergent path is then of major importance. Within this setting, I now wish to consider the effect of shocks which were previously unanticipated.

Consider first an unanticipated but permanent increase in the stock of nominal money balances at time t, the subsequent rate of growth θ being unaffected. Figure 8.4.1 remains relevant. At the instant the unanticipated increase in m_t occurs, we treat goods prices p_t as instantaneously predetermined, since they are less flexible than interest rates or the nominal exchange rate s_t. The impact effect is thus a shift to the right, denoting an increase in real money balances. The perfect foresight path then places the economy on the convergent path AA' vertically above this higher level of real money balances, for example at the point B in Figure 8.4.1, after which there is gradual convergence back to the original steady state; eventually, the only consequence of a permanently higher money stock is an equivalent rise in p_t and s_t, leaving all real variables unaltered.

Notice that the new information is immediately reflected in nominal interest rates and the spot exchange rate, the two variables which adjust most quickly. When the new information becomes available, nominal interest rates fall to ensure that the higher real money balances will be demanded, and the exchange rate depreciates to secure the rise in real competitiveness implied by the upward jump to the point B. Unanticipated movements in the interest rate and the nominal exchange rate are correlated as the conventional wisdom suggests. The rise in real competitiveness is expansionary in the goods market and provides an important channel through which unanticipated monetary expansion affects the demand for output.

Next suppose that at time t there is an unanticipated but permanent increase in θ the rate of nominal money growth.

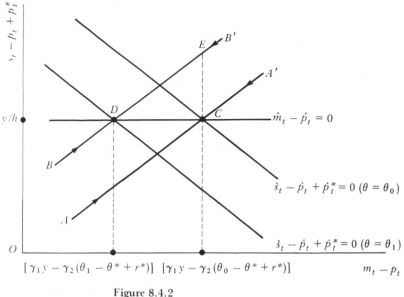

Figure 8.4.2

Higher steady state inflation now reduces the long-run demand for real money balances by raising nominal interest rates. If the original rate of money growth is θ_0, an unanticipated increase to θ_1 shifts both the steady state and the locus along which $\dot{s}_t - \dot{p}_t + \dot{p}_t^* = 0$ as equation (8.4.15) makes clear. The new locus is depicted in Figure 8.4.2.

The original steady state at the point C has shifted left to the point D reflecting the lower demand for real balances when inflation and interest rates are higher. The new convergent path is BB'. If the economy begins in the steady state C, the stock of real money balances is instantaneously unaffected at the date a higher rate of money growth is adopted: prices are instantaneously predetermined and the faster money growth has not yet taken effect. The new information is immediately reflected in asset prices and the economy jumps vertically to the point E on the new convergent path.

Again, unanticipated monetary expansion secures an increase in real competitiveness and the exchange rate becomes a vital channel of monetary policy. The converse result also applies. If governments adopt a tighter monetary policy in an attempt to reduce the inflation rate, there will be an immediate loss of real competitiveness with deflationary implications for aggregate goods demand. Unless goods market clearing is close to instantaneous a significant recession may ensue, although the economy will eventually return to the full employment steady state.

Finally, I consider the consequences of an unanticipated real shock. To be specific, how should the discovery of North Sea oil affect the Pound Sterling? I simplify by supposing that at time t there is an unanticipated discovery which allows an immediate and permanent flow of oil. More complicated dynamics ensue if the information that the oil exists precedes the ability to extract the oil or if the oil supply is known to be temporary. I amend the aggregate demand equation for domestic non-oil output to read

$$y_t^d = h(s_t - p_t + p_t^*) + h_1 \qquad (8.4.16)$$

where the positive constant h_1 denotes the Permanent Income gain implied by the oil which I assume to translate into a constant additional demand for non-oil output. Maintaining a transactions demand interpretation of the demand for money, the existing money stock must service not only the previous level y of non-oil output, but also the additional level of oil output. I therefore amend equation (8.4.3) to

$$m_t - p_t = \gamma_1(y + h_2) - \gamma_2 r_t \qquad (8.4.17)$$

where the positive constant h_2 reflects this additional oil output.

The steady state level of real competitiveness is now given by

$$s - p + p^* = \frac{y - h_1}{h} \qquad (8.4.18)$$

which is lower than the level of competitiveness implied by equation (8.4.10). A worsening in the non-oil current account is required to offset the higher Permanent Income consumption demand if the market for domestic non-oil output is eventually to clear. As UK manufacturers will attest, the discovery of oil is not an unmitigated blessing. Since the steady state

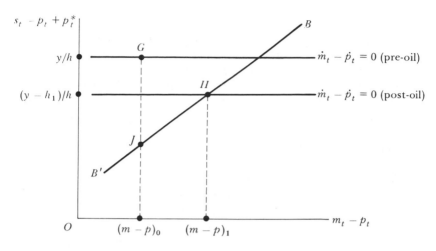

Figure 8.4.3

nominal interest rate is still given by $(\theta - \theta^* + r^*)$ from equation (8.4.12), the new steady state level of real money balances is given by

$$m - p = \gamma_1(y + h_2) - \gamma_2(\theta - \theta^* + r^*) \qquad (8.4.19)$$

which exceeds the level implied by equation (8.4.13) because of the additional transactions demand for money.

The phase diagram may now be constructed, and is shown in Figure 8.4.3. Suppose the economy begins in the original steady state G before the discovery of oil. For notational convenience I use $(m-p)_0$ to describe the steady state level of real money balances implied by equation (8.4.13) and $(m-p)_1$ to describe the higher level of steady state real money balances implied by equation (8.4.19).

After the discovery of oil the new steady state is at the point H through which the new downward sloping locus $\dot{s}_t - \dot{p}_t + \dot{p}_t^* = 0$ must pass. By drawing in the new arrows of motion we could confirm that the unique convergent path to the new steady state is BB'. The discovery of oil therefore leads to a vertical jump to the point J on this convergent locus, after which the economy gradually proceeds along BB' towards the point H.

The important implication of this analysis is that the discovery of oil not only requires a permanent reduction in real competitiveness, but also requires an even stronger appreciation of the currency in the short run to place the economy on the convergent path at the point J which lies below H. Foreseeing that oil output will increase the demand for money and increase interest rates, foreign exchange speculators will immediately bid up the foreign value of the currency generating a domestic recession. More sophisticated dynamics of the kind mentioned above are studied by Eastwood and Venables (1980) and Buiter and Miller (1981) and typically augment the speculative appreciation of the currency and make the short-term domestic recession more severe.

The assumption of Rational Expectations again allows insights into phenomena which are not easily explained within previous analyses and implies that quite rich dynamic behaviour may be derived even within simple models. Before turning to the empirical evidence on floating exchange rates I wish to indicate how the simple model in which I embedded Rational Expectations might be extended. The reader may feel uneasy that the current account plays such a limited role in the above analysis. Given the assumption that international assets are perfect substitutes, the only role for the current account is to affect the demand for output and hence the inflation rate, which feeds through the price level to real money balances and hence the interest rates which directly determine spot exchange rates.

A number of authors, particularly Branson (1977) and his subsequent collaborators Branson and Halttunen (1978), Branson, Halttunen and Masson (1977), have examined the implications of relaxing the assumption that international assets are perfect substitutes. Given the discussion of Sections 8.2 and 8.3, one might also expect participants in international bond markets to display risk aversion. Asset demands are then less than perfectly elastic with respect to the expected real return whose equilibrium value now depends partly on relative asset supplies. A current account surplus must be matched by a capital account deficit if exchange rates float freely. By increasing the supply of foreign assets held in the portfolios of domestic residents, a current account surplus will alter the expected real return on those assets and hence the equilibrium spot exchange rate. Such portfolio balance models still place the determination of floating exchange rates within an asset market equilibrium approach and will still exhibit the dynamic behaviour which characterises Efficient asset markets under Rational Expectations, even though the current account plays a more direct role in exchange rate determination. However, such models are more complicated than models making the simpler assumption that international assets are perfect substitutes, so the elaboration of this approach remains a challenging research problem.

A second class of extensions to the basic perfect substitutes model develops the role of wealth in the analysis. Wealth effects may be admitted either in goods demand or in asset demand. Current account imbalances imply net transfers of wealth between countries and these have two implications. In the short run, these transfers provide a mechanism by which the current account changes wealth and hence the equilibrium interest rates which directly determine spot exchange rates in asset market models of exchange rate determination, a mechanism which operates whether or not international assets are perfect substitutes. However, the longer-run implications must also be studied. Dornbusch (1980b) and Dornbusch and Fischer (1980) point out that the model analysed earlier in this section treats long-run real competitiveness only as a determinant of goods market clearing; there is no independent requirement that the current account balances in the steady state. A model which allows perpetual wealth transfers may not be very appealing. By modelling the endogenous transfer of wealth between countries and providing a mechanism by which this feeds back to the domestic equilibrium through wealth effects on demand, these new models allow a definition of the steady state in which both the domestic goods market and the current account are in balance. Dornbusch and Fischer show that simple models of this type are quite tractable, deriving phase diagrams in which previously unanticipated shocks, whether from policy or exogenous events, can be analysed under Rational Expectations.

I now summarise the discussion of this section before proceeding to the empirical evidence. Current Account

Monetarist models of floating exchange rates use money demand equations to predict relative goods prices from which nominal exchange rates may be inferred if Purchasing Power Parity obtains. In our subsequent terminology, we might say that this requires goods market efficiency when international commodities are perfect substitutes. Models of this type suggest a Natural Rate of real competitiveness and are essentially an extension of previous Natural Rate models to the open economy. The capital account of the balance of payments is usually ignored.

By contrast, asset market theories of exchange rate determination emphasise stock equilibrium in the market for international assets. While the exchange rate which secures this equilibrium has implications for competitiveness and the current account, the current account does not directly determine the equilibrium condition for foreign exchange. If international assets are perfect substitutes, expected real returns must be equated across countries and these returns include the expected capital gain or loss in the value of the currency over the holding period. A known positive interest differential is thus associated with a depreciating currency, though unanticipated rises in interest rates will be associated with unanticipated appreciation of the currency. Unless the goods market clears as quickly as the markets for bonds and foreign exchange, the economy will follow the unique convergent path to the Saddlepoint equilibrium, a path along which output is not generally at its steady state or Natural Rate. Changes in real competitiveness then become an important channel of monetary policy in the short and medium term, even though such effects eventually die out as the economy converges to the steady state.

The current account may be assigned various indirect roles in determining the level of exchange rates. If international assets are perfect substitutes and wealth effects are ignored, the only role for the current account is to influence goods market clearing, but relaxation of either assumption allows a more extensive though still indirect role. Notice finally that if the assumption of perfect substitutes is correct, intervention by central banks to buy or sell foreign exchange will have no direct effect on exchange rates, since asset demands are perfectly elastic at the required expected rate of return; only if intervention is thought to convey new information about the future path of interest rates and future money supply targets will such a policy be successful.

8.5 Empirical Evidence on Floating Exchange Rates

I begin with a brief review of the direct evidence of Purchasing Power Parity. Frenkel (1976)(1978)(1980c)(1981), Dornbusch (1978), Krugman (1978) and many other authors test a stochastic version of equation (8.4.2)

$$s_t = \alpha_0 + \alpha_1 (p_t - p_t^*) + u_t \qquad (8.5.1)$$

where u_t is a random disturbance. The weak version of PPP is taken to imply that the estimate of α_1 should equal unity; the strong version implies in addition that α_0 equals zero. If this model completely describes the short-run evolution of exchange rates, the random disturbance u_t should have mean zero and be serially uncorrelated.

Authors frequently use data from two distinct periods, the 1920s and the 1970s. The earlier period of floating exchange rates is of interest because it is a period of very large nominal shocks — Germany experienced a hyperinflation, while prices actually fell in the UK. If PPP does not adequately explain exchange rate changes when nominal variables are so volatile, it is unlikely to explain exchange rates during any other period. Krugman (1978) provides the earliest careful discussion of econometric issues and his results have been confirmed by subsequent studies. Estimates of α_0 are close to zero and estimates of α_1 are roughly unity, although some discrepancies occur. However, the behaviour of the unexplained part u_t is not favourable to the PPP hypothesis. An estimate of this unobservable variable may be obtained by evaluating $(s_t - \alpha_0 - \alpha_1 (p_t - p_t^*))$ at the estimated values of α_0 and α_1. Instead of behaving in a purely random manner, these residuals suggest that u_t obeys the relation

$$u_t = \rho u_{t-1} + v_t$$

where v_t is purely random and the positive constant ρ is only slightly less than unity. For example, taking the value for ρ

to be 0.9, 90% of any unexplained deviation u_t from PPP at time t persists at time $t+1$, 81% still persists at time $t+2$, 73% at time $t+2$, and so on. Deviations from short-run PPP are therefore much too important to be ignored.

The asset market models studied in the previous section are interesting because they predict long run PPP in the absence of any real shocks, but explain why exchange rates depart from short-run PPP as interest rates fail to keep pace exactly with inflation. To investigate this possibility, Frankel (1979a) extends the previous analysis by Dornbusch (1976a) which translates the phase diagram analysis of equation (8.4.4) into algebraic equations which can be fitted to the data.

Frankel assumes the perfect substitutes model of the previous section, but treats the domestic and foreign countries symmetrically: to pretend that foreign variables are exogenous is a legitimate theoretical simplification but not a promising basis for empirical work. In the Appendix to this chapter I give a formal derivation of the Perfect Foresight solution which has the property

$$\dot{s}_t - \dot{p}_t + \dot{p}_t^* = \lambda[(s_t - p_t + p_t^*) - \alpha_0] \qquad \lambda < 0 \quad (8.5.2)$$

where α_0 is the steady state level of real competitiveness $(s - p + p^*)$ and λ is a negative parameter determining the rate of convergence to the steady state and whose value may be derived from underlying parameters of the model. For example, when ϕ is infinite and goods market clearing instantaneous, the implied value of λ is minus infinity. From equation (8.5.2), this implies that the level of real competitiveness must never deviate from its steady state level if explosive behaviour is to be avoided. Conversely, maintaining the earlier assumption that ϕ is finite and goods market clearing sluggish, a finite negative value of λ is implied.

Using equation (8.5.2), equation (8.4.9) which describes asset market equilibrium, the LM equation (8.4.3) and a similar equation for the foreign country, we obtain

$$s_t = \alpha_0 + (m_t - m_t^*) - \gamma_1(y_t - y_t^*) +$$

$$(\frac{\gamma_2 \lambda + 1}{\lambda})(r_t - r_t^*) - (\frac{1}{\lambda})(\dot{p}_t - \dot{p}_t^*) + u_t \qquad (8.5.3)$$

where I include a random term u_t to capture elements of exchange rate determination not described by the theory. Thus the model implies a unit coefficient on relative money supplies $(m_t - m_t^*)$ in the domestic and foreign countries, a negative coefficient on relative output $(y_t - y_t^*)$, a coefficient of ambiguous sign on short-term interest rates $(r_t - r_t^*)$ and a positive coefficient on relative inflation rates $(\dot{p}_t - \dot{p}_t^*)$. This general specification includes the special case in which λ is minus infinity and goods market clearing instantaneous, in which case the model may be written

$$s_t = \alpha_0 + (m_t - m_t^*) - \gamma_1 (y_t - y_t^*) + \gamma_2 (r_t - r_t^*) + u_t$$
$$(8.5.4)$$

which is precisely the equation implied by the Current Account Monetarist model of exchange rate determination discussed in the previous section. Hence, equation (8.5.3) not only allows us to implement empirically the asset model of the previous section it also allows us to test the alternative hypothesis of Current Account Monetarism. Indeed, equation (8.5.3) also provides empirical evidence on the issue of goods market clearing discussed in Chapter 6.

Although equation (8.5.3) is derived under the simplifying assumption of Perfect Foresight, we intend this analysis to apply in a random world in which individuals form Rational Expectations. At time t, the one period interest rates r_t and r_t^* are known, but the relevant inflation rate over the coming period cannot yet be known with certainty. Frankel uses long bond yields as a proxy for current inflation expectations.[2] Thus the final deterministic term in equation (8.5.3) is not

2. Since long bond yields are an imperfect proxy for expected inflation, Frankel recognises the technical econometric problem caused by 'errors in variables' and uses instrumental variables to estimate the equation. He does not recognise the endogeneity of current money stocks and short-term interest rates, so his estimates are nevertheless suspect. Dornbusch (1978) obtains broadly similar estimates, even when the estimation takes account of these difficulties, but Dornbusch (1980b) obtains much less satisfactory results. Frankel (1980) also reports less satisfactory results.

Table 8.5.1

Exchange Rate	α_0	Coefficient on:			
		$(m_t - m_t^*)$	$(y_t - y_t^*)$	$(r_t - r_t^*)$	$(R_t - R_t^*)$
Deutsche Mark/Dollar	1.39	0.97	−0.52	−5.40	29.40

$(\dot{p}_t - \dot{p}_t^*)$ but $(R_t - R_t^*)$, where R_t and R_t^* denote domestic and foreign yields on long bonds at time t. Using monthly observations for July 1974—February 1978, Frankel examines the relation between the Deutsche Mark/Dollar exchange rate and the relevant variables in equation (8.5.3). His estimates are reported in Table 8.5.1.

As predicted, the estimate of the coefficient on relative money supplies is very close to unity and the coefficient on relative output is negative. Of more importance, the coefficient on short-term interest rates has a sign which is negative and significantly different from zero and the coefficient on bond yield is significantly positive. Neither result is compatible with equation (8.5.4), but both are consistent with equation (8.5.3) and suggest that goods market clearing is far from rapid. The empirical evidence thus supports the view that convergence to the steady state is only sluggish and that the analysis of Section 8.4 provides an important explanation for short-term deviations from Purchasing Power Parity.

Nevertheless, the simple model does not provide a complete solution to the problem of explaining exchange rate movements in the short run. Using the estimated coefficients to calculate the residuals which estimate u_t, the unexplained component of exchange rate movements, Frankel shows that these residuals may be fitted by the model

$$u_t = 0.46\, u_{t-1} + v_t$$

where v_t has mean zero and is serially uncorrelated. The serial correlation of u_t is much lower than the estimates obtained in the simple PPP models discussed earlier, but there is still a tendency for unexplained shocks at time t to have effects which persist for many periods. A yet more general model is required.

One possibility is to attempt to model real shocks which alter the steady state level of competitiveness α_0, for example by modelling the effect of changes in oil prices or oil reserves. A second possibility lies in modelling the risk premia which arise once the assumption that international assets are perfect substitutes is relaxed. A first step is to test empirically the assumption that assets are perfect substitutes and it is to this question that I now turn.

In Section 8.4 I argued that the joint assumptions of perfect substitutes and Rational Expectations imply that *ex post* returns on domestic and foreign assets should differ only because of forecasting errors reflecting information which cannot be anticipated at the date individuals make portfolio decisions. Rearranging equation (8.4.5)

$$s_t - s_{t-1} - r_{t-1} + r^*_{t-1} = \eta_t \tag{8.5.5}$$

where η_t is a serially uncorrelated random disturbance with mean zero which should be uncorrelated with any information available at time $t-1$ when one period portfolio decisions were made. A research strategy might involve adding to the right hand side of equation (8.5.5) variables known at time $t-1$, estimating equation (8.5.5) in this augmented form, and testing whether the coefficients on these additional variables are zero. Confirmation of this prediction would support both the assumption of Rational Expectations and the hypothesis of perfect substitutes. Rejection of this prediction would imply the failure of at least one of the joint hypotheses, though researchers have often exercised the *a priori* judgment that such a failure is more plausibly interpreted as evidence in favour of a risk premium than evidence against Rational Expectations.

Frankel (1979c) reports that in over one hundred attempts to implement this strategy using quarterly data for the USA and West Germany, he did not find a single specification in which the additional variables had coefficients which differed significantly from zero in the direction implied by the portfolio balance model of imperfect substitutability. This striking result has not been confirmed by other authors. Hacche and Townend (1981) using monthly data for the effective exchange rate of the Pound Sterling between June 1972 and February

1980 find significant coefficients on the variables $(s_{t-2} - s_{t-3})$ and Domestic Credit Expansion at time $t-1$.

Cumby and Obstfeld (1980) show that it is possible to take a sophisticated extrapolation of past values of $(s_t - s_{t-1} - r_{t-1} + r^*_{t-1})$ knowable at time $t-1$ and systematically predict part of the random variable η_t, reinforcing the earlier evidence of serial correlation of this disturbance. Using weekly data from July 5 1974 to June 27 1978, Cumby and Obstfeld find that their extrapolation of the previous sixteen weeks significantly contributes to explaining the deviation η_t for all six currencies they study — the US Dollar exchange rate against the Canadian Dollar, French Franc, Dutch Guilder, Swiss Franc, Deutsche Mark and Pound Sterling.

Hooper and Morton (1980) argue that the explanation for this serial correlation should be sought in a variable risk premium and in the possibility that individuals at time t may revise their estimate of the steady state real exchange rate as new information about real shocks becomes available. They add two variables to the right hand side of equation (8.5.3). First, to capture changing views about the steady state they use an extrapolation of past unanticipated components of the current account, arguing that the new information in any one set of figures is likely to be small, but that cumulatively such data allows us to model changing perceptions of the steady state. Having estimated the systematic dependence of the net current account position on information previously available, they use the residuals from the estimated equation to proxy unanticipated components of the current account. Secondly, they model the portfolio balance emphasis on changing asset supplies by cumulating past values of $(CB_t + I_t)$, the sum of the net current balance and official intervention as reflected by changes in foreign exchange reserves.

This augmented version of equation (8.5.3) is estimated using quarterly data for the US Dollar against other currencies from 1973 I to 1978 IV. Hooper and Morton find that the proxy for changing perceptions of the steady state real exchange rate has a significant coefficient of the expected sign, but that the proxy for the varying risk premium is insignificantly different from zero when the equation is estimated by the appropriate econometric technique of instrumental variables. Moreover, the residuals from this augmented equation no longer display the serial correlation found in the earlier work of Frankel (1979a) and Dornbusch (1978).

To summarise the empirical evidence of this section, the data does not provide strong support for Purchasing Power Parity in the 1970s, either when this hypothesis is tested directly, or when it is incorporated within Current Account Monetarism. A more promising approach is based on the role of exchange rates in clearing international asset markets.

If international assets are perfect substitutes, changes in the value of the currency should deviate only randomly from the interest rate differential if expectations are Rational. Direct tests of this proposition find that it is broadly supported by the data, but that more sophisticated empirical analysis is capable of establishing some departures from this rule of thumb. Where these tests are directly based on equation (8.5.5) rather than equation (8.5.3), a rejection of the theoretical prediction must be attributed to a violation either of the assumption of Rational Expectations, or of the assumption of perfect substitutes. Given the discussion of earlier sections of this chapter, the existence of a risk premium seems quite plausible, so proponents of Rational Expectations need not be unduly disturbed about these results. The empirical research does indicate that it is quite hard to pin down these risk premia but that they are quantitatively small, in which case theoretical results based on the simpler assumption of perfect substitutes may not be too misleading.

Empirical studies on the effects of real shocks remain scanty, although these may be of some importance as the analysis of Section 8.4 demonstrates. Hooper and Morton's study suggests that further work in this area may prove fruitful and may resolve the puzzle remaining in empirical work based on equation (8.5.3). Indirect evidence in favour of this position is also provided in Hacche and Townend (1981) who find that changes in oil prices have important effects on the Pound Sterling.

(**) Mathematical Appendix: Explicit Solution to the Frankel Model under Perfect Foresight

For notational convenience I use e_t to denote $(s_t - p_t + p_t^*)$ and rm_t to denote relative real money stocks $(m_t - p_t - m_t^* + p_t^*)$. Since variables are measured in logarithms, e_t denotes the level of real competitiveness of the domestic country and $(-e_t)$ denotes the real competitiveness of the foreign country. If $\theta*$ is the rate of foreign nominal money growth, corresponding to equation (8.4.8) we have

$$\dot{p}_t^* = \phi[h(-e_t) - y^*] + \theta*$$

Subtracting this equation from equation (8.4.8) we obtain

$$\phi(2he_t - y + y^*) = (\dot{p}_t - \theta) - (\dot{p}_t^* - \theta^*) = -\dot{rm}_t$$
$$(8.5.6)$$

Using equation (8.4.9) and the definition of e_t

$$\dot{e}_t = \dot{s}_t - (\dot{p}_t - \dot{p}_t^*) = (r_t - r_t^*) - \phi(2he_t - y + y^*)$$
$$- (\theta - \theta^*) \qquad (8.5.7)$$

From the domestic LM equation (8.4.3) and the analogous equation for the foreign country

$$r_t - r_t^* = \frac{rm_t - \gamma_1(y - y^*)}{-\gamma_2}$$

Substituting into equation (8.5.7) we obtain

$$\dot{e}_t = (-1/\gamma_2)\, rm_t - 2h\phi\, e_t$$
$$+ [\theta^* - \theta + (\phi + \gamma_1/\gamma_2)(y - y^*)] \qquad (8.5.8)$$

Letting $\bar{e}$ and $\bar{rm}$ denote the steady state values of these variables, equations (8.5.6) and (8.5.8) may be rewritten

$$\dot{rm}_t = -2h\phi\,(e_t - \bar{e})$$
$$\dot{e}_t = (-1/\gamma_2)(rm_t - \bar{rm}) - 2h\phi(e_t - \bar{e})$$

or, in matrix notation,

$$\begin{bmatrix} \dot{rm}_t \\ \dot{e}_t \end{bmatrix} = \begin{bmatrix} 0 & -2h\phi \\ (-1/\gamma_2) & -2h\phi \end{bmatrix} \begin{bmatrix} rm_t - \bar{rm} \\ e_t - \bar{e} \end{bmatrix} \qquad (8.5.9)$$

Applying the result given in equation (3.2.3) in the Mathematical Digression in Section 3.2, we wish to solve for the eigenvalues λ of the coefficient matrix in equation (8.5.9), verify that only one eigenvalue is negative, and select this negative eigenvalue as the solution to the simple first order differential equation system (8.5.9). These eigenvalues solve the characteristic equation

$$\lambda^2 + 2h\phi\lambda - 2h\phi/\gamma_2 = 0$$

whence

$$\lambda = -h\phi \left\{ 1 \pm \sqrt{(1 + \frac{1}{\gamma_2})} \right\}$$

confirming that the two eigenvalues have opposite sign. The stable root relevant to the unique convergent path is the negative root

$$\lambda = -h\phi \left\{ 1 + \sqrt{(1 + \frac{1}{\gamma_2})} \right\} \qquad (8.5.10)$$

and the unique convergent path, following the discussion in Section 3.2, then satisfies

$$\dot{rm}_t = \lambda(rm_t - \overline{rm}) \qquad (8.5.11)$$

$$\dot{e}_t = \lambda(e_t - \bar{e})$$

as asserted in the text in equation (8.5.2). Equation (8.5.10) also makes clear the dependence of λ on the underlying structural parameters as pointed out in the text.

Notes on the Literature

Fama (1970) provides a clear introduction to the literature on Efficient Markets and also surveys much of the early evidence. Fama (1976a) provides an introduction to portfolio theory. Grossman and Stiglitz (1980) emphasise the process by which new information is reflected in asset prices and the bibliography at the end of their paper is a useful reference list of articles questioning the most literal interpretation of Efficient Markets.

The Term Structure of interest rates has been studied by many authors. Prior to Rational Expectations, these include Meiselman (1962), Kessel (1965), Malkiel (1966), Modigliani and Sutch (1966)(1967), Masera (1972), and Burman and White (1972). The Rational Expectations approach is followed in Sargent (1972) (1979), Modigliani and Shiller (1973), Shiller (1979), and Mishkin (1978a). Friedman (1980) argues that survey evidence on interest rate expectations of bond market participants violates Rational Expectations, a conclusion challenged in Mishkin (1981a).

Authors studying the Efficiency of the forward market for foreign exchange include Frenkel (1977) (1979) (1980a) (1980c), Clements and Frenkel (1980), and Hansen and Hodrick (1980). Levich (1978) (1979) surveys much of this literature.

Floating exchange rates are extensively discussed in the textbook by Dornbusch (1980a). Dornbusch (1978) (1980b) and Frenkel (1980c) provide very useful summaries of the literature. The Monetary Approach to exchange rate determination is well presented by the selection of papers in the *Scandinavian Journal of Economics*, 78, No 2 (1976), and in Frenkel and Johnson (1978). The analysis of Section 8.4 draws most heavily on Dornbusch (1976a), Frankel (1979a), Eastwood and Venables (1980), and Buiter and Miller (1981). Wealth effects and current account extensions of the asset market model are studied in Dornbusch and Fischer (1980), and Hooper and Morton (1980). The Portfolio Balance approach owes much to Branson (1977), Branson, Halttunen and Masson (1977), and Branson and Halttunen (1978), but has also been studied by Dornbusch (1975) (1980b), Dooley and Isard (1979), and Kouri and de Macedo (1978).

If international capital is almost perfectly mobile, interventions by central banks to buy and sell currency in exchange for foreign exchange reserves will have little effect, since asset demands are almost perfectly elastic. Tobin (1978) proposes a tax on capital movements to allow domestic governments to pursue independent monetary policies without having to fear the international repercussions on exchange rates. This idea is taken up in Liviatan (1979), Dornbusch (1980b), and Buiter and Miller (1981).

9
Conclusions

In this book I have aimed to provide a comprehensive introduction to macroeconomic analysis under Rational Expectations. Macroeconomics must confront the real world, an uncertain world in which the dynamic implications of intertemporal decisions can be studied only when the process of expectations formation has been made explicit. In Chapter 2 I explained the shortcomings of previous attempts to treat this issue. In Chapters 3–5 I set out the Rational Expectations approach to theoretical and empirical macroeconomic analysis. Some readers may have wondered why specific applications were not discussed until Chapter 6. It is important to establish that these applications are not an *ad hoc* collection of research papers, but represent a coherent programme designed to elaborate and test the key ideas of Chapters 3–5. The prior discussion of more abstract issues thus has two advantages: it encourages the view that the analysis of Chapters 6–8 has a clear and consistent foundation, and it allows the reader to form a judgment about the wide applicability of the approach. In choosing the material to be covered in Chapters 6–8 I have necessarily had to be selective. The analysis of Chapters 3 and 4 should provide the reader with sufficient introduction to follow the original literature in areas which I have not had the space to discuss.

Section 9.1 summarises the argument of previous chapters. Section 9.2 offers an assessment of the Rational Expectations approach to macroeconomics. Finally, the implications for future research are discussed in Section 9.3.

253

9.1 Summary of the Preceding Chapters

In Chapter 2 I argued that Keynes recognised the importance of views about the future as determinants of current behaviour, foresaw many difficulties in the attempt to construct a theory of endogenous expectations formation, and therefore preferred to sidestep the issue by supposing that expectations were given but capable of exogenous shifts. The Adaptive Expectations hypothesis provided an operational theory of expectations revision and was used for many years by theoretical and empirical macroeconomists. Not only did this hypothesis offer no theory for the precise nature of the extrapolation it supposed, but it also had the disturbing implication that individuals would continue to use the same expectations rule when its past performance had been unsatisfactory. The Adaptive Expectations hypothesis does not rule out persistent forecasting errors which could have been perceived at the date expectations were formed.

The Rational Expectations hypothesis rules out systematic forecasting errors. In Chapter 3 I developed the formal structure of a dynamic model with Rational Expectations. To illustrate the forward looking solution procedure I first considered the simpler case of Perfect Foresight. A diagrammatic analysis was used to emphasise the importance of the Saddlepoint property without which a unique solution cannot be established. Equivalent mathematical derivations of the solution were given, for continuous time in the Mathematical Digression in Section 3.2, and for discrete time in Sections 3.3 and 5.1. The extension to linear stochastic models is conceptually straightforward; future variables are replaced by their expectations conditional on information currently available.

Section 3.4 considered possible objections to the Rational Expectations hypothesis. It is not necessary that all individuals explicitly perform the forward solution calculation, nor even that they understand the model itself. Rational Expectations may be given an 'as if' interpretation, a device which is useful to economists who wish to model the behaviour of individuals whose forecasts are on average correct. In any case, the predictions of professional economists are available to the public.

Other objections should be viewed not as criticisms of the approach but merely of the degree of sophistication of early efforts to explore that approach. For example, Rational Expectations analysis may easily be extended to models in which individuals have access to different information because they are faced with different costs of acquiring information. Thus many criticisms refer to the simplicity of the models in which Rational Expectations has so far been embedded. The objections which I take to have the most force will be discussed in Section 9.2.

Chapter 4 developed the foundations for empirical research on models with Rational Expectations. The fundamental properties of these models were set out. Two properties have formed the basis of much empirical investigation. *Ex post* forecasting errors should be uncorrelated with any information available at the date expectations were formed, and individuals at time t should not be able to predict how expectations of a variable y_{t+i} conditional on information available at some intermediate date will differ from the expectations of y_{t+i} given information currently available at time t. These properties are testable. However, the complete set of structural parameters can be estimated only if these parameters are statistically identified. This need not be the case. Identification problems were illustrated using simple examples. Rational Expectations are formed by extrapolating the past in the particular way which the model suggests is relevant. Any change in the structure of the model will alter the nature of the extrapolation and it is the great merit of Rational Expectations that it tells us exactly how these amendments should be undertaken. The previous failure of economists to appreciate this forms the basis of Lucas' criticism of policy evaluation. In practice, the new solution can be recomputed only if we have prior estimates of all the structural parameters of the model. When these are not fully identified it will not be possible to avoid completely the Lucas Problem.

In Chapter 5 I discussed the extension of conventional econometric theory to recognise the implications of Rational Expectations in dynamic models. Section 5.1 presented a general statement of the solution to a Rational Expectations model, emphasising once more the conditions implicit in the

Saddlepoint property. Section 5.2 presented a formal treatment of identification. This differed in two respects from the usual discussion of static simultaneous equation models: Rational Expectations at time t are statistically predetermined but not observable; and the Rational Expectations solution imposes a large number of cross equation restrictions on observable equations, a possibility recognised but not emphasised in the usual discussion of static models. Limited Information estimation was extensively discussed, since it forms the basis of much of the empirical work studied in Chapters 6–8. However, I argued that Full Information estimation would yield more useful evidence, since it exploits the cross equation restrictions which the theory implies. Similarly, empirical research frequently estimates equations which are at least partial reduced forms, but future research should concentrate on estimation of structural parameters. Tests of the Rational Expectations hypothesis were also discussed. It is straightforward to test the fundamental properties of Section 4.1, but more powerful tests may be derived by examining in addition the cross equation restrictions.

Chapter 6 examined the voluminous literature on the effectiveness of systematic stabilisation policy in Rational Expectations models. In classical models with continuous market clearing, anticipatable stabilisation policy can cause real variables to deviate from their Natural Rates only if the government has an informational advantage. However, except under very restrictive assumptions, systematic policy may gradually change the Natural Rates themselves. Market clearing should not be taken for granted. It is possible to specify models, and provide them with plausible microfoundations, which allow involuntary unemployment and other disequilibrium phenomena. Systematic stabilisation will then be effective, even if expectations are Rational. Although Rational Expectations analysis was pioneered in classical models with market clearing, the two assumptions should be distinguished. Empirically, fluctuations in output do not depend very strongly on current forecasting errors, but the cumulative effect of past errors may be important. The evidence is compatible with this model but also with more

Keynesian models. As yet, we have no convincing way of distinguishing them empirically.

Chapter 7 reconsidered the specification of consumption and investment functions under Rational Expectations. Under the strongest version of the Permanent Income hypothesis, consumption follows a Random Walk because all information previously available has already been reflected in past consumption. Only new information leads to revisions in Permanent Income. The data shows that consumption is approximately, but not exactly, a Random Walk, but this may be evidence against the simple Permanent Income hypothesis rather than evidence against Rational Expectations. Dynamic investment adjustment lends itself to Rational Expectations analysis and the phase diagram approach was used to suggest that interesting dynamics may be derived even within very simple models. Preliminary empirical work suggests that this approach should be developed further. The analysis of consumption and investment functions under Rational Expectations suggests that conventional descriptions of these functions will be very vulnerable to Lucas' criticism about policy analysis.

Chapter 8 examined the Efficient Market hypothesis in which Rational Expectations of future asset returns are assumed to be fully reflected in current asset prices. It was shown that asset prices should follow a Random Walk: only new information changes asset prices. A large number of empirical studies confirm this proposition, but the tests to which they subject the hypothesis are not always very powerful. There is also some evidence that the assumption of risk neutrality cannot be pushed too far: if risk premia do exist it is important that they be modelled, since changes in these premia over time would destroy the Random Walk prediction even where markets were Efficient. Section 8.3 extended this analysis to the forward market for foreign exchange. Apart from the variation in risk premia, current forward rates should differ only randomly from future spot rates. This prediction was broadly confirmed by empirical studies.

Analysis of floating exchange rates no longer emphasises goods market considerations. Purchasing Power Parity does not seem supported by the empirical evidence. Asset market models regard .the exchange rate as clearing international asset markets in which expectations of exchange rate changes form an important component of capital gain calculations. The Random Walk model applies only when international interest rates are identical; otherwise, exchange rates should be expected to change to produce capital gains or losses to offset interest differentials. Again, one would expect risk premia to complicate the analysis, although empirical specifications have not been very successful in modelling this phenomenon. Current account movements may enter this analysis through several channels: effects on the steady state exchange rate from which the Rational Expectations solution is derived; wealth effects induced by international asset transfers; or effects induced by changing the relative supplies of international assets which are imperfect substitutes. Empirical work in this area looks promising, but is not yet conclusive.

9.2 A Final Assessment

I have argued that one challenge Keynes left his successors was the elaboration of a theory of endogenous expectations formation. Although recognising the importance of such a theory, Keynes repeatedly argues that economics may have little to say about the process of expectations revision, a belief which seems to have been derived from his experience as an active investor in financial markets. Before evaluating the extent to which the Rational Expectations hypothesis meets his challenge, it is interesting to reflect that Keynes may have confused the possibility of modelling expectations with the possibility of modelling changes in expectations. Rational Expectations provides a neat solution to Keynes' dilemma by explaining the current level of expectations while simultaneously maintaining that revisions in expectations cannot be currently foreseen. A specific application of this general principle is the Random Walk model of asset pricing. Provided we interpret Keynes' 'given state of expectation' to mean the current assessment of the Rational Expectations path over the future, there is nothing in the treatment of expectations in the *General Theory* which could not be recast explicitly as Rational Expectations. This argument is developed in Begg (1982).

I turn now to an assessment of the Rational Expectations approach itself, and I begin with the plausibility of the hypothesis. In Chapter 3 I argued that the great strength of the hypothesis is that it is not *ad hoc*, but is based instead on the sound optimising principle that individuals do the best they can. I showed how many common objections to the approach can be countered. There are two objections which are less easily met. The first relates to the problem of uniqueness. If Rational Expectations models cannot guarantee to deliver unique solutions, can they provide a useful framework for macroeconomic analysis? In Chapter 3, I offered a limited riposte: the models of Chapters 6–8 suggest that there are many applications in which uniqueness may be established. I now wish to give a more general reply. If the real world is not characterised by expectational confusions, then it is legitimate to argue that the Rational Expectations approach is somehow deficient in failing to replicate the real world. However, the truth may be different. If the world is truly characterised by expectational confusions, it cannot be a criticism of Rational Expectations that it draws attention to this reality. Rather than adopt convenient expectations assumptions which erroneously deliver unique solutions to economic models, it is preferable that we understand the source of this confusion. For example, the simple macroeconomic model of Section 3.2 allows a unique equilibrium under a money supply rule, but not under an interest rate rule. The Saddlepoint property depends on the underlying economic structure of which policy rules form an important component. By understanding the source of the uniqueness problem we may be able to design policies which avoid the problem. If individuals do care about uncertainty itself, we could reasonably claim that Rational Expectations analysis might lead to better policies.

The second criticism which I take seriously relates to the problem of identification. Unless the structural parameters of the model can be disentangled from economic data, economists cannot implement the Rational Expectations solution procedure. Even if we adopt the 'as if' interpretation of Rational Expectations, so that individuals are not themselves required to undertake this process, the presumption that individuals on average guess correctly must be considerably weakened. Moreover, the problem is not static. Even if the parameters of the model can in principle be disentangled from a sufficiently long data sample, individuals may have begun from an incorrect view of the true model, forming mistaken expectations which, by affecting their current actions, contaminate the data from which they seek to discover more about the underlying structure. Changes in policy rule, by altering that structure, complicate this problem still further.

It is not yet possible to say whether all these difficulties can be overcome. The principle that individuals do not make perceivable errors in forecasting the future is sufficiently attractive that it will form the basis of research for some time to come. The process by which individuals learn is discussed more fully in the next section. It is not essential to assume that individuals know, or act as if they know, the full structure of the underlying model. That is a convenient assumption with which to begin the analysis of endogenous expectations formation, but the approach can be and will be extended.

The Rational Expectations approach has yet to be fully developed, but I suggest that we are now concentrating on the right issues. If anyone seriously disputes this, let them recall the previous treatment of expectations and indeed of all intertemporal considerations in macroeconomics, and let them propose an alternative research strategy. The Rational Expectations approach will be extended to model learning which is imperfect, because the world is random and information collection is costly. Nevertheless, models are intended as simplifications and strong assumptions may allow useful rules of thumb. In Chapters 6–8 we have seen that simple versions of the Rational Expectations hypothesis may be applied to simple models of the underlying economic structure to derive interesting results which should be taken seriously.

The idea that policy changes may induce revision of individuals' behaviour dates back to Marschak (1953). In the light of recent research discussed in Chapter 6, the stabilisation analysis of the 1950s and 1960s now seems rather sterile. Rational Expectations analysis has changed forever the debate about economic policy. It is unfortunate that Rational Expectations is popularly confused with the Natural Rate models in which it has often been embedded. The latter should be assessed in their own right and no reader should neglect the collected papers of Lucas (1981). Once it is agreed that Rational Expectations, or some appropriate generalisation of this hypothesis, provides the correct framework for dynamic macroeconomics, the debate about stabilisation policy can return to the central issue — whether or not markets clear — without being vulnerable to the elementary criticisms raised by Lucas, Sargent and Wallace, and others. Macroeconomic analysis of stabilisation policy should recognise that private sector expectations are endogenous and depend on the private sector's perception of the government policies in operation.

The new analysis of consumption and investment behaviour provides a striking example of what I have called the Lucas Problem. This insight is more important than the specific results which have been derived in simple models. The interesting dynamic behaviour which even those models allow is sufficient incentive to undertake an extended programme of research, both to capture more accurately the constraints which intertemporal decision makers actually face and to model more realistically the information they can acquire when forming expectations. However this research progresses, the Lucas insight will remain. It has changed forever the way we think about dynamic macroeconomics.

The analysis of asset markets has proved a particularly fruitful area for research for two reasons. First, the market clearing paradigm is readily accepted so that the framework is reasonably robust. Secondly, the relevant data is usually reliable and is available almost continuously. Empirical investigation of the Rational Expectations hypothesis has accordingly been most extensive in this area. I repeat an earlier conclusion. if proponents of Rational Expectations had been forced to make a Faustian pact with the devil before seeing any of the evidence, I believe they would happily have settled for the empirical research which has subsequently been undertaken. It is hard to discover obvious profitable opportunities for speculation. This may seem an astounding conclusion, but it is only recently that economists have begun to realise the implications for the analysis of bond and foreign exchange markets. As in the stabilisation debate, an important part of the Rational Expectations revolution has now been accomplished; economists can revert to the study of more difficult problems such as the modelling of risk.

9.3 Suggestions for Future Research

In my view, the Rational Expectations approach is now firmly established. It is no longer a postscript to be appended to conventional discussions of stabilisation policy or asset market behaviour, but part of the methodology of macroeconomics. Several problems remain, but the preceding discussion offers many hints about a possible way forward. The full richness of the approach has yet to be exploited. In this final section, I outline a programme for further research. The four areas I consider are: the elaboration of the process of information collection and expectations revision; the development of more sophisticated dynamic structures in which to embed the expectations assumption; the implications for econometric methodology; and the consequences for macroeconometric modelling and policy analysis.

Muth's definition of Rational Expectations requires individuals to know the relevant economic model and use it to form expectations. Given the simplicity of the models with which economists typically work, this may not be a convincing account of the expectations individuals actually form. I have argued that the Rational Expectations approach should be interpreted more generally. The process by which information is acquired should be studied so that the analysis may extend the basic principle that individuals do not remain satisfied with rules which generate perceivable errors. Until this process has been modelled explicitly, it cannot be said that Rational Expectations are rational in the usual sense of conforming with individual optimisation. We do not yet know how much costly information it is optimal to acquire. In this book, I have chiefly discussed a paradigm in which we pretend that individuals act as if they already know the structure of the model we are analysing. However useful, that cannot be the end of the story. The research which I am advocating will yield a more plausible account of the process of expectations formation and enable us to study phenomena which at present we neglect. Diversity of expectations is one example: if expectations are unanimous, there will never be an incentive to trade in Efficient asset markets, since the price will always fully reflect the shared information. Even if risk neutral individuals form estimates only of the means of statistical distributions describing future random variables, a disaggregated model would then have to analyse the dispersion of different expectations according to the different information individuals were assumed to acquire. Even then, we have adopted a particularly simple view of the way in which the future impinges on the present. Individuals may care not just about the mean of future random variables, but also about other measures of their statistical distributions. The Rational Expectations approach can be extended to allow individuals to form estimates of other measures of these distributions, such as their variances. These extensions would destroy the simplicity of the Certainty–Equivalence results obtained in the models examined in this book. Stochastic models with Rational Expectations would then yield solutions which were different in structure from the solutions obtained under Perfect Foresight in the corresponding models with complete certainty. However, linearity is a necessary condition for Certainty–Equivalence, so these problems will have to be confronted in any case when the Rational Expectations hypothesis is extended to non-linear models. Whilst these extensions of the Rational Expectations approach may prove technically tricky, they are not conceptually difficult. We have rather a good idea of the direction future research must take if the first generation of Rational Expectations models is to be generalised.

It is also natural that initial research should have embedded the expectations hypothesis in models with a simple underlying structure. We must now pay some attention to the underlying economic structure itself. By emphasising the dangers of *ad hoc* expectations rules, the Rational Expectations approach has encouraged a more general reconsideration of the microfoundations of macroeconomics. Sargent (1981) considers one way in which intertemporal decisions may be more adequately modelled in a stochastic framework. I would expect to see more research of this kind. The analysis of the preceding chapters suggests two other examples of areas in which more research is required on the economic structure itself. More sophisticated disequilibrium Rational Expectations models should be analysed: there is nothing in the Rational Expectations approach which asserts that individuals may not realise that markets may not clear and form expectations accordingly. Similarly, the analysis of asset markets should embrace the results of portfolio theory more fully. The traditional questions of macroeconomics have partly been neglected in the initial phase of research, where a premium has been placed on deriving striking new results using the exciting new methodology.

Similar remarks apply to econometric analysis. Much of the early empirical literature uses Limited Information estimation on equations which collapse the full structure. Quasi reduced form equations may allow quick tests of certain implications of Rational Expectations, but it is the structural parameters which are of most economic interest. Since Rational Expectations imposes precise cross equation restrictions, these should be imposed *a priori* to obtain more efficient estimates and more powerful tests. As computer time becomes increasingly cheap and non-linear estimation procedures become more familiar, computational difficulties should not be allowed to deter econometricians from adopting the procedures which are most appropriate.

The most widely used macroeconometric models have taken years, even decades, to construct. It is one thing to write a new paper on some particular aspect of Rational Expectations, but quite another to re-specify and re-estimate a complete macroeconometric model. If progress has been slow in this area, it is understandable. On the other hand, it is by the output of such models that the economics profession is often judged by the public. Expectations cannot continue to be treated in an *ad hoc* manner which differs from equation to equation. Individual equations must be recast to reflect developments elsewhere in macroeconomics. The Lucas critique must be recognised. A forecast or simulation should involve a series of iterations, until the future evolution of the economy is consistent with the expectations it assumes. This sounds technically difficult, but it is now feasible. For example, Lipton, Poterba, Sachs and Summers (1980) show how to solve a non-linear model to determine the initial jump when a change in policy shifts the convergent path under Rational Expectations.

To paraphrase a politician whose foresight proved better than that of others with access to the same information, we have not reached the end of the Rational Expectations revolution in macroeconomics, nor yet the beginning of the end, but the developments I have discussed in this book may mark the end of the beginning.

Reference Bibliography

Abel, A.B. (1980) Empirical investment equations, in K. Brunner & A.H. Meltzer (eds), *On the State of Macro-Economics*, Supplement to the *Journal of Monetary Economics*.

Abel, A.B. (1979) *Investment and the Value of Capital*, Garland Publishing, New York.

Akerlof, G.A. (1969) Relative wages and the rate of inflation, *Quarterly Journal of Economics*, 83, pp. 353—74.

Akerlof, G.A. (1970) The market for lemons: qualitative uncertainty and the market mechanism, *Quarterly Journal of Economics*, 84, pp. 488—500.

Akerlof, G.A. (1979) The case against conservative macroeconomics, *Economica*, 46, pp. 219—38.

Alexander, S.S. (1961) Price movements in speculative markets: trends or random walks, *Industrial Management Review*, 2, pp. 7—26.

Almon, S. (1965) The distributed lag between capital appropriations and expenditures, *Econometrica*, 33, pp. 178—96.

Anderson, P.A. (1979) Rational expectations forecasts from 'Nonrational' models, *Journal of Monetary Economics*, 5, pp. 67—80.

Ando, A. and Modigliani, F. (1963) The life cycle hypothesis of saving: aggregate implications and tests, *American Economic Review*, 53, pp. 55—84.

Aoki, M. and Canzoneri, M. (1979) Reduced forms of rational expectations models, *Quarterly Journal of Economics*, 93, pp. 59—71.

Archibald, G.C. and Lipsey, R.G. (1958) Monetary and value theory: a critique of Lange and Patinkin, *Review of Economic Studies*, 26, pp. 1—22.

Arrow, K.J. (1978) The future and the present in economic life, *Economic Inquiry*, 16, pp. 157—169.

Artus, J.R. and Young, J.H. (1979) Fixed and flexible exchange rates: a renewal of the debate, *Working Paper* 367, National Bureau of Economic Research.

Attfield, C.L.F., Demery, D. and Duck, N.W. (1982a) A quarterly model of unanticipated monetary growth, output and the price level in the UK 1963–78, *Journal of Monetary Economics* (forthcoming).

Attfield, C.L.F., Demery, D. and Duck, N.W. (1982b) Unanticipated monetary growth, output and the price level, *European Economic Review* (forthcoming).

Azariadis, C. (1975) Implicit contracts and underemployment equilibria, *Journal of Political Economy*, 83, pp. 1183–1202.

Azariadis, C. (1976) On the incidence of unemployment, *Review of Economic Studies*, 43, pp. 115–25.

Bachelier, L. (1900) Théorie de la Speculation reprinted in English in P. Cootner (ed.) (1964) *op. cit.*

Baily, M.N. (1974) Wages and employment under uncertain demand, *Review of Economic Studies*, 41, pp. 37–50.

Baily, M.N. (1977) On the theory of layoffs and unemployment, *Econometrica*, 45, pp. 1054–63.

Barro, R.J. (1974) Are government bonds net wealth, *Journal of Political Economy*, 82, pp. 1095–1117.

Barro, R.J. (1976) Rational expectations and the role of monetary policy, *Journal of Monetary Economics*, 2, pp. 1–33.

Barro, R.J. (1977a) Unanticipated money growth and unemployment in the United States, *American Economic Review*, 67, pp. 101–15.

Barro, R.J. (1977b) Long term contracting, sticky prices, and monetary policy, *Journal of Monetary Economics*, 3, pp. 305–16.

Barro, R.J. (1978) Unanticipated money, output and the price level in the United States, *Journal of Political Economy*, 86, pp. 549–80.

Barro, R.J. (1981) The equilibrium approach to business cycles, in *Money, Expectations and Business Cycles*, Academic Press, New York.

Barro, R.J. and Fischer, S. (1976) Recent developments in monetary theory, *Journal of Monetary Economics*, 2, pp. 133–67.

Barro, R.J. and Grossman, H.I. (1971) A general disequilibrium model of income and employment, *American Economic Review*, 61, pp. 82–93.

Barro, R.J. and Grossman, H.I. (1976) *Money, Employment and Inflation*, Cambridge University Press.

Barro, R.J. and Rush, M. (1980) Unanticipated money and economic activity, in S. Fischer (ed.) (1980a) *op. cit.*

Beenstock, M. (1980) *A Neoclassical Analysis of Macroeconomic Policy*, Cambridge University Press.

Begg, D.K.H. (1980) Rational expectations and the nonneutrality of systematic monetary policy, *Review of Economic Studies*, 47, pp. 293–303.

Begg, D.K.H. (1982) Rational expectations, wage rigidity, and involuntary unemployment, *Oxford Economic Papers* (forthcoming).

Bell, S. and Beenstock, M. (1980) An application of rational expectations to the UK foreign exchange market, in D. Currie and W. Peters (eds), *Studies in Contemporary Economic Analysis II*, Croom Helm.

Bernanke, B. (1977) Estimation of a macroeconomic model under the hypothesis of rational expectations, Mimeograph, Massachussetts Institute of Technology.

Bierwag, G.O. and Grove, M.A. (1971) A model of the structure of prices of marketable US Treasury securities, *Journal of Money Credit and Banking*, 3, pp. 605—29.

Bilson, J.F.O. (1978a) Rational expectations and the exchange rate in J.A. Frenkel and H.G. Johnson (eds) (1978) *op. cit.*

Bilson, J.F.O. (1978b) The monetary approach to the exchange rate: Some empirical evidence, *IMF Staff Papers*, 25, pp. 48—75.

Bilson, J.F.O. (1980) The rational expectations approach to the consumption function, *European Economic Review*, 13, pp. 273—99.

Bischoff, C.W. (1969) Hypothesis testing and the demand for capital goods, *Review of Economics and Statistics*, 51, pp. 354—68.

Bischoff, C.W. (1971) Business investment in the 1970s: a comparison of models, *Brookings Papers on Economic Activity*, 1, pp. 13—58.

Black, F. (1974) Uniqueness of the price level in monetary growth models, *Journal of Economic Theory*, 7, pp. 53—65.

Blanchard, O.J. (1976) The non-transition to rational expectations, Mimeograph, Massachussetts Institute of Technology.

Blanchard, O.J. (1979) Backward and forward solutions for economies with rational expectations, *American Economic Review, Papers and Proceedings*, 69, pp. 114—18.

Blanchard, O.J. (1980) The monetary mechanism in the light of rational expectations, in S. Fischer (ed.) (1980a) *op. cit.*

Blanchard, O.J. (1981) Output, the stock market, and interest rates, *American Economic Review*, 71, pp. 132—43.

Blanchard, O.J. and Kahn, C.M. (1980) The solution of linear difference models under rational expectations, *Econometrica*, 48, pp. 1305—11.

Blejer, M.I. and Fernandez, R.B. (1979) The effects of unanticipated money growth on prices, output, and its composition in a fixed exchange rate economy, Mimeograph, Hebrew University of Jerusalem.

Blinder, A.S. and Fischer, S. (1978) Inventories, rational expectations, and the business cycle, *Working Paper* 381, National Bureau of Economic Research.

Box, C.E.P. and Jenkins, G.M. (1970) *Time Series Analysis, Forecasting and Control*, Holden-Day, San Francisco.

Boyce, W.E. and DiPrima, R.C. (1977) *Elementary Differential Equations and Boundary Value Problems*, 3rd edition, John Wiley.

Brainard, W.C. and Tobin, J. (1968) Pitfalls in financial model building, *American Economic Review, Papers and Proceedings*, 58, pp. 99—122.

Branson, W.H. (1977) Asset markets and relative prices in exchange rate determination, *Sozialwissenschaftliche Annalen*, Band 1, pp. 69—89.

Branson, W.H., Halttunen, H. and Masson, P. (1977) Exchange rates in the short run: the Dollar-Deutchemark rate, *European Economic*

Review, 10, pp. 303—324.

Branson, W.H. and Halttunen, H. (1978) Asset determination of the exchange rate: initial empirical and policy results, in J.P. Martin & A. Smith (eds): *Trade and Payments Adjustment under Flexible Exchange Rates*, Macmillan.

Branson, W.H., Halttunen, H. and Masson, P. (1979) Exchange rates in the short run: some further results, *European Economic Review*, 12, pp. 395—402.

Bray, M. (1981) Futures trading, rational expectations and the efficient markets hypothesis, *Econometrica*, 49, pp. 575—96.

Brock, W.A. (1974) Money and growth: the case of long run perfect foresight, *International Economic Review*, 15, pp. 750—77.

Brock, W.A. (1975) A simple perfect foresight monetary model, *Journal of Monetary Economics*, 1, 133—50.

Brown, B.W. and Maital, S. (1981) What do economists know? An empirical study of experts' expectations, *Econometrica*, 49, pp. 491—504.

Buiter, W.H. (1980a) The macroeconomics of Dr. Pangloss, *Economic Journal*, 90, pp. 34—50.

Buiter, W.H. (1980b) Real effects of anticipated and unanticipated money: some problems of estimation and hypothesis testing, *Working Paper* 601, National Bureau of Economic Research.

Buiter, W.H. (1982) The superiority of contingent rules over fixed rules in models with rational expectations, *Economic Journal*, 91, (forthcoming).

Buiter, W.H. and Jewitt, I. (1980) Staggered wage setting without money illusion: variations on a theme of Taylor, *Working Paper* 545, National Bureau of Economic Research.

Buiter, W.H. and Miller, M. (1981) Monetary policy and international competitiveness: the problems of adjustment, *Oxford Economic Papers*, 33, pp. 143—75.

Burman, J.P. and White, W.R. (1972) Yield curves for gilt edged stocks, *Bank of England Quarterly Bulletin*, pp. 467—86.

Burmeister, E. (1980a) *Capital Theory and Dynamics*, Cambridge University Press.

Burmeister, E. (1980b) On some conceptual issues in rational expectations modelling, *Journal of Money Credit and Banking*, 12, pp. 800—16.

Burmeister, E., Caton, C., Dobell, A.R. and Ross, S. (1973) The saddlepoint property and the structure of dynamic heterogeneous capital goods models, *Econometrica*, 41, pp. 79—96.

Cagan, P. (1956) The monetary dynamics of hyperinflation in M. Friedman (ed.), *Studies in the Quantity Theory of Money*, University of Chicago Press.

Calvo, G.A. (1978) On the time inconsistency of optimal policy in a monetary economy, *Econometrica*, 46, pp. 1411—28.

Calvo, G.A. (1979) On models of money and perfect foresight, *International Economic Review*, 20, pp. 83—103.

Calvo, G.A. and Phelps, E.S. (1977) Appendix: employment — contingent wage contracts, in K. Brunner and A.H. Meltzer, *Stabilisation of the Domestic and International Economy*, Carnegie Rochester Conference Series, Supplement to the *Journal of Monetary Economics*.

Calvo, G.A. and Rodriguez, C.A. (1977) A model of exchange rate determination under currency substitution and rational expectations, *Journal of Political Economy*, 85, pp. 617—26.

Carlson, J.A. (1977a) Short term interest rates as predictors of inflation: comment, *American Economic Review*, 67, pp. 469—75.

Carlson, J.A. (1977b) A study of price forecasts, *Annals of Economics and Social Measurement*, 6, pp. 27—56.

Caves, D.W. and Feige, E.L. (1980) Efficient foreign exchange markets and the monetary approach to exchange rate determination, *American Economic Review*, 70, pp. 120—34.

Chiang, A.C. (1974) *Fundamental Methods of Mathematical Economics*, 2nd edition, McGraw-Hill.

Chow, G.C. (1975) *Analysis and Control of Dynamic Economic Systems*, John Wiley.

Chow, G.C. (1980) Estimation of rational expectations models, *Journal of Economic Dynamics and Control*, 2, pp. 241—55.

Christ, C.F. (1968) A simple macroeconomic model with a government budget restraint, *Journal of Political Economy*, 76, pp. 53—67.

Clark, K.B. and Summers, L.H. (1979) Labour market dynamics and unemployment: a reconsideration, *Brookings Papers on Economic Activity*, 1, pp. 13—60.

Clements, K.W. and Frenkel, J.A. (1980) Exchange rates, money and relative prices: the Dollar-Pound in the 1920s, *Journal of International Economics*, 10, pp. 249—62.

Cootner, P. (ed.) (1964) *The Random Character of Stock Market Prices*, MIT Press.

Cornell, W.B. and Dietrich, J.K. (1979) The efficiency of the market for foreign exchange under floating exchange rates, *Review of Economics and Statistics*, 60, pp. 111—20.

Cuddington, J.T. (1980) Simultaneous-equations tests of the natural rate and other classical hypotheses, *Journal of Political Economy*, 88, pp. 539—49.

Cumby, R.E. and Obstfeld, M. (1980) Exchange rate expectations and nominal interest differentials: a test of the Fisher hypothesis, *Working Paper* 537, National Bureau of Economic Research.

Davidson, J.E.H., Hendry, D.F., Srba, F. and Yeo, S. (1978) Econometric modelling of the aggregate time-series relationship between consumers' expenditure and income in the UK, *Economic Journal*, 88, pp. 661—93.

Davidson, J.E.H. and Hendry, D.F. (1981) Interpreting econometric evidence: the behaviour of consumers' expenditure in the UK, *European Economic Review*, 16, pp. 177—92.

DeCanio, S. (1979) Rational expectations and learning from experience, *Quarterly Journal of Economics*, 93, pp. 47—57.

Diller, S. (1969) Expectations and the term structure of interest rates, in J. Mincer (ed.), *Economic Forecasts and Expectations*, National Bureau of Economic Research.

Dooley, M.P. and Isard, P. (1979) The portfolio balance model of exchange rates, *International Finance Discussion Paper* 141, Board of Governors, Federal Reserve System, Washington DC.

Dooley, M.P. and Isard, P. (1980) Capital controls, political risk, and deviations from interest rate parity, *Journal of Political Economy*, 88, pp. 370–84.

Dornbusch, R. (1975) A portfolio balance model of the open economy, *Journal of Monetary Economics*, 1, pp. 3–20.

Dornbusch, R. (1976a) Expectations and exchange rate dynamics, *Journal of Political Economy*, 84, pp. 1161–76.

Dornbusch, R. (1976b) Capital mobility, flexible exchange rates and macroeconomic equilibrium, in E. Classen and P. Salin (eds), *Recent Issues in International Monetary Economics*, North-Holland.

Dornbusch, R. (1976c) The theory of flexible exchange regimes and macroeconomic policy, *Scandinavian Journal of Economics*, 78, pp. 255–75, reprinted in J.A. Frenkel and H.G. Johnson (eds) (1978) *op. cit.*

Dornbusch, R. (1978) Monetary policy under exchange rate flexibility, in *Managed Exchange Rate Flexibility: The Recent Experience*, Federal Reserve Bank of Boston Conference Series, 20, pp. 90–122.

Dornbusch, R. (1980a) *Open Economy Macroeconomics*, Basic Books.

Dornbusch, R. (1980b) Exchange rate economics: where do we stand?, *Brookings Papers on Economic Activity*, 1, pp. 143–85.

Dornbusch, R. and Fischer, S. (1978) *Macroeconomics*, McGraw-Hill.

Dornbusch, R. and Fischer, S. (1980) Exchange rates and the current account, *American Economic Review*, 70, pp. 960–71.

Dornbusch, R. and Frenkel, J.A. (1979) *International Economic Policy: Theory and Evidence*, Johns Hopkins University Press.

Durbin, J. (1970) Testing for serial correlation in least squares regression when some of the regressors are lagged dependent variables, *Econometrica*, 38, pp. 410–21.

Eastwood, R.K. and Venables, A.J. (1980) The macroeconomic implications of a resource discovery, *Economic Journal* (forthcoming).

Eisner, R. and Nadiri, M.I. (1968) Investment behaviour and neoclassical theory, *Review of Economics and Statistics*, 52, pp. 369–82.

Eisner, R. and Strotz, R.H. (1963) Determinants of business investment, in Commission on Money and Credit, *Impacts of Monetary Policy* Prentice-Hall.

Ezekial, M. (1938) The cobweb theorem, *Quarterly Journal of Economics*, 52, pp. 255–80.

Fair, R.C. (1970) The estimation of simultaneous equations models with lagged endogenous variables and first order serially correlated errors, *Econometrica*, 38, pp. 507–516.

Fair, R.C. (1978) A criticism of one class of macroeconomic models with rational expectations, *Journal of Money Credit and Banking*,

10, pp. 411—17.

Fair, R.C. (1979a) An analysis of the accuracy of four macroeconomic models, *Journal of Political Economy*, 67, pp. 701—18.

Fair, R.C. (1979b) An analysis of a macroeconometric model with rational expectations in the bond and stock market, *American Economic Review*, 69, pp. 539—52.

Fair, R.C. (1979c) On modelling the effects of government policies *American Economic Review, Papers and Proceedings*, 69, pp. 86—91.

Fair, R.C. and Taylor, J.B. (1980) Solution and maximum likelihood estimation of dynamic nonlinear rational expectations models, *Technical Paper* 5, National Bureau of Economic Research.

Fama, E.F. (1970) Efficient capital markets: a review of theory and empirical work, *Journal of Finance*, 25, pp. 383—417.

Fama, E.F. (1975) Short term interest rates as predictors of inflation *American Economic Review*, 65, pp. 269—82.

Fama, E.F. (1976a) *Foundations of Finance*, Basil Blackwell.

Fama, E.F. (1976b) Forward rates as predictors of future spot rates, *Journal of Financial Economics*, 3, pp. 361—77.

Fama, E.F. (1977) Interest rates and inflation: the message in the entrails, *American Economic Review*, 67, pp. 487—96.

Fama, E.F., Fisher, L., Jensen, M. and Roll, R. (1969) The adjustment of stock prices to new information, *International Economic Review*, 10, pp. 1—21.

Feige, E.L. and Pierce, D.K. (1976) Economically rational expectations: are innovations in the rate of inflation independent of innovations in measures of monetary and fiscal policy?, *Journal of Political Economy*, 84, pp. 499—522.

Feldstein, M.S. (1976) Temporary layoffs in the theory of unemployment, *Journal of Political Economy*, 84, pp. 937—57.

Fellner, W. (1979) The credibility effect and rational expectations: implications of the Gramlich study, *Brookings Papers on Economic Activity*, 1, pp. 167—78.

Fellner, W. (1980) The valid core of rationality hypotheses in the theory of expectations, *Journal of Money Credit and Banking*, 12, pp. 763—87.

Fischer, S. (1977) Long term contracts, rational expectations and the optimum money supply rule, *Journal of Political Economy*, 85, pp. 191—205.

Fischer, S. (1979a) Anticipations and the nonneutrality of money, *Journal of Political Economy*, 87, pp. 225—52.

Fischer, S. (1979b) Capital accumulation on the transition path in a monetary optimising economy, *Econometrica*, 47, pp. 1433—40.

Fischer, S. (ed.) (1980a) *Rational Expectations and Economic Policy*, University of Chicago Press.

Fischer, S. (1980b) On activist monetary policy with rational expectations, in S. Fischer (ed.) (1980a) *op. cit.*

Fisher, F.M. (1966) *The Identification Problem in Econometrics*, McGraw-Hill.

Fisher, I. (1930) *The Theory of Interest*, Macmillan, New York.

Flavin, M. (1978) Comment on 'Rational expectations, econometric exogeneity, and consumption' by T.J. Sargent, Mimeograph, Massachusetts Institute of Technology.

Flemming, J.S. (1973) The consumption function when capital markets are imperfect: the permanent income hypothesis reconsidered, *Oxford Economic Papers*, 25, pp. 160–72.

Flemming, J.S. (1976) *Inflation*, Oxford University Press.

Flood, R.P. (1979) Capital mobility and the choice of exchange rate system, *International Economic Review*, 20, pp. 405–16.

Flood, R.P. and Garber, P.M. (1980a) Market fundamentals versus price level bubbles: the first tests, *Journal of Political Economy*, 88, pp. 745–70

Flood, R.P. and Garber P.M., (1980b) A pitfall in the estimation of models with rational expectations, *Journal of Monetary Economics*, 6, pp. 433–5.

Frankel, J.A. (1979a) On the Mark: a theory of floating exchange rates based on real interest differentials, *American Economic Review*, 69, pp. 610–22.

Frankel, J.A. (1979b) The diversifiability of exchange rate risk, *Journal of International Economics*, 9, pp. 379–94.

Frankel, J.A. (1979c) A test of the existence of the risk premium in the foreign exchange market versus the hypothesis of perfect substitutability, *International Finance Discussion Paper* 149, Board of Governors, Federal Reserve System, Washington DC.

Frankel, J.A. (1980) Monetary and portfolio balance models of exchange rate determination, presented at World Congress of the Econometric Society, Aix-en-Provence, France.

Fraser, D.R. (1977) On the accuracy and usefulness of interest rate forecasts, *Business Economics, 12, pp. 38–44.*

Frenkel, J.A. (1976) A monetary approach to the exchange rate: doctrinal aspects and empirical evidence, *Scandinavian Journal of Economics*, 78, pp. 255–76.

Frenkel, J.A. (1977) The forward exchange rate, expectations and the demand for money: the German hyperinflation, *American Economic Review*, 70, pp. 771–5.

Frenkel, J.A. (1980c) Flexible exchange rates, prices and the role of the 'News': lessons from the 1970s, presented at the International Seminar in Macroeconomics, Oxford. (Revised version forthcoming *Journal of Political Economy*, 1982.)

Frenkel, J.A. (1981) The collapse of purchasing power parities during the 1970s, *European Economic Review*, 16, pp. 145–65.

Frenkel, J.A. and Johnson, H.G. (1976) *The Monetary Approach to the Balance of Payments*, George Allen & Unwin.

Frenkel, J.A. and Johnson, H.G. (ed) (1978) *The Economics of Exchange Rates: Selected Studies* , Addison-Wesley.

Frenkel, J.A. and Levich, R.M. (1975) Covered interest arbitrage: unexploited profits?, *Journal of Political Economy*, 83, pp. 325–9.

Frenkel, J.A. and Levich, R.M. (1977) Transactions costs and interest arbitrage: tranquil versus turbulent periods, *Journal of Political*

Economy, 85, pp. 1209—26.

Frenkel, J.A. and Mussa, M. (1980) Efficiency of foreign exchange markets and measures of turbulence, *American Economic Review*, 70, pp. 374—81.

Friedman, B.M. (1979) Optimal expectations and the extreme information assumptions of rational expectations macromodels, *Journal of Monetary Economics*, 5, pp. 23—41.

Friedman, B.M. (1980) Survey evidence on the 'rationality' of interest rate expectations, *Journal of Monetary Economics*, 6, pp. 153—65.

Friedman, M. (1957) *A Theory of the Consumption Function*, Princeton University Press.

Friedman, M. (1968) The role of monetary policy, *American Economic Review*, 58, pp. 1—17.

Friedman, M. (1977) Nobel Lecture: Inflation and Unemployment, *Journal of Political Economy*, 85, pp. 451—72.

Futia, C. (1981) Rational expectations in linear models, *Econometrica*, 49, pp. 171—92.

Genberg, H. (1978) Purchasing power parity under fixed and floating exchange rates, *Journal of International Economics*, 8, pp. 247—76.

Gordon, D.F. (1974) A neoclassical theory of Keynesian unemployment, *Economic Inquiry*, 12, pp. 431—59.

Gordon, R.J. (1976a) Recent developments in the theory of inflation and unemployment, *Journal of Monetary Economics*, 2, pp. 185—219.

Gordon, R.J. (1976b) Can econometric policy evaluation be salvaged?, in K. Brunner and A.H. Meltzer (eds) *The Phillips Curve and Labour Markets*, Supplement to the *Journal of Monetary Economics*.

Gordon, R.J. (1979) New evidence that fully anticipated monetary changes influence real output after all, *Working Paper* 361, National Bureau of Economic Research.

Gourieroux, C., Laffont, J.J. and Monfort, A. (1979) Rational expectations models: analysis of the solutions, Ecole Polytechnique, Paris.

Gramlich, E.M. (1979) Macroeconomic policy responses to price shocks, *Brookings Papers on Economic Activity*, 1, pp. 125—66.

Granger, C.W.J. (1969) Investigating causal relations by econometric models and cross spectral methods, *Econometrica*, 37, pp. 424—38.

Green, J.R. (1977) The nonexistence of informational equilibria, *Review of Economic Studies*, 44, pp. 451—64.

Grossman, H.I. (1979) Why does aggregate employment fluctuate?, *American Economic Review*, 69, pp. 64—9.

Grossman, H.I. (1980) Rational expectations, business cycles and government behaviour, in S. Fischer (ed.) (1980a) *op. cit.*

Grossman, S.J. (1976) On efficiency of competitive stock markets when traders have diverse information, *Journal of Finance*, 31, pp. 573—85.

Grossman, S.J. (1977) The existence of futures markets, noisy rational expectations, and informational externalities, *Review of Economic Studies*, 64, pp. 431—9.

Grossman, S.J. (1978) Further results on the informational efficiency of competitive stock markets, *Journal of Economic Theory*, 18, pp. 81—101.

Grossman, S.J. and Stiglitz, J.E. (1976) Information and competitive price systems, *American Economic Review*, 66, pp. 246—53.

Grossman, S.J. and Stiglitz, J.E. (1980) On the impossibility of informationally efficient markets, *American Economic Review*, 70, pp. 393—407.

Haberler, G. (1980) Critical notes on rational expectations, *Journal of Money Credit and Banking*, 12, pp. 833—6.

Hacche, G. and Townend, J. (1981) Exchange rates and monetary policy: modelling sterling's effective exchange rate, *Oxford Economic Papers*, 33, pp. 201—47.

Hahn, F.H. (1966) Equilibrium dynamics with heterogeneous capital goods, *Quarterly Journal of Economics*, 80, pp. 633-46.

Hahn, F.H. (1971) Professor Friedman's views on money, *Economica*, 38, pp. 61—80.

Hahn, F.H. (1980) Monetarism and economic theory, *Economica*, 47, pp. 1—17.

Hakkio, C. (1980) Expectations and the forward exchange rate,*Working Paper* 439, National Bureau of Economic Research.

Hall, R.E. (1975) The rigidity of wages and the persistence of unemployment,*Brookings Papers on Economic Activity*, 2,pp. 301—50.

Hall, R.E. (1978) Stochastic implications of the lifecycle-permanent income hypothesis: theory and evidence, *Journal of Political Economy*, 86, pp. 971—88.

Hall, R.E. (1980a) Employment fluctuations and wage rigidity,*Brookings Papers on Economic Activity*, 1, 1980, pp. 91—123.

Hall, R.E. (1980b) Comment on Bilson, *European Economic Review*, 13, pp. 301—3.

Hall, R.E. (1980c) Labour supply and aggregate fluctuations, in K. Brunner and A.H. Meltzer (ed.), *Policies for Employment, Prices and Exchange Rates*, Supplement to the *Journal of Monetary Economics*.

Hall, R.E. and Lilien, D. (1979) Efficient wage bargains under uncertain supply and demand, *American Economic Review*, 69, pp. 869—79.

Hansen, L.P. (1979) Asymptotic distribution of least squares estimators with endogenous regressions and dependent residuals, Mimeograph, Carnegie-Mellon University.

Hansen, L.P. (1980) Large sample properties of generalised methods of moments estimators, Mimeograph, Carnegie-Mellon University.

Hansen, L.P. and Hodrick, R. (1980) Forward exchange rates as optimal predictors of future spot rates: an econometric analysis, *Journal of Political Economy*, 88, pp. 829—53.

Hansen, L.P. and Sargent, T.J. (1980a) Formulating and estimating dynamic linear rational expectations models, *Journal of Economic Dynamics and Control*, 2, pp. 7—46.

Hansen, L.P. and Sargent, T.J. (1980b) Linear rational expectations models for dynamically interrelated variables, in R.E. Lucas and T.J. Sargent (1980) *op. cit.*

Harvey, A.C. (1981) *Econometric Analysis of Time Series*, Philip Allan.

Hatanaka, M. (1975) On global identification of the dynamic simultaneous equation model with stationary disturbances, *International Economic Review*, 16, pp. 545—54.

Hayashi, F. (1980) Estimation of macroeconomic models under rational expectations: a survey, *Discussion Paper* 444, Northwestern University Economics Department.

Hayashi, F. and Sims, C.A. (1980) Efficient estimation of time series models with predetermined but not exogenous instruments, Mimeograph.

Hendry, D.F. (1980) Predictive failure and econometric modelling in macroeconomics: the transactions demand for money, in P. Ormerod (ed.) (1980), *Economic Modelling*, Heinemann.

Hicks, J.R. (1939) *Value and Capital*, Clarendon Press.

Hodrick, R.J. (1978) An empirical analysis of the monetary approach to the determination of the exchange rate, in J.A. Frenkel and H.G. Johnson (eds) (1978) *op. cit.*

Hoffman, D.L. and Schmidt, P. (1981) Testing the restrictions implied by the rational expectations hypothesis, *Journal of Econometrics*, 15, pp. 265—87.

Hooper, P. and Morton, J. (1980) Fluctuations in the dollar: a model of nominal and real exchange rate determination, *International Finance Discussion Paper* 168, Board of Governors, Federal Reserve System, Washington DC.

Howitt, P. (1981) Activist monetary policy under rational expectations, *Journal of Political Economy*, 89, pp. 249—69.

Isard, P. (1977) How far can we push the law of one price?, *American Economic Review* 67, pp. 942—48.

Isard, P. (1980a) Expected and unexpected changes in exchange rates: the role of relative price levels, balance of payment factors, interest rates and risk, *International Finance Discussion Paper* 156, Board of Governors, Federal Reserve System, Washington DC.

Isard, P. (1980b) Factors determining exchange rates: the roles of relative prices, balance of payments, interest rates and risk, *International Finance Discussion Paper* 171, Board of Governors, Federal Reserve System, Washington DC.

Jensen, M. (1968) The performance on mutual funds in the period 1945—64, *Journal of Finance*, 23, pp. 389—416.

Johnston, J. (1972) *Econometric Methods*, 2nd edition, McGraw-Hill.

Jorgenson, D.W. (1963) Capital theory and investment behaviour, *American Economic Review*, 53, pp. 247—59.

Jorgenson, D.W. (1971) Econometric studies of investment behaviour: a survey, *Journal of Economic Literature*, 9, pp. 1111—47.

Jorgenson, D.W. (1972) Investment behaviour and the production function, *Bell Journal of Economic and Management Science*, 3, pp. 220—51.

Kennan, J. (1979) The estimation of partial adjustment models with rational expectations, *Econometrica*, 47, pp. 1441—56.

Kessel, R. (1965) The cyclical behaviour of the term stucture of interest rates, *Occasional Paper* 91, National Bureau of Economic Research.

Keynes, J.M. (1921) *A Treatise on Probability*, Macmillan.

Keynes, J.M. (1936) *The General Theory of Employment, Interest and Money*, Macmillan.

Keynes, J.M. (1937) The general theory of employment, *Quarterly Journal of Economics*, 51, pp. 209–23.

Kouri, P.J.K. (1976) The exchange rate and the balance of payments in the short run and the long run, *Scandinavian Journal of Economics*, 78, pp. 280–304.

Kouri, P.J.K. and de Macedo, J.B. (1978) Exchange rates and the international adjustment process, *Brookings Papers on Economic Activity*, 1, pp. 111–50.

Krugman, P.R. (1978) Purchasing power parity and exchange rates, *Journal of International Economics*, 8, pp. 397–407.

Kuga, K. (1977) General saddlepoint property of the steady state of a growth model with heterogeneous capital goods, *International Economic Review*, 18, pp. 29–58.

Kuznets, S. (1946) *National Income, A Summary of Findings*, National Bureau of Economic Research.

Kydland, F.E. and Prescott, E.C. (1977) Rules rather than discretion: the inconsistency of optimal plans, *Journal of Political Economy*, 85, pp. 473–91.

Kydland, F.E. and Prescott, E.C. (1980) A competitive theory of fluctuations and the desirability of stabilisation policy, in S. Fischer (ed.) (1980a) *op. cit.*

Laffer, A.B. and Zecher, R. (1975) Some evidence on the formation, efficiency, and accuracy of anticipations of nominal yields, *Journal of Monetary Economics*, 1, pp. 329–42.

Lahiri, K. (1976) Inflationary expectations: their formation and interest rate effects, *American Economic Review*, 66, pp. 124–31.

Leiderman, L. (1980) Macroeconometric testing of the rational expectations and structural neutrality hypothesis for the United States, *Journal of Monetary Economics*, 6, pp. 69–82.

Levich, R.M. (1978) Further results on the efficiency of markets for foreign exchange, in *Managed Exchange Rate Flexibility: The Recent Experience*, Federal Reserve Bank of Boston Conference Series.

Levich, R.M. (1979) The efficiency of markets for foreign exchange, in R. Dornbusch and J.A. Frenkel (eds) (1979) *op. cit.*

Levich, R.M. (1978) Tests of forecasting models and market efficiency in the international money market, in J.A. Frenkel and H.G. Johnson (eds) (1978) *op. cit.*

Lipton, D., Poterba, J., Sachs, J. and Summers, L. (1980) Multiple shooting in rational expectations models, *Technical Paper* 3, National Bureau of Economic Research.

Liviatan, N. (1979) Neutral monetary policy and the capital import tax, Mimeograph, Hebrew University of Jerusalem.

Lucas, R.E. Jr. (1972a) Econometric testing of the natural rate hypothesis, in O. Eckstein (ed.), *Econometrics of Price Determination Conference*, Board of Governors, Federal Reserve System, Washington DC.‘

Lucas, R.E. Jr. (1972b) Expectations and the neutrality of money *Journal of Economic Thoery*, 4, pp. 103–24.

Lucas, R.E. Jr. (1973) Some international evidence on output – inflation tradeoffs, *American Economic Review*, 68, pp. 326–334.

Lucas, R.E. Jr. (1975) An equilibrium model of the business cycle, *Journal of Political Economy*, 83, pp. 1113–44.

Lucas, R.E. Jr. (1976) Econometric policy evaluation: a critique, in K. Brunner and A.H. Meltzer (eds), *The Phillips Curve and Labour Markets*, Supplement to the *Journal of Monetary Economics*.

Lucas, R.E. Jr. (1977) Understanding business cycles, in K. Brunner and A.H. Meltzer (eds), *Stabilisation of the Domestic and International Economy*, North-Holland.

Lucas, R.E. Jr. (1980a) Methods and problems in business cycle theory, *Journal of Money Credit and Banking*, 12, pp. 696–715.

Lucas, R.E. Jr. (1980b) Rules, discretion and the role of the economic advisor, in S. Fischer (ed) (1980a) *op. cit.*

Lucas, R.E. Jr. (1981) *Studies in Business-Cycle Theory*, Blackwell.

Lucas, R.E. Jr. and Rapping, L. (1969) Real wages, employment and inflation, *Journal of Political Economy*, 77, pp. 721–54.

Lucas, R.E. Jr. and Sargent, T.J. (1978) After Keynesian macroeconomics, in *After the Phillips Curve: Persistence of High Inflation and High Unemployment*, Federal Reserve Bank of Boston.

Lucas, R.E. Jr. and Sargent, T.J. (eds) (1980) *Rational Expectations and Econometric Practice*, University of Minnesota Press.

McCallum, B.T. (1975) Rational expectations and the natural rate hypothesis: some results for the United Kingdom, *Manchester School*, 43, pp. 55–67.

McCallum, B.T. (1976a) Rational expectations and the estimation of econometric models: an alternative procedure, *International Economic Review*, 17, pp. 484–90.

McCallum, B.T. (1976b) Rational expectations and the natural rate hypothesis: some consistent estimates, *Econometrica*, 46, pp. 43–52.

McCallum, B.T. (1977) Price level stickiness and the feasibility of monetary stabilisation policy under rational expectations, *Journal of Political Economy*, 85, pp. 627–34.

McCallum, B.T. (1978) Price level adjustments and the rational expectations approach to macroeconomic stabilisation policy, *Journal of Money Credit and Banking*, 10, pp. 418–36.

McCallum, B.T. (1979a) Topics concerning the formulation, estimation and use of macroeconomic models with rational expectations, *American Statistical Association, Proceedings of the Business and Economic Statistics Section*, pp. 65–72.

McCallum, B.T. (1979b) The current state of the policy ineffectiveness debate, *American Economic Review, Papers and Proceedings*, 69, pp. 240–5.

McCallum, B.T. (1979c) On the observational inequivalence of classical and Keynesian models, *Journal of Political Economy*, 87, pp. 395–402.

McCallum, B.T. (1979d) Monetarism, rational expectations, oligopolistic pricing, and the MPS econometric model, *Journal of Political Economy*, 87, pp. 57–74.

McCallum, B.T. (1980a) Price Level determinacy with an interest rate policy rule and rational expectations, *Working Paper* 559, National Bureau of Economic Research.

McCallum, B.T. (1980b) Rational expectations and macroeconomic stabilisation policy, *Journal of Money Credit and Banking*, 12, pp. 716–46.

McCallum, B.T. (1981) On non-uniqueness in rational expectations models: an attempt at perspective, *Working Paper* 684, National Bureau of Economic Research.

McCallum, B.T. and Whittaker, J.K. (1979) The effectiveness of fiscal feedback rules and automatic stabilisers under rational expectations, *Journal of Monetary Economics*, 5, pp. 171–86.

McCormick, F. (1979) Covered interest arbitrage: unexploited profits? comment, *Journal of Political Economy*, 87, pp. 411–7.

Maital, S. (1979) Inflation expectations and the monetarist black box, *American Economic Review*, 69, pp. 429–34.

Malkiel, B. (1966) *The Term Structure of Interest Rates*, Princeton University Press.

Mandelbrot, B. (1966) Forecasts of future prices, unbiased markets and Martingale models, *Journal of Business*, 39, pp. 242–55.

Markowitz, H. (1959) *Portfolio Selection: Efficient Diversification of Investment*, John Wiley.

Marschak, J. (1953) Economic measurements for policy and prediction, in W.C. Hood and T.C. Koopmans (eds), *Studies in Econometric Method*, Yale University Press.

Masera, R.S. (1972) *The Term Structure of Interest Rates*, Clarendon Press.

Meese, R.A. and Singleton, K.J. (1980) Rational expectations, risk premia, and the market for spot and forward foreign exchange, *International Finance Discussion Paper* 165, Board of Governors, Federal Reserve System, Washington DC.

Meiselman, D. (1962) *The Term Structure of Interest Rates*, Prentice-Hall.

Minford, A.P.L. (1979) A rational expectations model of the United Kingdom under fixed and floating exchange rates, in K. Brunner and A.H. Meltzer (eds), *On the State of Macro-Economics*, Supplement to the *Journal of Monetary Economics*.

Minford, A.P.L. and Peel, D. (1981) The role of monetary stabilisation policy under rational expectations, *Manchester School*, 69, pp. 39–50.

Mishkin, F.S. (1978a) Efficient markets theory: implications for monetary policy, *Brookings Papers on Economic Activity*, 3, pp. 707–52.

Mishkin, F.S. (1978b) Simulation methodology in macroeconomics: an innovation technique, *Journal of Political Economy*, 87, pp. 816–36.

Mishkin, F.S. (1980) Is the Preferred Habitat model of the term structure inconsistent with financial market efficiency? *Journal of Political Economy*, 88, pp. 406—11.

Mishkin, F.S. (1981a) Are market forecasts rational? *American Economic Review*, 71, pp. 295—306.

Mishkin, F.S. (1981b) Monetary policy and long term interest rates: an efficient markets approach, *Journal of Monetary Economics*, 7, pp. 29—56.

Modigliani, F. (1977) The monetarist controversy, or should we forsake stabilisation policies?, *American Economic Review*, 67, pp. 1—19.

Modigliani, F. and Grunberg, E. (1954) The predictability of social events, *Journal of Political Economy*, 62, pp. 465—78.

Modigliani, F. and Shiller, R.J. (1973) Inflation, rational expectations, and the term structure of interest rates, *Economica*, 40, pp. 12—43.

Modigliani, F. and Sutch, R. (1966) Innovations in interest rate policy, *American Economic Review, Papers and Proceedings*, 56, pp. 178—97.

Modigliani, F. and Sutch, R. (1967) Debt management and the term structure of interest rates, *Journal of Political Economy*, 75, pp. 569—89.

Mullineaux, D.J. (1978) On testing for rationality: another look at the Livingstone price expectations data, *Journal of Political Economy*, 86, pp. 329—36.

Mussa, M. (1979) Empirical regularities in the behaviour of exchange rates and theories of the foreign exchange market, in K. Brunner and A.H. Meltzer (eds), *Policies for Employment, Prices and Exchange Rates*, Supplement to the *Journal of Monetary Economics*.

Muth, J.F. (1961) Rational expectations and the theory of price movements, *Econometrica*, 29, pp. 315—35.

Neary, P. and Stiglitz, J.E. (1982) Towards a reconstruction of Keynesian economics: expectations and constrained equilibria, *Quarterly Journal of Economics* (forthcoming).

Neftci, S. and Sargent, T.J. (1978) A little bit of evidence on the natural rate hypothesis in the United States, *Journal of Monetary Economics*, 4, pp. 315—19.

Neiderhoffer, V. and Osborne, M.F.M. (1966) Market making and reversal on the stock exchange, *Journal of the American Statistical Association*, 61, pp. 897—916.

Nelson, C.R. (1972) *The Term Structure of Interest Rates*, Basic Books.

Nelson, C.R. (1975a) Rational expectations and the estimation of econometric models, *International Economic Review*, 16, pp. 555—61.

Nelson, C.R. (1975b) Rational expectations and the predictive efficiency of economic models, *Journal of Business*, 48, pp. 331—43.

Nelson, C.R. (1979) Granger causality and the natural rate hypothesis, *Journal of Political Economy*, 87, pp. 390—4.

Nelson, C.R. and Schwert, G.W. (1977) Short term interest rates as predictors of inflation: on testing the hypothesis that the real interest rate is constant, *American Economic Review*, 67, pp. 478—86.

Nerlove, M. (1958) Adaptive expectations and Cobweb phenomena,

Quarterly Journal of Economics, 72, pp. 227–40.

Obstfeld, M., Cumby, R. and Huizinga, J. (1981) Two step two stage least squares estimation in models with rational expectations, *Technical Paper* 11, National Bureau of Economic Research.

Patinkin, D. (1956) *Money, Interest and Prices,* Harper and Row.

Pesando, J.E. (1975) A note on the rationality of the Livingstone price expectations, *Journal of Political Economy*, 83, pp. 849–58.

Pesando, J.E. (1978) On the efficiency of the bond market: some Canadian evidence, *Journal of Political Economy*, 86, pp. 1057–76.

Phelps, E.S. (ed.) (1970) *Microeconomic Foundations of Employment and Inflation Theory*, Norton, New York.

Phelps, E.S. and Taylor, J.B. (1977) The stabilising powers of monetary policy under rational expectations, *Journal of Political Economy*, 85, pp. 163–90.

Poole, W. (1976) Rational expectations in the macro model, *Brookings Papers on Economic Activity*, 2, pp. 463–505.

Porter, M.G. (1979) Exchange rates, current accounts and economic activity: a survey of some theoretical and empirical issues, Board of Governors, Federal Reserve System, Washington DC

Precious, M. (1979) *Supply Factors in Investment: A Keynesian Approach*, M. Phil. Thesis, University of Oxford.

Prell, M.J. (1973) How well do experts forecast interest rates? *Federal Reserve Bank of St. Louis, Monthly Bulletin*, pp. 3–13.

Prescott, E.C. (1975) Efficiency of the natural rate, *Journal of Political Economy*, 83, pp. 1229–36.

Radner, R. (1979) Rational expectations equilibrium: generic existence and the information revealed by prices, *Econometrica*, 47, pp. 655–788.

Revankar, N.S. (1980) Testing of the rational expectations hypothesis, *Econometrica*, 48, pp. 1347–65.

Roll, R. (1979) Violations of purchasing power parity and their implication for efficient international capital markets, in M. Sarnat and G. Szego (eds), *International Trade and Finance*, Ballinger.

Rosen, H.S. and Quandt, R.E. (1978) Estimation of a disequilibrium aggregate labour market, *Review of Economics and Statistics*, 60, pp. 371–5.

Salemi, M. and Sargent, T.J. (1979) The demand for money during hyperinflation under rational expectations, *International Economic Review*, 20, pp. 741–58.

Salop, S. (1978) Parables on information transmission, in A. A. Mitchell (ed.), *The Effect of Information on Consumer and Market Behaviour*, American Marketing Association.

Salop, S. (1979) A model of the natural rate of unemployment, *American Economic Review*, 69, pp. 117–25.

Samuelson, P.A. (1965) Proof that properly anticipated prices fluctuate randomly, *Industrial Management Review*, 6, pp. 41–9.

Sargent, T.J. (1972) Rational expectations and the term structure of interest rates, *Journal of Money Credit and Banking*, 4, pp. 74–97.

Sargent, T.J. (1973) Rational expectations, the real rate of interest, and the natural rate of unemployment, *Brookings Papers on Economic Activity*, 2, pp. 429–72.

Sargent, T.J. (1976a) A classical macroeconomic model of the United States, *Journal of Political Economy*, 84, pp. 207–38.

Sargent, T.J. (1976b) The observational equivalence of natural and unnatural rate theories of macroeconomics, *Journal of Political Economy*, 84, pp. 631–40.

Sargent, T.J. (1977) The demand for money during hyperinflations under rational expectations, *International Economic Review*, 18, pp. 59–72.

Sargent, T.J. (1978a) Rational expectations, econometric exogeneity, and consumption, *Journal of Political Economy*, 86, pp. 673–700.

Sargent, T.J. (1978b) Estimation of dynamic labour demand schedules under rational expectations, *Journal of Political Economy*, 86, pp. 1009–44.

Sargent T.J. (1979a) *Macroeconomic Theory*, Academic Press, New York.

Sargent, T.J. (1979b) A note on the maximum likelihood estimation of the rational expectations model of the term structure, *Journal of Monetary Economics*, 5, pp. 133–43.

Sargent, T.J. (1979c) Causality, exogeneity, and natural rate models: reply to C.R. Nelson and B.T. McCallum, *Journal of Political Economy*, 87, pp. 403–9.

Sargent, T.J. (1980) Tobin's q and the rate of investment in general equilibrium, in K. Brunner and A.H. Meltzer (eds), *On the State of Macroeconomics*, Supplement to the *Journal of Monetary Economics*.

Sargent, T.J. (1981) Interpreting economic time series, *Journal of Political Economy*, 89, pp. 213–48.

Sargent, T.J, and Sims, C.A. (1977) Business cycle modelling without pretending to have much *A Priori* economic theory, in C.A. Sims (ed.), *New Methods in Business Cycle Research*, Federal Reserve Bank of Minneapolis.

Sargent, T.J. and Wallace, N. (1973a) The stability of models of money and growth with perfect foresight, *Econometrica*, 41, pp. 1043–8.

Sargent, T.J. and Wallace, N. (1973b) Rational expectations and the dynamics of hyperinflation, *International Economic Review*, 14, pp. 328–50.

Sargent, T.J. and Wallace, N. (1975) Rational expectations, the optimal monetary instrument and the optimal money supply rule, *Journal of Political Economy*, 83, pp. 241–54.

Sargent, T.J. and Wallace, N. (1976) Rational expectations and the theory of economic policy, *Journal of Monetary Economics*, 2, pp. 169–83.

Schmidt, P. (1976) *Econometrics*, Dekker, New York.

Shell, K. and Stiglitz, J.E. (1967) The allocation of investment in a dynamic economy, *Quarterly Journal of Economics*, 81, pp. 592–609.

Shiller, R. J. (1978) Rational expectations and the dynamic structure of macroeconomic models, *Journal of Monetary Economics*, 4, pp.1—44.

Shiller, R.J. (1979) The volatility of long term interest rates and expectations models of the term structure, *Journal of Political Economy*, 87, pp. 1190—219.

Shiller, R.J. (1980) Can the Fed control real interest rates? in S. Fischer (ed.) (1980a) *op. cit.*

Shiller, R.J. (1981) Do stock prices move too much to be justified by subsequent changes in dividends? *American Economic Review*, 71, pp. 421—36.

Sims, C.A. (1972) Money, income, and causality, *American Economic Review*, 62, pp. 540—552.

Sims, C.A. (1979) Macroeconomics and reality, *Econometrica*, 48, pp.1—48.

Sims, C.A. (1980) Comparison of interwar and postwar cycles: monetarism reconsidered, *American Economic Review, Papers and Proceedings*, 70, pp. 250—57.

Singleton, K.J. (1980) Expectations models of the term structure and implied variance bounds, *Journal of Political Economy*, 88, pp. 1159—76.

Small, D. (1979) A comment on Robert Barro's 'Unanticipated Money Growth and Unemployment in the United States', *American Economic Review*, 69, pp. 996—1003.

Solow, R.M. and Stiglitz, J.E. (1968) Output, employment and wages in the short run, *Quarterly Journal of Economics*, 82, pp. 537—60.

Stewart, J. (1976) *Understanding Econometrics*, Hutchinson.

Taylor, J.B. (1975) Monetary policy during the transition to rational expectations, *Journal of Political Economy*, 83, pp. 1009—21.

Taylor, J.B. (1977) Conditions for unique solutions to stochastic macroeconomic models with rational expectations, *Econometrica*, 45, pp. 1377—85.

Taylor, J.B. (1979a) Estimation and control of a macroeconomic model with rational expectations, *Econometrica*, 47, pp. 1267—86.

Taylor, J.B. (1979b) Staggered wage setting in a macroeconomic model, *American Economic Review, Papers and Proceedings*, 69, pp. 108—13.

Taylor, J.B. (1980a) Aggregate dynamics and staggered contracts, *Journal of Political Economy*, 88, pp. 1—23.

Taylor, J.B. (1980b) Output and price stability: an international comparison, *Journal of Economic Dynamics and Control*, 2, pp. 109—32.

Theil, H. (1971) *Principles of Econometrics*, John Wiley.

Tinbergen, J. (1956) *Economic Policy: Principles and Design*, North-Holland.

Tobin, J. (1961) Money, capital and other stores of value, *American Economic Review, Papers and Proceedings*, 51, pp. 26—37.

Tobin, J. (1969) A general equilibrium approach to monetary theory, *Journal of Money Credit and Banking*, 1, pp. 15—29.

Tobin, J. (1978) A proposal for international monetary reform, *Cowles*

Foundation Discussion Paper 506.

Tobin, J. (1980) *Asset Accumulation and Economic Activity*, Basil Blackwell.

Turnovsky, S.J. (1969) A Bayesian approach to the theory of expectations, *Journal of Economic Theory*, 1, pp. 220—7.

Turnovsky, S.J. (1970) Empirical evidence on the formation of price expectations, *Journal of the American Statistical Association*, 65, pp. 1441—54.

Turnovsky, S.J. (1980) The choice of monetary instruments under alternative forms of price expectations, *Manchester School*, 48, pp. 39—63.

Turnovsky, S.J. and Wachter, M. (1972) A test of the expectations hypothesis using directly observed wage and price expectations, *Review of Economics and Statistics*, 54, pp. 47—54.

Waldo, D.G. (1981) Sticky nominal wages and the optimal employment rule, *Journal of Monetary Economics*, 7, pp. 339—53.

Wallace, N. (1980) The overlapping generations model of fiat money, in J. Kareken and N. Wallace (eds), *Models of Monetary Economics*, Federal Reserve Bank of Minneapolis.

Wallis, K.F. (1980) Econometric implications of the rational expectations hypothesis, *Econometrica*, 48, pp. 49—72.

Walters, A.A. (1971) Consistent expectations, distributed lags, and the quantity theory, *Economic Journal*, 81, pp. 273—81.

Weiss, L. (1980) The role for active monetary policy in a rational expectations model, *Journal of Political Economy*, 88, pp. 221—33.

Wickens, M.R. (1977) The efficient estimation of econometric models with rational expectations, Mimeograph, University of Essex.

Wilson, C. (1979) Anticipated shocks and exchange rate dynamics, *Journal of Monetary Economics*, 6, pp. 55—68.

Wogin, G. (1980) Unemployment and monetary policy under rational expectations: some Canadian evidence, *Journal of Monetary Economics*, 6, pp. 59—68.

Woglom, G. (1979) Rational expectations and the role of monetary policy in a simple macroeconomic model, *Quarterly Journal of Economics*, 93, pp. 91—105.

Author Index

285

Subject Index

288